T0321962

Multi–Criteria Decision–Making Models for Website Evaluation

Kemal Vatansever
Alanya Alaaddin Keykubat University, Turkey

Yakup Akgül
Alanya Alaaddin Keykubat University, Turkey

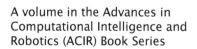

A volume in the Advances in
Computational Intelligence and
Robotics (ACIR) Book Series

Published in the United States of America by
    IGI Global
    Engineering Science Reference (an imprint of IGI Global)
    701 E. Chocolate Avenue
    Hershey PA, USA 17033
    Tel: 717-533-8845
    Fax: 717-533-8661
    E-mail: cust@igi-global.com
    Web site: http://www.igi-global.com

Library of Congress Cataloging-in-Publication Data

Names: Vatansever, Kemal, 1979- editor. | Akgul, Yakup, 1977- editor.
Title: Multi-criteria decision-making models for website evaluation / Kemal
   Vatansever and Yakup Akgul, editors.
Description: Hershey PA : Engineering Science Reference, [2019] | Includes
   bibliographical references.
Identifiers: LCCN 2018052156| ISBN 9781522582380 (hardcover) | ISBN
   9781522582397 (ebook)
Subjects: LCSH: Web sites--Design. | Web site development--Evaluation. | Web
   sites--Evaluation. | Multiple criteria decision making. | Decision support
   systems. | Decision making--Mathematical models.
Classification: LCC TK5105.888 .H36356 2019 | DDC 006.7/8--dc23 LC record available at
https://lccn.loc.gov/2018052156

This book is published in the IGI Global book series Advances in Computational Intelligence and Robotics (ACIR) (ISSN: 2327-0411; eISSN: 2327-042X)

British Cataloguing in Publication Data
A Cataloguing in Publication record for this book is available from the British Library.

All work contributed to this book is new, previously-unpublished material.
The views expressed in this book are those of the authors, but not necessarily of the publisher.

For electronic access to this publication, please contact: eresources@igi-global.com.

Advances in Computational Intelligence and Robotics (ACIR) Book Series

ISSN:2327-0411
EISSN:2327-042X

Editor-in-Chief: Ivan Giannoccaro, University of Salento, Italy

MISSION

While intelligence is traditionally a term applied to humans and human cognition, technology has progressed in such a way to allow for the development of intelligent systems able to simulate many human traits. With this new era of simulated and artificial intelligence, much research is needed in order to continue to advance the field and also to evaluate the ethical and societal concerns of the existence of artificial life and machine learning.

The **Advances in Computational Intelligence and Robotics (ACIR) Book Series** encourages scholarly discourse on all topics pertaining to evolutionary computing, artificial life, computational intelligence, machine learning, and robotics. ACIR presents the latest research being conducted on diverse topics in intelligence technologies with the goal of advancing knowledge and applications in this rapidly evolving field.

COVERAGE

- Agent technologies
- Fuzzy Systems
- Computational Logic
- Intelligent control
- Neural Networks
- Automated Reasoning
- Algorithmic Learning
- Pattern Recognition
- Adaptive and Complex Systems
- Natural Language Processing

IGI Global is currently accepting manuscripts for publication within this series. To submit a proposal for a volume in this series, please contact our Acquisition Editors at Acquisitions@igi-global.com or visit: http://www.igi-global.com/publish/.

Titles in this Series

For a list of additional titles in this series, please visit:
https://www.igi-global.com/book-series/advances-computational-intelligence-robotics/73674

Artificial Intelligence and Security Challenges in Emerging Networks
Ryma Abassi (University of Carthage, Tunisia)
Engineering Science Reference • ©2019 • 293pp • H/C (ISBN: 9781522573531) • US $195.00

Emerging Trends and Applications in Cognitive Computing
Pradeep Kumar Mallick (Vignana Bharathi Institute of Technology, India) and Samarjeet
Borah (Sikkim Manipal University, India)
Engineering Science Reference • ©2019 • 300pp • H/C (ISBN: 9781522557937) • US $215.00

Predictive Intelligence Using Big Data and the Internet of Things
P.K. Gupta (Jaypee University of Information Technology, India) Tuncer Ören (University
of Ottawa, Canada) and Mayank Singh (University of KwaZulu-Natal, South Africa)
Engineering Science Reference • ©2019 • 300pp • H/C (ISBN: 9781522562108) • US $245.00

Advanced Metaheuristic Methods in Big Data Retrieval and Analytics
Hadj Ahmed Bouarara (Dr. Moulay Tahar University of Saïda, Algeria) Reda Mohamed
Hamou (Dr. Moulay Tahar University of Saïda, Algeria) and Amine Rahmani (Dr. Moulay
Tahar University of Saïda, Algeria)
Engineering Science Reference • ©2019 • 320pp • H/C (ISBN: 9781522573388) • US $205.00

Nature-Inspired Algorithms for Big Data Frameworks
Hema Banati (Dyal Singh College, India) Shikha Mehta (Jaypee Institute of Information
Technology, India) and Parmeet Kaur (Jaypee Institute of Information Technology, India)
Engineering Science Reference • ©2019 • 412pp • H/C (ISBN: 9781522558521) • US $225.00

Novel Design and Applications of Robotics Technologies
Dan Zhang (York University, Canada) and Bin Wei (York University, Canada)
Engineering Science Reference • ©2019 • 341pp • H/C (ISBN: 9781522552765) • US $205.00

For an entire list of titles in this series, please visit:
https://www.igi-global.com/book-series/advances-computational-intelligence-robotics/73674

701 East Chocolate Avenue, Hershey, PA 17033, USA
Tel: 717-533-8845 x100 • Fax: 717-533-8661
E-Mail: cust@igi-global.com • www.igi-global.com

Table of Contents

Detailed Table of Contents

Chapter 1
Technology Acceptance Model-Based Website Evaluation of Service
Industry: An Application on the Companies Listed in BIST via Hybrid
Hasan Dinçer, Istanbul Medipol University, Turkey
Serhat Yüksel, İstanbul Medipol University, Turkey
Fatih Pınarbaşı, Istanbul Medipol University, Turkey

The aim of this chapter is to evaluate the website of Turkish companies in service industry which are listed in İstanbul Stock Exchange. Within this framework, two different dimensions are identified by considering technology acceptance model. On the other side, six different criteria are also defined based on SERVQUAL method. Fuzzy DEMATEL method is used to weight dimensions and criteria. Moreover, fuzzy VIKOR and fuzzy TOPSIS approaches are considered to rank the service companies according to the website overall performance. The findings show that being user friendly is the most significant criterion with respect to the website effectiveness. Another important result is that banks are on the first rank for this aspect whereas telecommunication companies have the lowest performance. Therefore, it is recommended that telecommunication companies should firstly focus on improving the factors that make the use of website very easily for the investors. This situation attracts the attention of these investors and it has a positive influence on the financial performance of these companies.

Chapter 2
The Criteria of Websites Quality on Consumers' Buying Behavior: An
Kemal Vatansever, Alanya Alaaddin Keykubat University, Turkey
Hatice Handan Öztemiz, Alanya Alaaddin Keykubat University, Turkey

The aim of this chapter is to investigate the effects of website quality criteria that affect the customer purchasing intentions. Website quality criteria are categorized as security, privacy, usability and web design, convenience, trust and confidence, product value, and product customization. In this study, the criteria are chosen in accordance with the two main criteria of the technology acceptance model. In this chapter, Decision-Making Trial and Evaluation Laboratory (DEMATEL) is used to evaluate the effects of criteria on each other from a causal perspective. According to the research findings, security, trust and trustworthiness, product value, and product customization criteria are more effective than privacy, usability, and web design convenience criteria.

Cengiz Gazeloğlu, Suleyman Demirel University, Turkey
Zeynep Hande Toyganözü, Suleyman Demirel University, Turkey
Cüneyt Toyganözü, Suleyman Demirel University, Turkey
Murat Kemal Keleş, Applied Sciences University of Isparta, Turkey

Wikipedia is a source that has been used at many universities around the world for students to gain some skills and be motivated positively. In higher education, some academicians have a positive view on the teaching usefulness of Wikipedia, and some of them are determined to use classical teaching. In this chapter, teaching use of Wikipedia in all faculty members of the Universitat Oberta de Catalunya are used as data. Then an entropy-based decision tree algorithm was developed. Wikipedia users and non-users are classified according to some aspects with this decision tree. Thus, it can be understood that whether Wikipedia has been used as a teaching tool by academicians or not. So, researchers can have information about the usefulness of Wikipedia in teaching and the intentions in use of it by academicians.

Himanshu Sharma, University of Delhi, India
Aakash Aakash, University of Delhi, India
Anu G. Aggarwal, University of Delhi, India

The digital revolution has transformed many offline retailers to perform their business activities online, resulting in tough competition in a dynamic marketing environment. A well-built, user friendly, and attractive e-commerce website will result in high traffic intensity and eventually impact the market position of the online vendor. Over the past few decades, a number of studies have been done to predict the key determinants of e-commerce system success. This chapter considers the criteria, namely system quality, content quality, use, trust, support, personalization, and electronic word-of-mouth. Evaluating objects based on a single criterion may pose to be subjective, which have shifted these decisions towards multiple criteria, and hence has popularized the concept of multi-criteria decision making (MCDM). This chapter combines Pythagorean fuzzy analytic hierarchy process (PFAHP) and complex proportional assessment of alternatives with grey relations (COPRAS-G), under multiple decision makers, to select the best e-commerce website from five alternatives.

Chapter 5

> *Günay Kılıç, Pamukkale Üniversity, Turkey*
> *Arzu Organ, Pamukkale Üniversity, Turkey*

The share of electronic commerce (e-commerce) in total trade is increasing. There are many kinds of services and products within the scope of e-commerce. These products and services are subdivided according to their sales forms and product groups. In this chapter, only the private shopping websites in the online sales group were examined. Private shopping sites are the sites where the members buy certain products with limited stock in limited time. In this chapter, six leading sites are defined as alternatives for the purpose of comparison. When the studies in the literature are examined, it is seen that multi-criteria decision making methods are used in order to sort the special shopping sites by taking into consideration the criteria. Entropy method was used to determine the weights of the criteria under each main topic determined in the study. Moosra method was chosen from multi-criteria decision making methods in order to rank alternative websites. As a result, alternative sites were listed separately and then examined as to whether there was a relationship between these groups.

Chapter 6

> *Burak Efe, Necmettin Erbakan University, Turkey*

This chapter uses intuitionistic fuzzy VIKOR (IFVIKOR) for the application of ERP software selection. First, priority values of criteria in ERP software selection problem have been determined by using the judgments of the experts. IFWA operator is utilized to integrate the judgments of the experts about the weights of criteria. Then, the result of the IFVIKOR can be employed to define the most appropriate ERP alternative in uncertain environment. Intuitionistic fuzzy numbers are presented in all phases in order to overcome any vagueness in the decision-making process. The final decision depends on the degree of importance of each decision so that wrong degree of importance causes the mistaken result. The researchers generally determine the degrees of importance of each decision makers according to special characteristics of each decision maker as subjectivity. In order to overcome this subjectivity in this chapter, the judgments of decision makers are degraded to unique decision by using the importance degree of each expert. There is no study about ERP software selection using IFVIKOR.

We cannot find any website without advertisements on it. As the number of websites has increased enormously, marketers are trying every niche to target the consumers. While designing a website, a lot of elements are kept in mind. Type of website, ad layout opted, type of internet ad, duration, and position of the ad on the website will be discussed. As the research is based on Harold Laswell model of communication (i.e., who says what, to whom, which channel, and with what effect), the role of the marketers and the way the message is communicated to the online consumers will be discussed. Earlier researches done under this topic will be discussed so as to understand the scope of the research conducted and model suggested. The chapter will include the model suggested at the end of the research and how the basic model of communication by Harold Laswell has diversified over a period of time.

The internet has become an indispensable tool for humanity to access any knowledge. Many companies use the internet to provide their customers with information about their organizations. Website development is a tiring process that requires huge investments. If the performance of the website falls below the expected performance, it will have a negative impact on the website owner. Therefore, the measurement of website performance is an important task for companies. Since many factors or criteria affects the website performance, the use of multi-criteria decision-making methods will be helpful to the performance measurement. In this chapter, fuzzy SWARA and WASPAS-F methods are used to evaluate the performance of 10 state universities' websites located in Turkey. According to the results, the website of Erciyes University has been determined to have the best performance among the 10 universities evaluated. Future research may extend the sample size of the websites of universities.

Chapter 9
Website Evaluation Using Interval Type-2 Fuzzy-Number-Based TOPSIS
Burak Efe, Necmettin Erbakan University, Turkey

In recent years, with the development of the internet, there has been an increase in interest in the internet thanks to other technological developments. In the face of increased user demand, educational institution websites have to maintain high quality of service for a sustainable success. The authors present the possibility degree based TOPSIS method with IT2F numbers as an extension of TOPSIS method to evaluate the educational institution websites. In contrast to precise numbers in TOPSIS method, the merit of fuzzy TOPSIS method is to handle the fuzzy numbers to evaluate the alternatives. Type-1 fuzzy numbers consider crisp membership degrees to express fuzzy numbers but IT2F numbers handle more uncertainties than type-1 fuzzy numbers. The subjective judgments of the decision makers are aggregated by using the IT2F number operations to determine the weights of these criteria. IT2TrF numbers-based TOPSIS phase is employed to rank alternatives based on criteria so that assessment process is completed. The proposed method is applied to evaluate the educational institution websites.

Preface

Decision making is the process of choosing one of the alternatives. The principal duties of the managerial positions in the public and private sectors are to decide. Decision-making is a process that requires a series of actions and needs to be considered with precision. Together with the process of globalization, competition between enterprises has increased. This increase in competition has brought about changing and differentiated customer demands and expectations. Customers have started to demand a higher quality product, faster delivery, more reliable, and lower prices. This situation also presents the concept of uncertainty. The future is uncertain. Businesses are struggling to survive against uncertainty of the future, increasing competition, and changing customer paradigm. Multi-criteria decision-making- MCDM is the most advanced techniques used by decision-makers in decision-making in uncertain environments.

The MCDM is a set of mathematical techniques in which the criteria affecting our decision are weighted and included in the model while making decisions among multiple alternatives. These techniques are now widely used in decision making in uncertain environments. MCDM techniques are not just for selection; sorting, weighting and thus performance measurement. The usage areas are different as well as their aimed areas. In the literature; It is seen that these techniques are used in many different subjects such as supplier selection, machine selection, selection of the most suitable location, measurement of performance of companies, and even selection of spouses.

The main focus of this book is the measurement of the performances of websites by using MCDM techniques. In order to survive in aggravated competition and uncertainty environments, enterprises make serious investments in technology in line with the requirements of the era. Many of their activities and services are provided to customers through the websites they have prepared. However, only the existence of websites is not enough. Continuous monitoring of this investment and performance should be measured at regular intervals. The use of MCDM techniques to measure the performance of the websites is a relatively new field of study, considering other areas of use. Therefore, we believe that this book will be an important resource for the managers in different fields of business in order to help the undergraduate and graduate students. We would like to thank the researchers who supported the completion of this project with the belief that this will be beneficial to the readers.

THE PURPOSE AND THE TARGET AUDIENCE OF THE BOOK

The main aim of the study is to perform the performance of the websites with multi-criteria decision making techniques and to provide decision support to decision makers. Nowadays, the activities of the companies with the Internet technologies to perform the measurement of the performance of websites has made more significant. Enterprises that want to provide more qualified and high quality services to their customers also increase their investments in internet technologies. While the profitability of the enterprises with high performance is high, other enterprises disappear in heavy competition environments. Measuring the performance of the websites is crucial not only for private sector enterprises, but also for public organizations. States reduce the bureaucracy in the public sector with the electronic services they offer to their citizens while at the same time gaining serious savings. As a result of an effective performance measurement, public decision makers will also use resources more optimally. In this context, making these evaluations from a multi-criteria point of view will reduce the effects of the uncertainty of the future.

This book serves the following broad audience:

- Researchers in academia
- Business Executives and IT Personnel
- Students studying towards Management Information Systems, Business Administration, Statistics and both undergraduate and post graduate levels
- Web Design Developers and Marketing and Sales Managers.

Kemal Vatansever
Alanya Alaaddin Keykubat University, Turkey

Yakup Akgül
Alanya Alaaddin Keykubat University, Turkey

Chapter 1
Technology Acceptance Model–Based Website Evaluation of Service Industry:
An Application on the Companies Listed in BIST via Hybrid MCDM

Hasan Dinçer
Istanbul Medipol University, Turkey

Serhat Yüksel
İstanbul Medipol University, Turkey

Fatih Pınarbaşı
ⓘD https://orcid.org/0000-0001-9005-0324
Istanbul Medipol University, Turkey

ABSTRACT

The aim of this chapter is to evaluate the website of Turkish companies in service industry which are listed in İstanbul Stock Exchange. Within this framework, two different dimensions are identified by considering technology acceptance model. On the other side, six different criteria are also defined based on SERVQUAL method. Fuzzy DEMATEL method is used to weight dimensions and criteria. Moreover, fuzzy VIKOR and fuzzy TOPSIS approaches are considered to rank the service companies according to the website overall performance. The findings show that being user friendly is the most significant criterion with respect to the website effectiveness. Another important result is that banks are on the first rank for this aspect whereas telecommunication companies have the lowest performance. Therefore, it is recommended that telecommunication companies should firstly focus on improving the factors that make the use of website very easily for the investors. This situation attracts the attention of these investors and it has a positive influence on the financial performance of these companies.

DOI: 10.4018/978-1-5225-8238-0.ch001

INTRODUCTION

Financial communication is a very significant aspect that has a direct effect on the financial performance of the companies. It refers to all news, strategies, tactics and other kind of information related to the companies which are aimed to be transferred to the shareholders (Rensburg and Botha, 2014). As it can be understood from these definitions that it plays a crucial role to build an effective relationship with the investors (Yüksel et al., 2018). Owing to this issue, it can be possible to attract the attention of the potential investors. Thus, it can have a positive influence on the profitability of the companies (Mayew, 2012).

Effective website is also important point for these companies with respect to the building strong communication with the shareholders (Tan and Wei, 2006). The main reason behind this situation is that website of the company is the first way of the investors to make analysis. If the website of a company is user-friendly and it is possible to reach all necessary information on this website easily, it can provide a competitive advantage for this company in comparison with its rivals. Because of this issue, most of the companies have a department of website management in order to provide an effective website to the shareholders (Pallud and Straub, 2014).

This situation gives information that having an effective website for the companies is a crucial aspect for the sustainable growth (Sreedhar et al., 2010). It also explains that websites of the companies should be evaluated periodically so as to understand the ways to make improvement. Otherwise, ineffective website has a reducing effect on the motivations of the investors. It can be seen that the method, which is used in the evaluation process, has a key role for this purpose. In other words, an effective methodology should be considered in this process to have better evaluation of the website (Yen et al., 2007).

Technology acceptance model is accepted as a successful methodology to evaluate the performance of the website. It was developed by Davis (1986) and it mainly gives information that how users accept the technology. In other words, regarding the website usage of the companies, this approach explains how customers think about the websites of the companies. This methodology considers two main factors which are perceived usefulness and perceived ease of use (Legris et al., 2003). With respect to the perceived usefulness, it focuses on the possibility of the technology to increase the performance (Ersoy, 2011). On the other side, as for perceived ease of use, it explains whether this technology can be used without too much effort (Pavlou, 2003).

In addition to the technology acceptance model, SERVQUAL is also an important methodology to understand customer expectations. This method was developed by Parasuraman et al. (1988) and five different dimensions are taken into the consideration. With respect to the dimension of reliability, the accuracy of the service is considered. Moreover, the dimension of assurance gives information about the knowledge of the employees (Cronin and Taylor, 1994). Additionally, physical facilities of the companies are taken into the consideration in tangibles dimension. Furthermore, empathy refers to the paying attention to the customers whereas the willingness of help to the customers is considered in the dimension of the responsiveness (Basfirinci and Mitra, 2015).

Parallel to these aspects, in this study, it is aimed to evaluate the website of service companies. Within this scope, 5 significant Turkish companies in service industry are taken into the consideration. The main reason behind this aspect is that investor relationship is significant for the companies that are listed in the stock exchanges. In addition to this situation, the reason of selecting service companies is that the nature of service industry makes personnel communication very important. Within this framework, 2 different dimensions are identified by considering the factors emphasized in technology acceptance model. In this circumstance, "perceived ease of use" referrers to the situation in which people can use the website without much effort. Similarly, "perceived usefulness" is the second dimension which gives information that the usage of this website increases productivity. On the other side, 6 different criteria are also defined for these dimensions. In this process, SERVQUAL methodology is considered.

With respect to the weighting dimensions and criteria, fuzzy DEMATEL method is taken into the consideration. Moreover, fuzzy VIKOR and fuzzy TOPSIS approaches are also taken into the consideration in order to rank the service companies according to the website overall performance. As a result of this evaluation, it can be possible to understand which factors have powerful impacts on this performance for service companies in Turkey. Hence, necessary recommendations can be proposed for these companies to improve the website overall performance.

This study has many different novelties. First of all, multicriteria decision making methodology is taken into the consideration firstly regarding website evaluation. Because these methods give effective results for decision making under uncertain environment, it is aimed to reach more meaningful results with the help of these approaches. In addition to this issue, technology acceptance model and SERVQUAL methodology are used together in this study to reach the objective. While considering these aspects, it is thought that this study makes a significant contribution to the literature.

This study has five different sections. In this introduction section, general information about the key concepts are given. Moreover, the second section includes literature review in which some important studies related to this subject are detailed. Furthermore, the third section explains the theoretical background of different methods used in this study. Additionally, the fourth section includes the application on Turkish service industry. In the final section, necessary recommendations according to the analysis results are given.

LITERATURE REVIEW

Technology acceptance model (TAM) is a method which measures the performance of the technology used by the companies. In the literature, it is accepted as a valid methodology in comparison with others. This approach was generated by Davis (1986). The main purpose of this approach is to give information that how users accept the technology. That is to say, this method evaluates the thoughts of the customers with respect to the technology effectiveness of the companies. two main factors are mainly taken into the consideration in technology acceptance model. Regarding the perceived usefulness, this method analyzes whether the technology increases the performance of the company. On the other hand, with respect to the perceived ease of use, it explains whether this technology can be used without too much effort.

In the literature, technology acceptance model was evaluated in many different ways. Some of the studies aimed to analyze the performance of this approach. For example, King and He (2006) examines 88 related studies about technology acceptance model in the literature. They reached a conclusion that TAM is valid and robust model which can be widely used. Ukpabi and Karjaluoto (2017) also emphasized this situation by focusing on 71 different studies in period 2005-2016. Similar to these studies, Ayeh (2015), Kim et al. (2008) and Cheung and Vogel (2013) also concluded that technology acceptance model is very beneficial in many different industries. In spite of them, Legris et al. (2003) identified some aspects that can be very helpful to improve technology acceptance model.

In addition to these studies, it can be seen that technology acceptance model was mainly used to evaluate the performance of some issues. For instance, Brandon-Jones and Kauppi (2018) made a study to measure e-procurement performance of the companies by using this approach. Within this framework, structural equation model is taken into the consideration to reach the objective. Similarly, Ha and Stoel (2009) measured the performance of e-shopping activities with technology acceptance model. For this purpose, a survey was conducted with 298 different participants about the quality, enjoyment and trust of the users. Furthermore, Pai and Huand (2011) examined the quality of healthcare information system with the help of this approach.

Moreover, the internet connection performance was also analyzed by technology acceptance model in many different studies. As an example, Maditinos et al. (2013) used this approach with the aim of measuring internet connection quality of online banking system. In this circumstance, the dimensions of technology acceptance model are taken into the consideration. Similar to this study, Gao and Bai (2014) made another analysis in order to assess the internet connection effectiveness. In this study, perceived ease of use, perceived usefulness and trust are identified as the variables that give information about the quality of internet connection.

Furthermore, mobile commerce is also another factor that was examined by using technology acceptance model in the literature. For instance, Wu and Wang (2005) made an analysis to evaluate mobile commerce acceptance. In this study, the dimensions of technology acceptance model are taken into the consideration. Similar to this study, Park and Kim (2014) conducted a study to evaluate the mobile cloud services. In order to reach this objective, a survey was conducted with 1,099 people. In this survey, the questions are prepared by considering technology acceptance model dimensions. Additionally, Verma et al. (2018) used this approach for big data analysis and Carlos Martins Rodrigues Pinho and Soares (2011) conducted a survey with 150 university students about the quality of social networks.

In addition to the technology acceptance model, website evaluation is also a very popular subject in the literature. For example, Díaz and Martín-Consuegra (2016) made an analysis to measure the websites of airline companies. In this study, content analysis is taken into the consideration. Ass a result, three airline segments are concluded, these segments were influential, follower and passive. Also, Chiou et al. (2010) made a literature of website evaluation concept by focusing on 83 different articles for the periods between 1995 and 2006. Moreover, Kang et al. (2016) and Tanjung and Dhewanto (2014) considered fuzzy TOPSIS approach in order to evaluate the website performance of e-commerce companies.

Furthermore, Tsai et al. (2010) made an analysis to measure the quality of the websites of national parks. For this purpose, DEMATEL, ANP and VIKOR methods are taken into the consideration. In addition to this study, Sun et al. (2017) used content analysis in order to evaluate the quality of the websites of tourism companies. User interface, marketing effectiveness and website quality are the topics mostly discussed in this article. Moreover, Lin (2010) used fuzzy AHP approach to measure course website quality. Similarly, Rocha (2012), Tan and Tung (2003) and Seock and Chen-Yu (2007) are other studies which focused on the website evaluations.

While considering all these studies, it can be understood that technology acceptance model and website evaluation are important topics. With respect to the technology acceptance model, many different studies were conducted in various concepts, such as analyzing the performance of e-procurement, e-shopping, internet connection quality and social networks. On the other side, regarding website evaluation subject, a lot of studies were made with the help of different methodologies like structural equation model, fuzzy DEMATEL and content analysis. Nonetheless, it is identified that there is a need for a new study which focuses on website evaluation by considering the dimensions of technology acceptance model.

METHODOLOGY

Fuzzy DEMATEL

The term "The Decision-Making Trial and Evaluation Laboratory" refers to the DEMATEL. The main purpose of this approach is the decision making under uncertain environment. By weighting the different alternatives, the more important ones can be identified. In addition to this situation, causality relationship between these alternatives can be defined. DEMATEL approach is also considered with fuzzy logic in many different studies in the literature (Nosratabadi et al., 2011; Vafadarnikjoo et al., 2015; Dinçer et al., 2016).

In the first step of the analysis, the purpose is defined. Additionally, in the second step, there is an identification of the criteria. Within this framework, fuzzy linguistic scales ("no", "low", "medium", "high", "very high") are used. In the third step, these criteria are assessed. In the evaluation process, firstly, average fuzzy matrix is created with the help of decision makers' assessment (Dinçer et al., 2018). This matrix is demonstrated on equation (1)-(2)

$$\breve{Z} = \frac{\breve{Z}^1 \oplus \breve{Z}^2 \oplus \ldots \oplus \breve{Z}^p}{p} \tag{1}$$

$$\breve{Z} = \begin{bmatrix} 0 & \cdots & \breve{Z}_{1n} \\ \vdots & \ddots & \vdots \\ \breve{Z}_{n1} & \cdots & 0 \end{bmatrix} \tag{2}$$

As it can be understood, there are p different decision makers in the analysis. Furthermore, $\breve{Z}$ refers to the fuzzy matrixes. In the fourth step, there is a normalization of the direct relation fuzzy matrix (Yüksel et al., 2017). The details of this step are given on the equations (3)-(5).

$$\bar{X} = \begin{bmatrix} \bar{X}_{11} & \cdots & \bar{X}_{1n} \\ \vdots & \ddots & \vdots \\ \bar{X}_{n1} & \cdots & \bar{X}_{nn} \end{bmatrix} \tag{3}$$

$$\bar{X}_{ij} = \frac{Z_{ij}}{r} \left(\frac{l_{ij}}{r}, \frac{m_{ij}}{r}, \frac{u_{ij}}{r} \right) \tag{4}$$

Moreover, on the equations (6)-(11), total relation fuzzy matrix is created, and this process is called as the fifth step.

$$\hat{T} = \begin{bmatrix} \breve{t}_{11} & \cdots & \breve{t}_{1n} \\ \vdots & \ddots & \vdots \\ \breve{t}_{n1} & \cdots & \breve{t}_{nn} \end{bmatrix} \tag{6}$$

$$\breve{t}_{ij} = (l''_{ij}, m''_{ij}, u''_{ij}) \tag{7}$$

$$l''_{ij} = X_l \times (1 - X_l)^{-1} \tag{8}$$

$$m''_{ij} = X_m \times (1 - X_m)^{-1} \tag{9}$$

$$u''_{ij} = X_u \times (1 - X_u)^{-1} \tag{10}$$

$$X_l = \begin{bmatrix} 0 & \cdots & l'_{1n} \\ \vdots & \ddots & \vdots \\ l'_{n1} & \cdots & 0 \end{bmatrix} \qquad X_m = \begin{bmatrix} 0 & \cdots & m'_{1n} \\ \vdots & \ddots & \vdots \\ m'_{n1} & \cdots & 0 \end{bmatrix} \qquad X_u = \begin{bmatrix} 0 & \cdots & u'_{1n} \\ \vdots & \ddots & \vdots \\ u'_{n1} & \cdots & 0 \end{bmatrix} \tag{11}$$

In the last step, there is a calculation of the values of $\left(\breve{D}_i + \breve{R}_i \right)^{def}$ and $\left(\breve{D}_i - \breve{R}_i \right)^{def}$. In order to reach this objective, there is the defuzzification of the fuzzy numbers (Tadić et al., 2014). This situation is detailed on the following matrix.

$$\breve{T}^{def} = \begin{bmatrix} \breve{t}_{11}^{def} & \cdots & \breve{t}_{1n}^{def} \\ \vdots & \ddots & \vdots \\ \breve{t}_{n1}^{def} & \cdots & \breve{t}_{nn}^{def} \end{bmatrix} \tag{12}$$

Fuzzy DEMATEL approach preferred in some studies in the literature. For instance, Raut et al. (2011), Chang et al. (2011), and Mavi and Shahabi (2015) aimed to analyze the best supplier with the help of fuzzy DEMATEL. In addition to these studies, Jeong and Ramírez-Gómez (2018) and Yeh and Huang (2014) tried to find the best location by considering this approach.

Fuzzy TOPSIS

The term "Technique for Order Preference by Similarity to Ideal Solution" explains the TOPSIS. This approach was developed by Hwang and Yoon (1981) with the aim of finding the ideal solution. Within this framework, different alternatives are determined, and they are ranked according to the importance level. In this process, the similarity with the ideal solution is identified. Thus, the shortest distance to the positive ideal solution gives information about the best alternative.

In the first step, fuzzy decision matrix is developed. The details of the calculation of this matrix are demonstrated on the equations (13) and (14).

$$\tilde{x}_{ij} = \frac{1}{K}\left[\tilde{x}_{ij}^1 + \tilde{x}_{ij}^2 + \ldots + \tilde{x}_{ij}^K\right] \tag{13}$$

$$C_1 \, C_2 \, C_3 \ldots C_n$$

$$\tilde{D} = \begin{matrix} A_1 \\ A_2 \\ A_3 \\ \vdots \\ A_m \end{matrix} \begin{bmatrix} \tilde{x}_{11} & \tilde{x}_{12} & \tilde{x}_{13} & \cdots & \tilde{x}_{1n} \\ \tilde{x}_{21} & \tilde{x}_{22} & \tilde{x}_{23} & \cdots & \tilde{x}_{2n} \\ \tilde{x}_{31} & \tilde{x}_{32} & \tilde{x}_{33} & \cdots & \tilde{x}_{3n} \\ \vdots & \vdots & \vdots & \ddots & \cdots & \vdots \\ \tilde{x}_{m1} & \tilde{x}_{m2} & \tilde{x}_{m3} & \cdots & \tilde{x}_{mn} \end{bmatrix} \tag{14}$$

In the second step, the criteria are weighted. In this process, equation (15) is taken into the consideration.

$$\tilde{w}_j = \frac{1}{K} \left[\tilde{w}_j^1 + \tilde{w}_j^2 + \dots + \tilde{w}_j^K \right] \tag{15}$$

In equation (15), there are K different experts. Moreover, in the third step, the normalized fuzzy decision matrix is created with the help of following equations (16)-(17).

$$\tilde{r}_{ij} = \left(\frac{l_{ij}}{u_j^*}, \frac{m_{ij}}{u_j^*}, \frac{u_{ij}}{u_j^*} \right), \text{where } u_j^* = \underset{i}{max} \, u_{ij}$$

$$\tilde{r}_{ij} = \left(\frac{l_j^-}{u_{ij}}, \frac{l_j^-}{m_{ij}}, \frac{l_j^-}{l_{ij}} \right), \text{where } l_j^- = \underset{i}{min} \, l_{ij}$$

Furthermore, the fourth step includes the normalization of fuzzy decision matrix. On the other side, the distances from positive (d_i^*) and negative (d_i^-) ideal solutions are computed by using following equations.

$$d_i^* = \sum_{j=1}^{n} d\left(\tilde{v}_{ij}, \tilde{v}_j^* \right), i = 1, 2, \dots, m \tag{18}$$

$$d_i^- = \sum_{j=1}^{n} d\left(\tilde{v}_{ij}, \tilde{v}_j^- \right), i = 1, 2, \dots, m \tag{19}$$

In the final step, the closeness coefficient is identified with the help of equation (20) (Şengül et al., 2015).

$$CC_i = \frac{d_i^-}{d_i^* + d_i^-} \qquad i = 1, 2, \dots, m \tag{20}$$

Fuzzy TOPSIS methodology was considered by different researchers in the literature. For example, Chu (2002), Chu and Lin (2003), Dagdeviren et al. (2009), Kannan et al. (2014), Oenuet and Soner (2008), Taylan et al. (2014), Yong (2016) and Wang et al. (2009) used fuzzy TOPSIS methodology in order to select the best alternatives, such as green supplier, facility location, robot, weapon, logistic provider, construction project and plant location.

Fuzzy VIKOR

VIKOR method has been developed for multi-criteria optimizations in complex systems. In this method, a weighted distance is determined for a compatible ranking list. The VIKOR method focuses on ranking alternatives. There are 3 stages in the VIKOR methodology (Opricovic and Tzeng, 2004;2007). In the first stage, the best (f^{*}_{j}) and the worst (f_{j}) criteria are identified. These are given on equation (21).

$$\tilde{f}^{*}_{J} = \overset{mak}{\underset{i}{}} \tilde{x}_{ij} \ and \ \tilde{f}^{*}_{J} = \overset{min}{\underset{i}{}} \tilde{x}_{ij} \tag{21}$$

In the second stage, S_i and R_i values are calculated with the following equations (22)-(23).

$$\tilde{S}_i = \sum_{i=1}^{n} \tilde{w}_j \frac{\left(\left| \tilde{f}^{*}_j - \tilde{x}_{ij} \right| \right)}{\left(\left| \tilde{f}^{*}_j - \tilde{f}^{-}_j \right| \right)} \tag{22}$$

$$\tilde{R}_i = mak \ j \left[\tilde{w}_j \frac{\left(\left| \tilde{f}^{*}_j - \tilde{x}_{ij} \right| \right)}{\left(\left| \tilde{f}^{*}_j - \tilde{f}^{-}_j \right| \right)} \right] \tag{23}$$

In the last stage, index value (Q_i) is calculated. In this process equation (24) is taken into the consideration (Rostamzadeh et al., 2015).

$$\tilde{Q}_i = \frac{v \left(\tilde{S}_i - \tilde{S}^{*} \right)}{\left(\tilde{S}^{-} - \tilde{S}^{*} \right)} + \left(1 - v \right) \frac{\left(\tilde{R}_i - \tilde{R}^{*} \right)}{\left(\tilde{R}^{-} - \tilde{R}^{*} \right)} \tag{24}$$

Similar to the other approaches, fuzzy VIKOR is also a very popular methodology in the literature. Many studies such as decision making to improve airport quality of service (Liou et al., 2011), improvement of information security risk (Ou Yang et al., 2009), decision about insurance company selection (Yucenur and Demirel, 2012) in the delivery phase were conducted by using fuzzy VIKOR method.

AN APPLICATION ON THE FIRMS LISTED IN BIST

In this study, it is aimed to assess the website of Turkish service companies. Within this framework, 2 different dimensions are identified by considering the factors emphasized in technology acceptance model that are "perceived ease of use" and "perceived usefulness". In addition to this condition, 6 different criteria are determined by considering SERVQUAL dimensions. The details of these dimensions and criteria are shown on Table 1.

Table 1 gives information that user friendly (C1) is the first criterion that gives information about how easy to use the website (Mulfari et al., 2015; Moritz et al., 2017). Moreover, for the accessibility (C2) criterion, the different possible ways to access the companies' websites, such as computer and mobile phone are taken into the consideration (Čáslavová and Čmakalová, 2015; Hamzah et al., 2015). Furthermore, the criterion of the responsiveness (C3) explains the effectiveness of the response to the problems by the companies (Tung et al., 2017; Bolumole et al., 2016; Naor and Coman, 2017).

With respect to the dimension of perceived usefulness (D2), assurance (C4) is selected as the first criterion which focuses on the accuracy of the information given by the companies (Izogo, 2017; Stamatis, 2015; Levy, 2015; Jordan, 2018). In addition to this aspect, image (C5) is another criterion regarding this dimension. It gives information about the company perception in the eyes of the customer

Table 1. The details of dimensions and criteria

Dimensions	Criteria	Supported Literature
Perceived Ease of Use (D1)	User Friendly (C1)	Tonidandel and LeBreton (2015), Mulfari et al. (2015), Moritz et al. (2017)
	Accessibility (C2)	Čáslavová and Čmakalová (2015), Hamzah et al. (2015), Wuyts et al. (2015)
	Responsiveness (C3)	Tung et al. (2017), Bolumole et al. (2016), Naor and Coman (2017)
Perceived Usefulness (D2)	Assurance (C4)	Izogo (2017), Stamatis (2015), Levy (2015), Jordan (2018)
	Image (C5)	Zameer et al. (2015), Steinhoff et al. (2018), Dachyar and Rusydina (2015)
	Experience (C6)	Filardi et al. (2015), Gupta (2016), Bombiak and Marciniuk-Kluska (2018)

(Steinhoff et al. (2018; Dachyar and Rusydina, 2015). On the other side, the last criterion of perceived usefulness is the experience (C6). This criterion mainly explains that there is a positive correlation between the experience of the company with technology usage effectiveness and customer satisfaction (Filardi et al., 2015; Gupta, 2016; Bombiak and Marciniuk-Kluska, 2018).

Weighting the Dimensions and Criteria With Fuzzy DEMATEL

In the first phase of the analysis, dimensions and criteria are weighted according to the decision makers' evaluations. In this circumstance, fuzzy DEMATEL methodology is taken into the consideration. Firstly, the initial direct relation fuzzy matrix is calculated. The details of this matrix are given on Table 2.

After this process, this matrix is normalized. The details of normalized direct relation fuzzy matrix are demonstrated on Table 3.

In the next process, the total relation fuzzy matrix for the dimensions is created which is given on Table 4.

In the last process of fuzzy DEMATEL analysis, total impact relationship degrees are identified. In addition to this situation, weights for the dimensions can be calculated in this process. The results are shown on Table 5.

Table 2. The initial direct-relation fuzzy matrix for the dimensions

Dimensions	D1			D2		
Perceived Ease of Use (D1)	0.000	0.000	0.000	0.500	0.750	1.000
Perceived Usefulness (D2)	0.250	0.500	0.750	0.000	0.000	0.000

Table 3. Normalized direct-relation fuzzy matrix for the dimensions

Dimensions	D1			D2		
Perceived Ease of Use (D1)	0.000	0.000	0.000	0.500	0.750	1.000
Perceived Usefulness (D2)	0.250	0.500	0.750	0.000	0.000	0.000

Table 4. The total-relation fuzzy matrix for the dimensions

Dimensions	D1			D2		
Perceived Ease of Use (D1)	0.143	0.600	3.000	0.571	1.200	4.000
Perceived Usefulness (D2)	0.286	0.800	3.000	0.143	0.600	3.000

Table 5. Total impact-relationship degrees and the weights for the dimensions

Criteria	$\tilde{D}_i^{def}$	$\tilde{R}_i^{def}$	$\tilde{D}_i^{def} + \tilde{R}_i^{def}$	$\tilde{D}_i^{def} - \tilde{R}_i^{def}$	Weights
D1	2.632	2.145	4.777	0.488	0.503
D2	2.121	2.609	4.729	-0.488	0.497

Table 5 gives information that perceived ease of use (D1) is more important dimension than perceived usefulness (D2). The main reason is that its weight (0.503) is greater than the second dimension's weight (0.497). In this circumstance, the significant point is that there is no great difference between the weights of 0.503 and 0.497. In other words, although the weight of D1 is higher than D2, it can be said that their importance is quite similar. Table 5 explains the results for the dimensions. This process is performed for all criteria under these dimensions. The details of the calculation process are shown on the appendix. On the other side, the summary results of the weights for the criteria are demonstrated on Table 6.

Table 6 explains that user friendly (C1) is the most significant criteria with the weight of 0.178. In addition to this situation, image (C5) is the second most important criteria since it has a weight of 0.177. On the other side, responsiveness (C3) is the least significant criterion because it has the lowest weight (0.156). The results give information that service companies should mainly focus on the factors so that customers can easily use the website. For this purpose, a survey can be conducted with the customers of the companies to understand the expectations. By considering these expectations, companies should arrange their websites, so these customers can use them very easily. Owing to this situation, these companies can increase their competitive power because they are preferred by the customers. In the literature, Tonidandel and LeBreton (2015), Mulfari et al. (2015) and Moritz et al. (2017) also underlined the importance of this issue in their studies.

Table 6. Local and global weights of the dimensions and criteria

Dimensions	Local Weights	Criteria	Local Weights	Global Weights
D1	0.503	C1	0.354	0.178
		C2	0.335	0.169
		C3	0.311	0.156
D2	0.497	C4	0.322	0.160
		C5	0.356	0.177
		C6	0.322	0.160

RANKING THE ALTERNATIVES WITH
FUZZY TOPSIS AND FUZZY VIKOR

After weighting the dimensions and criteria, website effectiveness of the services companies is measured. Within this framework, 5 significant Turkish companies in service industry are taken into the consideration. The main reason behind this aspect is that investor relationship is significant for the companies that are listed in the stock exchanges. In addition to this situation, the reason of selecting service companies is that the nature of service industry makes personnel communication very important. The details of these companies are given on Table 7.

In addition to this condition, fuzzy TOPSIS and fuzzy VIKOR methods are taken into the consideration to rank these companies with respect to the website effectiveness. The first analysis is performed by using fuzzy TOPSIS approach and within this context, firstly, aggregated fuzzy decision matrix is created by considering the evaluations of the decision makers. The details of this matrix are given on Table 8.

After that, these services companies are ranked by calculating the values of D_i^*, D_i^- and CC_i. Analysis results are shared on Table 9.

Table 9 indicates that A4 and A5 have the highest performance with respect to the website effectiveness. On the other hand, A2 and A3 are the companies that have the lowest performance. This situation explains that banks are the most successful companies whereas telecommunication companies are the worst companies. In addition to the fuzzy TOPSIS methodology, similar analysis is also performed with the help of fuzzy VIKOR approach. Analysis results are demonstrated on Table 10.

Table 10 shows that the companies operating in the banking industry have the highest performance. On the other side, telecommunication companies are on the last rank. It can easily be understood that the results of fuzzy TOPSIS and fuzzy VIKOR are quite similar. This situation increases the validity of the results.

Table 7. The details of the companies

Companies / Alternatives	Industry Information
A1	Airline
A2	Telecommunication
A3	Telecommunication
A4	Banking
A5	Banking

Table 8. Aggregated fuzzy decision matrix

	C1			C2			C3			C4			C5			C6		
A1	6.67	9.17	10.00	5.00	7.50	10.00	5.00	7.50	10.00	4.17	6.67	9.17	5.00	7.50	10.0	5.00	7.50	10.00
A2	4.17	6.67	9.17	3.33	5.83	8.33	3.33	5.83	8.33	2.50	5.00	7.50	2.50	5.00	7.50	3.33	5.83	8.33
A3	4.17	6.67	9.17	3.33	5.83	8.33	4.17	6.67	9.17	4.17	6.67	9.17	3.33	5.83	8.33	3.33	5.83	8.33
A4	6.67	9.17	10.00	5.00	7.50	10.00	5.83	8.33	10.00	4.17	6.67	9.17	5.00	7.50	10.0	5.83	8.33	10.00
A5	6.67	9.17	10.00	6.67	9.17	10.00	5.83	8.33	10.00	6.67	9.17	10.0	6.67	9.17	10.0	5.00	7.50	10.00

Table 9. The values of D_i^*, D_i^- and CC_i and ranking the alternatives with fuzzy TOPSIS

Alternatives	D_i^*	D_i^-	CC_i	Ranking
A1	6.640	0.373	0.053	3
A2	6.729	0.289	0.041	5
A3	6.703	0.314	0.045	4
A4	6.632	0.380	0.054	2
A5	6.602	0.406	0.058	1

Table 10. The values of S_i, R_i and Q_i and ranking the alternatives with fuzzy VIKOR

Alternatives	S_i	R_i	Q_i	Ranking
A1	0.256	0.082	0.280	3
A2	1.000	0.178	1.000	5
A3	0.818	0.178	0.906	4
A4	0.185	0.082	0.243	2
A5	0.036	0.036	0.000	1

SOLUTIONS AND RECOMMENDATIONS

In this study, it is identified that user friendly is the most significant criteria with respect to the website evaluation. In addition to this issue, it is also defined that as a result of both fuzzy TOPSIS and fuzzy VIKOR analysis, the companies operating in the banking industry have the highest performance whereas telecommunication companies are the worst companies regarding this subject. Therefore, it can be said that telecommunication companies should mainly focus on the factors for the customers to use the website easily. For this purpose, they may conduct a survey among their customers in order to understand their expectations.

FUTURE RESEARCH DIRECTIONS

This study evaluates the website of 5 significant Turkish companies listed in İstanbul Stock Exchange. In order to reach this objective, fuzzy DEMATEL, fuzzy TOPSIS and fuzzy VIKOR approaches are taken into the consideration. Nevertheless, it the future studies, a new analysis can be conducted with an original methodology, such as interval type 2 fuzzy logic.

CONCLUSION

Effective financial communication has a significant effect on the financial performance of the companies. The main reason is that in case of having an effective relationship with the investors, the companies can be preferred more. In this circumstance, website design plays a very important role. Because website of the company is the first way of the investors to make analysis, it influences the thought of the investors about the companies. Due to this statement, many companies make a great effort to design and control their websites.

The aim of this study is to measure the website of service companies. For this purpose, 5 significant Turkish companies in service industry, which are listed in İstanbul Stock Exchange, are considered. Firstly, 2 different dimensions are identified by considering the factors emphasized in technology acceptance model. After that, 6 different criteria are also defined for these dimensions based on SERVQUAL methodology. In addition to these issues, fuzzy DEMATEL method is used to weight the dimensions and criteria and fuzzy VIKOR and fuzzy TOPSIS approaches are considered to rank these service companies.

As a result of fuzzy DEMATEL, it is defined that perceived ease of use is more important dimension than perceived usefulness. Moreover, it is also concluded that user friendly is the most significant criteria. Additionally, it is also identified that image is the second most important criteria. On the other side, according to the results of fuzzy TOPSIS and fuzzy VIKOR, it is determined that the companies operating in the banking industry have the highest performance. However, another important conclusion is that telecommunication companies are on the last rank with respect to the effectiveness of the website design.

While considering the aspects emphasized in this study, it can be said that telecommunication companies should give more importance to the website design. Within this scope, they should firstly focus on the factors which provide easy use for the investors. When investors think that the websites of these companies are user friendly, they can be preferred more. This situation has a positive influence on the financial performance of these companies. Otherwise, it can be very difficult for these companies to survive in competitive environment.

REFERENCES

Ayeh, J. K. (2015). Travellers' acceptance of consumer-generated media: An integrated model of technology acceptance and source credibility theories. *Computers in Human Behavior, 48*, 173–180. doi:10.1016/j.chb.2014.12.049

Basfirinci, C., & Mitra, A. (2015). A cross cultural investigation of airlines service quality through integration of Servqual and the Kano model. *Journal of Air Transport Management, 42*, 239–248. doi:10.1016/j.jairtraman.2014.11.005

Bolumole, Y. A., Grawe, S. J., & Daugherty, P. J. (2016). Customer service responsiveness in logistics outsourcing contracts: The influence of job autonomy and role clarity among on-site representatives. *Transportation Journal, 55*(2), 124–148. doi:10.5325/transportationj.55.2.0124

Bombiak, E., & Marciniuk-Kluska, A. (2018). Green Human Resource Management as a Tool for the Sustainable Development of Enterprises: Polish Young Company Experience. *Sustainability, 10*(6), 1739. doi:10.3390u10061739

Brandon-Jones, A., & Kauppi, K. (2018). Examining the antecedents of the technology acceptance model within e-procurement. *International Journal of Operations & Production Management, 38*(1), 22–42. doi:10.1108/IJOPM-06-2015-0346

Carlos Martins Rodrigues Pinho, J., & Soares, A. M. (2011). Examining the technology acceptance model in the adoption of social networks. *Journal of Research in Interactive Marketing, 5*(2/3), 116–129. doi:10.1108/17505931111187767

Čáslavová, E., & Čmakalová, H. (2015). Competition and customer loyalty of fitness centres in the Prague region compared to the Prague-West area. *Studia sportiva, 9*(1), 144-150.

Chang, B., Chang, C. W., & Wu, C. H. (2011). Fuzzy DEMATEL method for developing supplier selection criteria. *Expert Systems with Applications, 38*(3), 1850–1858. doi:10.1016/j.eswa.2010.07.114

Cheung, R., & Vogel, D. (2013). Predicting user acceptance of collaborative technologies: An extension of the technology acceptance model for e-learning. *Computers & Education, 63*, 160–175. doi:10.1016/j.compedu.2012.12.003

Chiou, W. C., Lin, C. C., & Perng, C. (2010). A strategic framework for website evaluation based on a review of the literature from 1995–2006. *Information & Management, 47*(5-6), 282–290. doi:10.1016/j.im.2010.06.002

Chu, T. C. (2002a). Facility location selection using fuzzy TOPSIS under group decisions. *International Journal of Uncertainty, Fuzziness and Knowledge-based Systems, 10*(6), 687–701. doi:10.1142/S0218488502001739

Chu, T. C., & Lin, Y. C. (2003). A fuzzy TOPSIS method for robot selection. *International Journal of Advanced Manufacturing Technology, 21*(4), 284–290. doi:10.1007001700300033

Cronin, J. J. Jr, & Taylor, S. A. (1994). SERVPERF versus SERVQUAL: Reconciling performance-based and perceptions-minus-expectations measurement of service quality. *Journal of Marketing, 58*(1), 125–131. doi:10.1177/002224299405800110

Dachyar, M., & Rusydina, A. (2015). Measuring customer satisfaction and its relationship towards taxi's service quality around capital City Jakarta. *IACSIT International Journal of Engineering and Technology, 15*(1), 24–27.

Dagdeviren, M. (2008). Decision making in equipment selection: An integrated approach with AHP and PROMETHEE. *Journal of Intelligent Manufacturing, 19*(4), 397–406. doi:10.100710845-008-0091-7

Davis, F. D. (1985). *A technology acceptance model for empirically testing new end-user information systems: Theory and results* (Doctoral dissertation). Massachusetts Institute of Technology.

Díaz, E., & Martín-Consuegra, D. (2016). A latent class segmentation analysis of airlines based on website evaluation. *Journal of Air Transport Management, 55,* 20–40. doi:10.1016/j.jairtraman.2016.04.007

Dincer, H., Hacioglu, U., & Yuksel, S. (2016). Balanced scorecard-based performance assessment of Turkish banking sector with analytic network process. *International Journal of Decision Sciences & Applications-IJDSA, 1*(1), 1–21.

Dinçer, H., Yuksel, S., & Bozaykut-Buk, T. (2018). Evaluation of Financial and Economic Effects on Green Supply Chain Management With Multi-Criteria Decision-Making Approach: Evidence From Companies Listed in BIST. In *Handbook of Research on Supply Chain Management for Sustainable Development* (pp. 144–175). IGI Global. doi:10.4018/978-1-5225-5757-9.ch009

Ersoy, İ. (2011). The impact of financial openness on financial development, growth and volatility in Turkey: Evidence from the ARDL bounds tests. Economic research-. *Ekonomska Istrazivanja, 24*(3), 33–44.

Filardi, F., Berti, D., & Moreno, V. (2015). Implementation analysis of Lean Sigma in IT applications. A multinational oil company experience in Brazil. *Procedia Computer Science*, *55*, 1221–1230. doi:10.1016/j.procs.2015.07.128

Gao, L., & Bai, X. (2014). A unified perspective on the factors influencing consumer acceptance of internet of things technology. *Asia Pacific Journal of Marketing and Logistics*, *26*(2), 211–231. doi:10.1108/APJML-06-2013-0061

Gupta, A. (2016). Redefining service quality scale with customer experience quality scale: A critical review. *International Journal of Services and Operations Management*, *25*(1), 48–64. doi:10.1504/IJSOM.2016.078070

Ha, S., & Stoel, L. (2009). Consumer e-shopping acceptance: Antecedents in a technology acceptance model. *Journal of Business Research*, *62*(5), 565–571. doi:10.1016/j.jbusres.2008.06.016

Hamzah, N., Ishak, N. M., & Nor, N. I. M. (2015). Customer satisfactions on Islamic banking system. *Journal of Economics. Business and Management*, *3*(1), 140–144.

Hwang, C. L., & Yoon, K. (1981). Methods for multiple attribute decision making. In *Multiple attribute decision making* (pp. 58–191). Berlin: Springer. doi:10.1007/978-3-642-48318-9_3

Izogo, E. E. (2017). Customer loyalty in telecom service sector: The role of service quality and customer commitment. *The TQM Journal*, *29*(1), 19–36. doi:10.1108/TQM-10-2014-0089

Jeong, J. S., & Ramírez-Gómez, Á. (2018). Optimizing the location of a biomass plant with a fuzzy-DEcision-MAking Trial and Evaluation Laboratory (F-DEMATEL) and multi-criteria spatial decision assessment for renewable energy management and long-term sustainability. *Journal of Cleaner Production*, *182*, 509–520. doi:10.1016/j.jclepro.2017.12.072

Jordan, T. (2018). Quality Assurance: Applying Methodologies for Launching New Products, Services and Customer Satisfaction. *Quality Progress*, *51*(2), 60–60.

Kang, D., Jang, W., & Park, Y. (2016). Evaluation of e-commerce websites using fuzzy hierarchical TOPSIS based on ES-QUAL. *Applied Soft Computing*, *42*, 53–65. doi:10.1016/j.asoc.2016.01.017

Kannan, D., Lopes de Sousa Jabbour, A. B., & Chiappetta Jabbour, C. J. (2014). Selecting green suppliers based on GSCM practices: Using fuzzy TOPSIS applied to a Brazilian electronics company. *European Journal of Operational Research, 233*(2), 432–447. doi:10.1016/j.ejor.2013.07.023

Kim, T. G., Lee, J. H., & Law, R. (2008). An empirical examination of the acceptance behaviour of hotel front office systems: An extended technology acceptance model. *Tourism Management, 29*(3), 500–513. doi:10.1016/j.tourman.2007.05.016

King, W. R., & He, J. (2006). A meta-analysis of the technology acceptance model. *Information & Management, 43*(6), 740–755. doi:10.1016/j.im.2006.05.003

Legris, P., Ingham, J., & Collerette, P. (2003). Why do people use information technology? A critical review of the technology acceptance model. *Information & Management, 40*(3), 191–204. doi:10.1016/S0378-7206(01)00143-4

Lin, H. F. (2010). An application of fuzzy AHP for evaluating course website quality. *Computers & Education, 54*(4), 877–888. doi:10.1016/j.compedu.2009.09.017

Liou, J. J., Tsai, C. Y., Lin, R. H., & Tzeng, G. H. (2011). A modified VIKOR multiple-criteria decision method for improving domestic airlines service quality. *Journal of Air Transport Management, 17*(2), 57–61. doi:10.1016/j.jairtraman.2010.03.004

Maditinos, D., Chatzoudes, D., & Sarigiannidis, L. (2013). An examination of the critical factors affecting consumer acceptance of online banking: A focus on the dimensions of risk. *Journal of Systems and Information Technology, 15*(1), 97–116. doi:10.1108/13287261311322602

Mavi, R. K., Goh, M., & Zarbakhshnia, N. (2017). Sustainable third-party reverse logistic provider selection with fuzzy SWARA and fuzzy MOORA in plastic industry. *International Journal of Advanced Manufacturing Technology, 91*(5-8), 2401–2418. doi:10.100700170-016-9880-x

Mayew, W. J. (2012). Disclosure Outlets and Corporate Financial Communication: A Discussion of "Managers' Use of Language Across Alternative Disclosure Outlets: Earnings Press Releases versus MD&A". *Contemporary Accounting Research, 29*(3), 838–844. doi:10.1111/j.1911-3846.2011.01126.x

Moritz, S., Berna, F., Jaeger, S., Westermann, S., & Nagel, M. (2017). The customer is always right? Subjective target symptoms and treatment preferences in patients with psychosis. *European Archives of Psychiatry and Clinical Neuroscience, 267*(4), 335–339. doi:10.100700406-016-0694-5 PMID:27194554

Mulfari, D., Celesti, A., & Villari, M. (2015). A computer system architecture providing a user-friendly man machine interface for accessing assistive technology in cloud computing. *Journal of Systems and Software, 100*, 129–138. doi:10.1016/j.jss.2014.10.035

Naor, M., & Coman, A. (2017). Offshore responsiveness: Theory of Constraints innovates customer services. *Service Industries Journal, 37*(3-4), 155–166. doi:10.1080/02642069.2017.1303047

Nosratabadi, H. E., Pourdarab, S., & Nadali, A. (2011). Credit Risk Assessment of Bank Customers using DEMATEL and Fuzzy Expert System. *Economics and Finance Research, 4*, 255–259.

Oenuet, S., & Soner, S. (2008). Transshipment site selection using the AHP and TOPSIS approaches under fuzzy environment. *Waste Management (New York, N.Y.), 28*(9), 1552–1559. doi:10.1016/j.wasman.2007.05.019 PMID:17768038

Opricovic, S., & Tzeng, G. H. (2004). Compromise solution by MCDM methods: A comparative analysis of VIKOR and TOPSIS. *European Journal of Operational Research, 156*(2), 445–455. doi:10.1016/S0377-2217(03)00020-1

Opricovic, S., & Tzeng, G. H. (2007). Extended VIKOR method in comparison with outranking methods. *European Journal of Operational Research, 178*(2), 514–529. doi:10.1016/j.ejor.2006.01.020

Ou Yang, Y. P., Shieh, H. M., Leu, J. D., & Tzeng, G. H. (2009). A VIKOR-based multiple criteria decision method for improving information security risk. *International Journal of Information Technology & Decision Making, 8*(02), 267–287. doi:10.1142/S0219622009003375

Pai, F. Y., & Huang, K. I. (2011). Applying the technology acceptance model to the introduction of healthcare information systems. *Technological Forecasting and Social Change, 78*(4), 650–660. doi:10.1016/j.techfore.2010.11.007

Pallud, J., & Straub, D. W. (2014). Effective website design for experience-influenced environments: The case of high culture museums. *Information & Management, 51*(3), 359–373. doi:10.1016/j.im.2014.02.010

Parasuraman, A., Zeithaml, V. A., & Berry, L. L. (1988). Servqual: A multiple-item scale for measuring consumer perc. *Journal of Retailing, 64*(1), 12.

Park, E., & Kim, K. J. (2014). An integrated adoption model of mobile cloud services: Exploration of key determinants and extension of technology acceptance model. *Telematics and Informatics, 31*(3), 376–385. doi:10.1016/j.tele.2013.11.008

Pavlou, P. A. (2003). Consumer acceptance of electronic commerce: Integrating trust and risk with the technology acceptance model. *International Journal of Electronic Commerce, 7*(3), 101–134. doi:10.1080/10864415.2003.11044275

Raut, R. D., Bhasin, H. V., & Kamble, S. S. (2011). Evaluation of supplier selection criteria by combination of AHP and fuzzy DEMATEL method. *International Journal of Business Innovation and Research, 5*(4), 359–392. doi:10.1504/IJBIR.2011.041056

Rensburg, R., & Botha, E. (2014). Is integrated reporting the silver bullet of financial communication? A stakeholder perspective from South Africa. *Public Relations Review, 40*(2), 144–152. doi:10.1016/j.pubrev.2013.11.016

Rostamzadeh, R., Govindan, K., Esmaeili, A., & Sabaghi, M. (2015). Application of fuzzy VIKOR for evaluation of green supply chain management practices. *Ecological Indicators, 49*, 188–203. doi:10.1016/j.ecolind.2014.09.045

Şengül, Ü., Eren, M., Shiraz, S. E., Gezder, V., & Şengül, A. B. (2015). Fuzzy TOPSIS method for ranking renewable energy supply systems in Turkey. *Renewable Energy, 75*, 617–625. doi:10.1016/j.renene.2014.10.045

Sreedhar, G., Chari, A. A., & Ramana, V. (2010). A qualitative and quantitative frame work for effective website design. *International Journal of Computers and Applications, 2*(1), 71–79. doi:10.5120/610-860

Stamatis, D. H. (2015). *Quality Assurance: Applying Methodologies for Launching New Products, Services, and Customer Satisfaction.* CRC Press. doi:10.1201/b18887

Steinhoff, L., Witte, C., & Eggert, A. (2018). Mixed Effects of Company-Initiated Customer Engagement on Customer Loyalty: The Contingency Role of Service Category Involvement. *SMR-Journal of Service Management Research, 2*(2), 22–35. doi:10.15358/2511-8676-2018-2-22

Tadić, S., Zečević, S., & Krstić, M. (2014). A novel hybrid MCDM model based on fuzzy DEMATEL, fuzzy ANP and fuzzy VIKOR for city logistics concept selection. *Expert Systems with Applications, 41*(18), 8112–8128. doi:10.1016/j.eswa.2014.07.021

Tan, G. W., & Wei, K. K. (2006). An empirical study of Web browsing behaviour: Towards an effective Website design. *Electronic Commerce Research and Applications, 5*(4), 261–271. doi:10.1016/j.elerap.2006.04.007

Taylan, O., Bafail, A. O., Abdulaal, R. M. S., & Kabli, M. R. (2014). Construction projects selection and risk assessment by fuzzy AHP and fuzzy TOPSIS methodologies. *Applied Soft Computing, 17*, 105–116. doi:10.1016/j.asoc.2014.01.003

Tonidandel, S., & LeBreton, J. M. (2015). RWA web: A free, comprehensive, web-based, and user-friendly tool for relative weight analyses. *Journal of Business and Psychology, 30*(2), 207–216. doi:10.100710869-014-9351-z

Tung, V. W. S., Chen, P. J., & Schuckert, M. (2017). Managing customer citizenship behaviour: The moderating roles of employee responsiveness and organizational reassurance. *Tourism Management, 59*, 23–35. doi:10.1016/j.tourman.2016.07.010

Vafadarnikjoo, A., Mobin, M., Allahi, S., & Rastegari, A. (2015, January). A hybrid approach of intuitionistic fuzzy set theory and DEMATEL method to prioritize selection criteria of bank branches locations. In *Proceedings of the International Annual Conference of the American Society for Engineering Management* (p. 1). American Society for Engineering Management (ASEM).

Wang, J.-W., Cheng, C.-H., & Kun-Cheng, H. (2009). Fuzzy hierarchical TOPSIS for supplier selection. *Applied Soft Computing, 9*(1), 377–386. doi:10.1016/j.asoc.2008.04.014

Wuyts, S., Rindfleisch, A., & Citrin, A. (2015). Outsourcing customer support: The role of provider customer focus. *Journal of Operations Management, 35*(1), 40–55. doi:10.1016/j.jom.2014.10.004

Yeh, T. M., & Huang, Y. L. (2014). Factors in determining wind farm location: Integrating GQM, fuzzy DEMATEL, and ANP. *Renewable Energy, 66*, 159–169. doi:10.1016/j.renene.2013.12.003

Yen, B., Hu, P. J. H., & Wang, M. (2007). Toward an analytical approach for effective Web site design: A framework for modeling, evaluation and enhancement. *Electronic Commerce Research and Applications, 6*(2), 159–170. doi:10.1016/j.elerap.2006.11.004

Yong, D. (2006). Plant location selection based on fuzzy TOPSIS. *International Journal of Advanced Manufacturing Technology, 28*(7–8), 839–844. doi:10.100700170-004-2436-5

Yücenur, G. N., & Demirel, N. Ç. (2012). Group decision making process for insurance company selection problem with extended VIKOR method under fuzzy environment. *Expert Systems with Applications, 39*(3), 3702–3707. doi:10.1016/j.eswa.2011.09.065

Yüksel, S., Dinçer, H., & Emir, Ş. (2017). Comparing the performance of Turkish deposit banks by using DEMATEL, Grey Relational Analysis (GRA) and MOORA approaches. *World Journal of Applied Economics, 3*(2), 26–47. doi:10.22440/wjae.3.2.2

Yüksel, S., Mukhtarov, S., Mammadov, E., & Özsarı, M. (2018). Determinants of Profitability in the Banking Sector: An Analysis of Post-Soviet Countries. *Economies, 6*(3), 1–15. doi:10.3390/economies6030041

Zameer, H., Tara, A., Kausar, U., & Mohsin, A. (2015). Impact of service quality, corporate image and customer satisfaction towards customers' perceived value in the banking sector in Pakistan. *International Journal of Bank Marketing, 33*(4), 442–456. doi:10.1108/IJBM-01-2014-0015

KEY TERMS AND DEFINITIONS

BIST: İstanbul Stock Exchange.

DEMATEL: It refers to the "decision making trial and evaluation laboratory."

MCDM: Multi-criteria decision making model.

TAM: Technology acceptance model.

TOPSIS: It is "technique for order preference by similarity to ideal solution."

VIKOR: It is an acronym for "Vise Kriterijumska Optimizacija I Kompromisno Resenje".

APPENDIX

Table 11. The initial direct-relation fuzzy matrix for the criteria of D1

Criteria	C1			C2			C3		
User Friendly (C1)	0.000	0.000	0.000	0.500	0.750	1.000	0.500	0.750	1.000
Accessibility (C2)	0.500	0.750	1.000	0.000	0.000	0.000	0.250	0.500	0.750
Responsiveness (C3)	0.250	0.500	0.750	0.250	0.500	0.750	0.000	0.000	0.000

Table 12. Normalized direct-relation fuzzy matrix for the criteria of D1

Criteria	C1			C2			C3		
User Friendly (C1)	0.000	0.000	0.000	0.250	0.375	0.500	0.250	0.375	0.500
Accessibility (C2)	0.250	0.375	0.500	0.000	0.000	0.000	0.125	0.250	0.375
Responsiveness (C3)	0.125	0.250	0.375	0.125	0.250	0.375	0.000	0.000	0.000

Table 13. The total-relation fuzzy matrix for the criteria of D1

Criteria	C1			C2			C3		
User Friendly (C1)	0.120	0.455	2.333	0.320	0.727	2.667	0.320	0.727	2.667
Accessibility (C2)	0.302	0.679	2.485	0.102	0.406	2.152	0.213	0.606	2.424
Responsiveness (C3)	0.178	0.533	2.182	0.178	0.533	2.182	0.067	0.333	1.909

Table 14. Total impact-relationship degrees and the weights for the criteria of D1

Criteria	$\tilde{D}_i^{def}$	$\tilde{R}_i^{def}$	$\tilde{D}_i^{def} + \tilde{R}_i^{def}$	$\tilde{D}_i^{def} - \tilde{R}_i^{def}$	Weights
C1	2.825	2.517	5.342	0.308	0.354
C2	2.550	2.517	5.066	0.033	0.335
C3	2.177	2.517	4.694	-0.341	0.311

Table 15. The initial direct-relation fuzzy matrix for the criteria of D2

Criteria	C4			C5			C6		
Assurance (C4)	0.000	0.000	0.000	0.500	0.750	1.000	0.250	0.500	0.750
Image (C5)	0.500	0.750	1.000	0.000	0.000	0.000	0.500	0.750	1.000
Experience (C6)	0.250	0.500	0.750	0.500	0.750	1.000	0.000	0.000	0.000

Table 16. Normalized direct-relation fuzzy matrix for the criteria of D2

Criteria	C4			C5			C6		
Assurance (C4)	0.000	0.000	0.000	0.250	0.375	0.500	0.125	0.250	0.375
Image (C5)	0.250	0.375	0.500	0.000	0.000	0.000	0.250	0.375	0.500
Experience (C6)	0.125	0.250	0.375	0.250	0.375	0.500	0.000	0.000	0.000

Table 17. The total-relation fuzzy matrix for the criteria of D2

Criteria	C4			C5			C6		
Assurance (C4)	0.111	0.467	3.364	0.333	0.800	4.000	0.222	0.667	3.636
Image (C5)	0.333	0.800	4.000	0.167	0.600	4.000	0.333	0.800	4.000
Experience (C6)	0.222	0.667	3.636	0.333	0.800	4.000	0.111	0.467	3.364

Table 18. Total impact-relationship degrees and the weights for the criteria of D2

Criteria	$\tilde{D}_i^{def}$	$\tilde{R}_i^{def}$	$\tilde{D}_i^{def} + \tilde{R}_i^{def}$	$\tilde{D}_i^{def} - \tilde{R}_i^{def}$	Weights
C4	3.457	3.457	6.914	-0.001	0.322
C5	3.817	3.816	7.633	0.001	0.356
C6	3.457	3.457	6.914	-0.001	0.322

Chapter 2
The Criteria of Websites Quality on Consumers' Buying Behavior:
An Applicaiton of DEMATEL Method

Kemal Vatansever
Alanya Alaaddin Keykubat University, Turkey

Hatice Handan Öztemiz
Alanya Alaaddin Keykubat University, Turkey

ABSTRACT

The aim of this chapter is to investigate the effects of website quality criteria that affect the customer purchasing intentions. Website quality criteria are categorized as security, privacy, usability and web design, convenience, trust and confidence, product value, and product customization. In this study, the criteria are chosen in accordance with the two main criteria of the technology acceptance model. In this chapter, Decision-Making Trial and Evaluation Laboratory (DEMATEL) is used to evaluate the effects of criteria on each other from a causal perspective. According to the research findings, security, trust and trustworthiness, product value, and product customization criteria are more effective than privacy, usability, and web design convenience criteria.

DOI: 10.4018/978-1-5225-8238-0.ch002

INTRODUCTION

As we begin to live in a digitalized world in all aspects, businesses cannot resist to this change. Even though the mobile apps are becoming current trend, websites are still the most common way of businesses' digital existence.

Technology, which is one of the biggest focuses of globalization, is one of the most important facts of today. First of all, it is almost impossible to ignore the effect of technology in people's communication with each other and trade. In addition to the fact that technology provides comfort in trade in many respects, it has shown as online purchase / online commerce that connects the customer directly to the company. For this reason, in order to provide more competitive advantage, parallel to the popularity of online commerce, firms must do what the platform needs. It is therefore important to have a better website and determine what criteria the customers are paying attention to on their website.

Websites' performances can be considered as an indicator of firm performance, thus website performances are one of the subject that is been studied by both researchers and business analysts, throughly. From that point, this study try to focus on website quality criteria that affect the customer purchasing intentions of the companies. By doing that, these criteria are not just mentioned but also discussed the effects on each other.

In order to draw a picture of the general trend of related studies, a through literature review had been conducted and this reiew takes place in second part. As a method that can analyze previously mentioned relations between criteria, DEMATEL has been chosen as the research method of this study and introduced in the third part.

RELATED LITERATURE

The Technology Acceptance Model developed by Davis (1986), describes how users accept technology, and consider customer reviews in relation to the technology effectiveness of the institutions. The two main criteria that cause people to accept and reject information teonology are the main factors of Technology Acceptance Model (Davis,1989). The first is the perceived usefullness, and the second is the perceived ease of use. Perceived usefullness states that people can use information technologies to the extent that they believe and improve their performance. Perceived ease of use, is that information technology can be used without too much effort and that is the reason for people to prefer.

In the literature, as regards the technology acceptance model which examines the behavior of the consumer engaged in internet shopping, there are different studies based on Technology Acceptance Model's main criterias, new criteria and application areas of technology acceptance. In addition to common application areas such as e-procurement, e-shopping, internet connection quality and analysis of social networks, it is also involved in differentiated applications such as e–declaration, Health Information Systems, effects of website quality on online purchase intention. Determining the factors that affect customer satisfaction and customer buying intention in online shopping websites is also an application of the mononology acceptance models.

Liu and Arnett (2000) evaluated the factors affecting the success of the website in electronic commerce. As a result of factor analysis, the four factors for the success of the website in electronic commerce, information and service quality, usability, entertainment, system design quality as stated.

Yang et al. (2004) developed a reliable and valid measurement to measure the quality of online service. In the study, the dimensions of online service quality were determined as reliability, responsiveness, competence, ease of use, confidentiality, product portfolio.

Schaupp & Bélanger (2005) showed that 3 criteria were the result of the conjoint analysis on customer satisfaction in online shopping: merchandising (product facade), privacy (technology factor) and convenience (shopping factor). The sub-factors of the main factors in research are respectively security, privacy, usability and web design; convenience, trust and trustworthiness, delivery ; mechandising, product value and product customization

Lee & Kozar (2006) identified website quality factors and examined the relative importance of choosing the most preferred website and the relationship between website preference and financial performance. In the study, the quality of the website is discussed in 4 dimensions: information quality, service quality, systems quality and vendor-specific quality. According to the findings of this study, system quality is seen as the most important factor and the website with the highest quality produced the highest business performance.

Yüksel (2007) evaluated the quality dimensions of internet sites and determined the quality dimensions as 5 factors, security, reaction, confidence, empathy and concrete objects as a result of the literature survey.

Bai et al. (2008) emphasized the increasing popularity of online shopping and China's effective market in online trading. In particular, researchers investigating the online buying behavior of Chinese customers have found that web site quality has positive effects on customer satisfaction and customer buying intent. In the research, the quality of the website is discussed in 5 functions as purchase information, service/products information, destination information, quality of information and contact information. Usability is another variable of the research model.

Al- Manasraa at al (2013) examined the impact of websites quality which was measured by usability, information quality and service interaction of four major Jordanian telecommunication organizations on the consumer's satisfaction. As a result of this study, it was found that there are very important factors that directly affect the satisfaction of consumers according to test model of usability and service interaction.

Nilashi & Bin İbrahim (2014) emphasized that the perception and attitude of people towards E-commerce and B2C websites significantly affect their online purchase intentions and determined the customer's purchase intent in online shopping by using Topsis and Fuzzy Logic Methods, using the criterias in the Schaupp & Bélanger's (2005) study.

Hasanov & Khalid (2015) examined the influence of website quality on consumers' intention to purchase organic food online based on the Malaysian perspective. In this study, which categorizes the quality of the website as security, satisfaction, information quality, ease of use and quality of service, it is concluded that the quality of the website has an indirect effect through the full mediation of customer satisfaction in online purchasing intentions of health foods in Malaysia.

Li at all (2017) investigated the potential theoretical relationships among economy hotel website quality,eTrust, and online booking intentions in China. In the study, the quality of the website is discussed in 4 dimensions: usability, ease of use, entertainment, and complementarity.

Kocabulut and Albayrak (2017) discussed the relationship between service quality and customer satisfaction of a national airline website in Turkey and examined the website service quality in four dimensions: entertainment, convenience and response time, private communication, confidence.

The evaluation criteria for website quality are summarized in Table 1. In the context of this brief summary, when determining criteria, delivery and merchandising criteria have been disabled from the Schaupp & Bélanger(2005) study, which has a wide range of criteria. Therefore web site quality criteria are defined as security, privacy, usability and web design, convenience, trust and trustworthiness, product value and product customization. Table 2 contains information about the criteria.

Table 1. Summarized result of the previous studies based on website quality criteria

References	Methodology	Criteria of Websites quality
Liu and Arnett (2000)	Factor Analysis	Information and service quality, usability, entertainment learning capability, system quality,
Yang et al. (2004)	SERVQUAL	Reliability, responsiveness, competence, ease of use, confidentiality, product portfolio
Schaupp & Bélanger (2005)	Conjoint Analysis	Security, privacy, usability and web design; convenience, trust and trustworthiness, delivery ; merchandising, product value and product customization
Lee & Kozar (2006)	Analytic Hierarchy Process	Information quality, service quality, systems quality and vendor-specific quality
Yüksel (2007)	SERVQUAL	security, reaction, confidence, empathy and concrete objects
Bai et al. (2008)	Confirmatory factor analysis and Structural Equation Modeling (SEM)	Purchase information, service/products information, destination information, quality of information and contact information
Al- Manasraa at al (2013)	Factor Analysis	Usability, information quality and service interaction
Nilashi & Bin Ibrahim (2014)	TOPSIS and Fuzzy Logic Model	Security, privacy, usability and web design; convenience, trust and trustworthiness, delivery ; merchandising, product value and product customization
Hasanov & Khalid (2015)	A WebQual Model Approach	Security, satisfaction, information quality, ease of use and quality of service
Li at all (2017)	Factor Analysis	Usability, ease of use, entertainment, and complementarity.
Kocabulut and Albayrak (2017)	Penalty-reward contrast analysis	Entertainment, convenience and response time, private communication, confidence.

METHODOLOGY

The Decision Making Trial And Evaluation Laboratory (DEMAEL) method was developed between 1972 and 1976 in the scope of the Geneva Battelle Memorial Institute, Science and Human Relations program, to be used in the solution of complex research and problem groups (Huang, Shyu ve Tzeng, 2007). DEMATEL method is used as a kind of structural modeling approach to analyze the cause and effect relationships between the components of a system (Si et all.2018). This method uses the knowledge of experts to regulate a structural model (Liou, Yen, and Tzeng, 2008). The Criteria weights are determined and criteria can be sorted according to their importance by using DEMATEL. In addition, the degree of influence between the criteria can be measured by DEMATEL.

Table 2. Criterias of website quality

Main Criteria	Feature
Security (C1)	(1) Encryption of information for data transmission provided by the website (Glass,1998; Schaupp & Bélanger 2005) (2) setting an account as required on the website of an account with an ID and password by the user (Ranganathan &Ganapathy,2002; Schaupp & Bélanger 2005) (3) the digital certificates that the website offers to verify the identity and consumer identities (Nilashi & Bin Ibrahim,2014)
Privacy (C2)	(1) The presenting a privacy statement (Schaupp & Bélanger 2005; Gordon, & Schoenbachler,2002 as cited in Nilashi & Bin Ibrahim, 2014) (2) Requesting customer consent to share or distribute private information (Ranganathan &Ganapathy,2002) (3) Customer request confirmation in cookie usage (Schaupp & Bélanger 2005)
Usability and Web Design (C3)	(1) Have a user-friendly interface and ease of use (Schaupp & Bélanger 2005) (2) Have the ability to search quickly and accurately (Schaupp & Bélanger 2005) (3) Providing rich content and interactive mechanisms (Schaupp & Bélanger 2005)
Convenience (C4)	To minimize the effort spent by the consumers during the shopping process and to save time with easy shopping presentation process ((1) Product categorization for ease of shopping (Schaupp & Bélanger 2005) (2) he existence of various payment methods (eg credit card, bank transfer and online money transfer) (Ranganathan &Ganapathy,2002) (3) product exchange and return services (Nilashi & Bin Ibrahim,2014) (4) online forum service that allows consumers to share information (Nilashi & Bin Ibrahim,2014)
Trust and Trustworthiness (C5)	(1) using a vendor-approved transaction platform (Bellanger et all,2002) (2) instant disclosure and online help provided by the seller in the event of problems encountered by the consumer (Nilashi & Bin Ibrahim,2014) (3) transaction contracts provided by the seller specifying the rights and responsibilities of trading organizations ((Nilashi & Bin Ibrahim,2014)
Product Value (C6)	(1) product characteristics, price and cost match the customer expectation (Brukcs et all.2000) (2) product pricing reflects the product brand (Turban et all.2006) (3) Continuous service before and after sales (Anand, 2007)
Product Customization (C7)	(1) presentation of special products by sellers (Schaupp & Bélanger 2005; Anand, 2007) (2) Wide range of products by venders (Schaupp & Bélanger 2005; Anand, 2007

After taking the opinions of the experts, the DEMATEL method in 5 steps is as follows (Sumrit & Anuntavoranich,2013; Vatansever and Akgül,2017):

Step 1: Create a direct relationship Matrix Z

Step 2: Create a direct relationship matrix to normalize D

Step 3: Prepare the total relationship Matrix T

Step 4: İdentify the sender and receiver group

Step 5: Adjust the threshold value and obtain the effect-oriented graph diagram

While determining the relations between the criteria by the expert group, The comparison scale used can be made between 0-3 or 0-4 (Karaoğlan,2016). The Comparison scale is shown in Table 3.

Step 1: If the number of experts evaluating the criteria is more than one, the arithmetic average of the points given is taken. Then, these values are placed in the diagonal of the matrix and "0" are obtained in an asymmetric matrix. This matrix is called the direct relationship matrix (Z).

$$Z = \begin{bmatrix} 0 & \cdots & Z_{1n} \\ \vdots & \ddots & \vdots \\ Z_{n1} & \cdots & 0 \end{bmatrix} \qquad i,j = 1,2,3,\ldots,n$$

Step 2: After obtaining the direct relationship matrix, the maximum sum of each row and column is obtained as shown in Equation 1

$$s = \max\left(\max \sum_{j=1}^{n} Z_{ij}, \sum_{i=1}^{n} Z_{ij} \right) \qquad (1)$$

Then each element of the matrix is divided by the value "s" and normalized direct relationship matrix (D) is generated.

$$D = Z \big/ s \qquad (2)$$

Table 3. The comparison scale

Numeric Value	Definition
0	Non-effective
1	Low effective
2	Mediun effective
3	Highly effective
4	Very highly effective

Source: Karaoğlan,2016:13

Step 3: Matrix D is subtracted from the unit matrix, the opposite is taken and multiplied by the matrix D again as shown in Equation 3. Thus, the total relationship Matrix (T) is obtained.

$$\lim_{K \to \infty} D + D^2 + D^3 + \ldots + D^K$$

$$T = D + D^2 + D^3 + \ldots + D^K = D\left(1 - D\right)^{-1}$$

Step 4: The sum of the total direct relationship matrix T is R and the column sum C is calculated:

$$R = \sum_{j=1}^{n} t_{ij} \ , \quad C = \sum_{i=1}^{n} t_{ij} \tag{3}$$

The R+C value indicates the positive or negative relationship between each criterion and the other criterion. The R-C value shows the net effect of the criteria on the system. These values are used to determine which receiver and sender criteria.

If R-C value is positive, that criterion is accepted as a cause or sender criterion as it has a higher effect on others than the combined effect of other on itself. On the other hand, if the R-C value is negative, this criterion is considered as the receiever criterion (Kaya, 2017).

Step 5: The effect-directional graph diagram is obtained by the points (R + C, R-C) on the coordinate plane that is the horizontal axis R+C and the vertical axis R-C.

The value of the threshold to be used can influence the relationship between the criteria and allows the solution to be simple or much more complex (Gürbüz & Çavdarcı,2018). The following equations are used to determine the criteria weights (Eroğlu,2014):

$$w_i = \sqrt{\left(R_i + C_i\right)^2 + \left(R_i - C_i\right)^2}$$

$$W_i = \frac{w_i}{\sum_{i=1}^{n} w_i}$$

RESULTS AND DISCUSSIONS

The criteria were evaluated by experts using the comparison scale in Table 3. As a result of the evaluations of the experts, The Direct Relationship Matrix (Z) in Table 4 is obtained.

It has determined that the S value mentioned in Equation (1) is 13.250 by the direct reletionship matrix (Z). Subsequently, the Normalized Direct Relationship Matrix (D) obtained in Table 5 is obtained by dividing each element of the matrix by this value.

Once the normalized Direct Relationship Matrix is established, the transaction in Equation 3 is performed and the Total Relationship Matrix (T) is shown in Table 6 is obtained.

After obtaining the Total Relationship Matrix, R, C, R+C and R-C is found and is shown in Table 7.

When Table 7 is examined, it is seen that negative R-C values are provided for Privacy, Usability and Web Design Convenience criteria. Each of these criteria is a receiver criteria. And similarly, it is seen that positive R-C values are provided for Security, Trust and Trustworthiness, Product Value and Product Customization. This shows that these criteria are sender criteria. It should not be forgotten that sender criteria are more effective in the system. The fact that the criteria remain in the positive zone of the distribution chart (see Figure 1) also shows that they are senders.

Table 4. The direct relationship matrix (Z)

	Security	Privacy	Usability and	Convenie	Trust and Trust	Product Val	Product Customiz	Total
Security	0,0000	3,0000	2,0000	2,2500	1,7500	1,5000	1,0000	11,5000
Privacy	1,7500	0,0000	2,0000	1,7500	2,5000	1,0000	0,7500	9,7500
Usability and We	0,7500	1,7500	0,0000	2,7500	1,2500	1,0000	0,7500	8,2500
Convenience	0,7500	3,0000	2,2500	0,0000	1,7500	1,5000	1,0000	10,2500
Trust and Trust	2,0000	3,0000	3,0000	2,2500	0,0000	1,2500	0,7500	12,2500
Product Value	1,5000	1,2500	2,2500	2,2500	0,7500	0,0000	1,5000	9,5000
Product Customi	0,7500	0,7500	0,7500	2,0000	1,0000	2,2500	0,0000	7,5000
Total	7,5000	12,7500	12,2500	13,2500	9,0000	8,5000	5,7500	

	Security	Privacy	Usability and	Convenie	Trust and Trust	Product Val	Product Customiz	Total
Security	0,0000	0,2264	0,1509	0,1698	0,1321	0,1132	0,0755	0,8679
Privacy	0,1321	0,0000	0,1509	0,1321	0,1887	0,0755	0,0566	0,7358
Usability and We	0,0566	0,1321	0,0000	0,2075	0,0943	0,0755	0,0566	0,6226
Convenience	0,0566	0,2264	0,1698	0,0000	0,1321	0,1132	0,0755	0,7736
Trust and Trust	0,1509	0,2264	0,2264	0,1698	0,0000	0,0943	0,0566	0,9245
Product Value	0,1132	0,0943	0,1698	0,1698	0,0566	0,0000	0,1132	0,7170
Product Customi	0,0566	0,0566	0,0566	0,1509	0,0755	0,1698	0,0000	0,5660
Total	0,5660	0,9623	0,9245	1,0000	0,6792	0,6415	0,4340	

Table 5. The normalized direct relationship matrix (D)

	C_1	C_2	C_3	C_4	C_5	C_6	C_7	Total
C_1	0,0000	0,2264	0,1509	0,1698	0,1321	0,1132	0,0755	0,8679
C_2	0,1321	0,0000	0,1509	0,1321	0,1887	0,0755	0,0566	0,7358
C_3	0,0566	0,1321	0,0000	0,2075	0,0943	0,0755	0,0566	0,6226
C_4	0,0566	0,2264	0,1698	0,0000	0,1321	0,1132	0,0755	0,7736
C_5	0,1509	0,2264	0,2264	0,1698	0,0000	0,0943	0,0566	0,9245
C_6	0,1132	0,0943	0,1698	0,1698	0,0566	0,0000	0,1132	0,7170
C_7	0,0566	0,0566	0,0566	0,1509	0,0755	0,1698	0,0000	0,5660
Total	0,5660	0,9623	0,9245	1,0000	0,6792	0,6415	0,4340	

Table 6. The total relationship matrix (T)

	C_1	C_2	C_3	C_4	C_5	C_6	C_7	Total
C_1	0,2958	0,6806	0,6014	0,6308	0,4848	0,4102	0,2918	3,3954
C_2	0,3771	0,4366	0,5476	0,5448	0,4825	0,3417	0,2479	2,9783
C_3	0,2707	0,4822	0,3488	0,5344	0,3581	0,3002	0,2187	2,5131
C_4	0,3199	0,6225	0,5649	0,4332	0,4437	0,3753	0,2671	3,0267
C_5	0,4423	0,7098	0,6864	0,6602	0,3892	0,4100	0,2873	3,5853
C_6	0,3358	0,4830	0,5252	0,5459	0,3499	0,2574	0,2858	2,7829
C_7	0,2487	0,3767	0,3677	0,4556	0,3063	0,3607	0,1535	2,2691
Total	2,2903	3,7914	3,6420	3,8049	2,8144	2,4556	1,7520	

Table 7. Affecting and affected factor groups

	R	C	R+C	R-C
Security	3,3954	2,2903	5,6857	1,1051
Privacy	2,9783	3,7914	6,7697	-0,8131
Usability and Web Design	2,5131	3,6420	6,1551	-1,1290
Convenience	3,0267	3,8049	6,8316	-0,7782
Trust and Trustworthiness	3,5853	2,8144	6,3998	0,7709
Product Value	2,7829	2,4556	5,2385	0,3273
Product Customization	2,2691	1,7520	4,0211	0,5170

Figure 1. Distribution chart

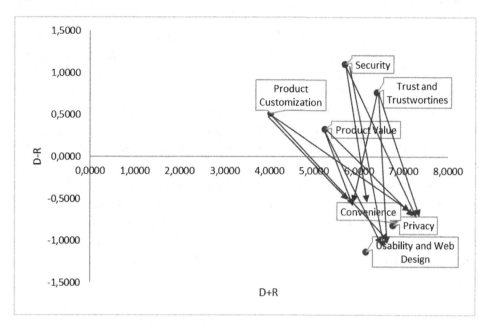

Finally, the benchmark weights are found in the final stage of the DEMATEL method and the criteria are listed according to their priority. The benchmark weights is shown in Table 8.

As seen in Table 8, the most leading factor in the ranking of criteria was conveinence with 0.16571 weight. It is followed by privacy criteria with a weight value of 0.16433.

Table 8. The criteria weights and criteria priorities table

	$(R+C)^2$	$(R-C)^2$	$\sqrt{(R+C)^2+(R-C)^2}$	The Criteria Weights	Criteria Priorities
Security	32,327	1,22121	5,79208	0,13959	5
Privacy	45,8292	0,6611	6,81838	0,16433	2
Usability and Web Design	37,8854	1,27453	6,25779	0,15082	4
Convenience	46,671	0,60567	6,87581	0,16571	1
Trust and Trustworthiness	40,957	0,59424	6,44602	0,15535	3
Product Value	27,4414	0,10712	5,24867	0,1265	6
Product Customization	16,1694	0,26733	16,4367	0,09771	7

CONCLUSION

The main purpose of the study is to determine the effectiveness levels of the website quality criteria that affect the purchasing tendency of the customer. In this study, it is emphasized that what are the web site quality criteria and which criteria are chosen by choosing from the studies in the literature.In this context, it can be said that the criteria set for the study are the website quality criteria accepted by many researchers and the criteria that lead the customer to buy for the performance of the company.

As a result of the research, Convenience, Privacy, Trust and Trustworthiness's have 0.116571, 0,16433 and 0,15535 weights respectively and they formed the first three rankings in severity. However, the sender criteria are more effective on the system: security, trust and reliability, product value and product customization.

Website quality criteria are considered for all companies providing online commerce services. It is not a sector application. There may be a limitation of this research. For this reason, it is recommended to evaluate websites of different sectors using criteria in the research.

REFERENCES

Al-Manasraa, E. A., Khair, M., Zaid, S.A., & TaherQutaishatc, F. (2013). Investigating the Impact of Website Quality on Consumers' Satisfaction in Jordanian Telecommunication Sector. *Arab Economic and Business Journal, 8*, 31–37.

Anand, A. (2007). E-satisfaction—A comprehensive framework. *Second international conference on internet and web applications and service (ICIW'07)*, 13–19, 55–60.

Bai, B., Law, R., & Wen, L. (2008). The impact of website quality on customer satisfaction and purchase intentions: Evidence from Chinese online visitors. *International Journal of Hospitality Management, 27*(3), 391–402. doi:10.1016/j.ijhm.2007.10.008

Brucks, M., Zeithaml, V. A., & Naylor, G. (2000). Price and Brand name as indicators of quality dimensions for consumer durables. *Journal of the Academy of Marketing Science, 25*, 139–374.

Eroğlu, Ö. (2014). *Assessment of Maintenance/Repair Alternatives With The Fuzzy Dematel And Smaa-2 Methods* (Unpublished Master dissertation). Turkish Military Academy Defense Science Institute, Department of Supply and Logistics Management, Ankara, Turkey.

Davis, F. D. (1985). *A technology acceptance model for empirically testing new end-user information systems: Theory and results* (Unpublished Doctoral dissertation). Massachusetts Institute of Technology, Cambridge, MA.

Davis, F. D. (1989). Perceived Usefulness, Perceived Ease of Use, and User Acceptance of Information Technology. *Management Information Systems Quarterly, 13*(3), 319–340. doi:10.2307/249008

Belanger, F., Hiller, J. S., & Smith, W. J. (2002). Trustworthiness in electronic commerce: The role of privacy, security, and site attributes. *The Journal of Strategic Information Systems, 11*(3-4), 245–270. doi:10.1016/S0963-8687(02)00018-5

Gabus, A., & Fontela, E. (1972). *World Problems, An Invitation to Further Thought within The Framework of DEMATEL.* Geneva, Switzerland: Battelle Geneva Research Centre.

Glass, A. D. (1998). A countdown to the age of secure electronic commerce. *Credit World, 86*, 29–31.

Gürbüz, F., & Çavdarcı, S. (2018). Evaluation of problem areas related to the recycling sector via DEMATEL and Grey DEMATEL Method. *Sakarya University Journal of the Institute of Science and Technology, 22*(2), 285–301.

Hasanov, J., & Khalid, H. (2015). The Impact of Website Quality on Online Purchase Intention of Organic Food in Malaysia: A WebQual Model Approach. *Procedia Computer Science, 72,* 382–389. doi:10.1016/j.procs.2015.12.153

Huang, C. Y., Shyu, J. Z., & Tzeng, G. H. (2007). Reconfiguring The Innovation Policy Portfolios For Taiwan's SIP Mall Industry. *Technovation, 27*(12), 744–765. doi:10.1016/j.technovation.2007.04.002

Kocabulut, Ö., & Albayrak, T. (2017). The E*ffect of Website Service Quality on Customer Satisfaction. Anatolia: Journal of Tourism Research, 28*(2), 293–303.

Kaya, R. (2017). *Integration Of Bayesian Networks With Dematel For Causal Risk Analysis: A Supplier Selection Case Study In Automotive Industry* (Unpublished doctoral dissertation). University of Hacettepe, Ankara, Turkey.

Lee, Y., & Kozar, K. A. (2006). Investigating the effect of website quality on e-business success: An analytic hierarchy process (AHP) approach. *Decision Support Systems, 42*(3), 1383–1401. doi:10.1016/j.dss.2005.11.005

Li, L., Peng, M., Jiang, N., & Law, R. (2017). An empirical study on the influence of economy hotel website quality on online booking intentions. *International Journal of Hospitality Management, 63,* 1–10. doi:10.1016/j.ijhm.2017.01.001

Liou, J. J. H., Yen, L., & Tzeng, G. H. (2008). Building An Effective Safety Management system for Airlines. *Journal of Air Transport Management, 14,* 20–26. doi:10.1016/j.jairtraman.2007.10.002

Liu, C., & Arnett, K. P. (2000). Exploring The Factors Associated With Web Site Success In the Context of Electronic Commerce. *Information & Management, 38*(1), 23–33. doi:10.1016/S0378-7206(00)00049-5

Ranganathan, C., & Ganapathy, S. (2002). Key dimensions of business to consumer web sites. *Information & Management, 39*(6), 457–465. doi:10.1016/S0378-7206(01)00112-4

Schaupp, L. C., & Belanger, F. (2005). A conjoint analysis of online consumer satisfaction. *Journal of Electronic Commerce Research, 6*(2), 95–111.

Si, S. L., You, X. Y., Liu, H. C., & Zhang, P. (2018). DEMATEL Technique: A Systematic Review of the State-of-the-Art Literature on Methodologies and Applications. *Mathematical Problems in Engineering*, 1–33.

Sumrit, D., & Anuntavoranich, P. (2013). Using DEMATEL method to analyze the causal relations on technological innovation capability evaluation factors in Thai technology-based firms. *International Transaction Journal of Engineering, Management, & Applied Sciences & Technologies*, 4(2), 81–103.

Vatansever, K., & Akgül, Y. (2017). Evaluation of Information Management Infrastructure and factors affecting process competencies with Demterial method. *International Symposium on Social Sciences*.

Wu, W. W., & Lee, Y. T. (2007). Developing Global Managers' Competencies Using The Fuzzy DEMATEL Method. *Expert Systems with Applications*, 32(2), 499–507. doi:10.1016/j.eswa.2005.12.005

Yang, Z., Jun, M., & Peterson, R. (2004). Measuring Customer Perceived Online Service Quality, Scale Development and Managerial Implications. *International Journal of Operations & Production Management*, 24(11), 1149–1174. doi:10.1108/01443570410563278

Yüksel, H. (2007). Evaluation Of Quality Dimensions Of Web Sites. *Anadolu University Journal of Social Sciences*, 7(1), 519–536.

Chapter 3

Classification of the Usage of Wikipedia as a Tool of Teaching in Higher Education With Decision Tree Model

Cengiz Gazeloğlu
Suleyman Demirel University, Turkey

Zeynep Hande Toyganözü
Suleyman Demirel University, Turkey

Cüneyt Toyganözü
Suleyman Demirel University, Turkey

Murat Kemal Keleş
Applied Sciences University of Isparta, Turkey

ABSTRACT

Wikipedia is a source that has been used at many universities around the world for students to gain some skills and be motivated positively. In higher education, some academicians have a positive view on the teaching usefulness of Wikipedia, and some of them are determined to use classical teaching. In this chapter, teaching use of Wikipedia in all faculty members of the Universitat Oberta de Catalunya are used as data. Then an entropy-based decision tree algorithm was developed. Wikipedia users and non-users are classified according to some aspects with this decision tree. Thus, it can be understood that whether Wikipedia has been used as a teaching tool by academicians or not. So, researchers can have information about the usefulness of Wikipedia in teaching and the intentions in use of it by academicians.

DOI: 10.4018/978-1-5225-8238-0.ch003

INTRODUCTION

In advance, people who referred to multi-volume encyclopedias, such as the Encyclopedia Britannica to access information have promoted to the online encyclopedia with easy and fast access to information as the internet begins to be in our lives recently. Wikipedia is one of the world's most visited and used online encyclopedia. Its content is jointly created by volunteers from all over the world. However, Wikipedia cannot be thought as a reliable source for academic writing or research, since its content can be changed at any time. On the other hand, in terms of providing easy access to information on any topic.

Wikipedia is a source that has been used at many universities around the world for students to gain some skills and be motivated positively. So, there are two different idea on the teaching use of Wikipedia in higher education: Some academicians have got a positive view on the teaching usefulness of Wikipedia, some of them are determined to use classical teaching use instead of Wikipedia use.

OpenCourseWare (OCW) is a project that is included the course lessons created at universities and published for free via the Internet. It allows students to become better prepared for classes. The OpenCourseWare (OCW) movement began in 2001 with the creation of the initiative OpenCourseWare (OCW) at MIT (Massachusetts Institute of Technology), then many universities have created this project. The Universitat Oberta de Catalunya (UOC) launched in 1994, is a pure virtual online university located in Barcelona. As a pioneering university, UOC provides all community members with a Virtual Campus where all teaching activities are carried on, including the use of web 2.0 tools such as blogs or wikis, among others (Aibar et al., 2013).

In this chapter, by using an entropy-based decision tree algorithm, it is investigated that whether Wikipedia has been used as a teaching tool by academicians or not. For this purpose, teaching use of Wikipedia in all faculty members of the Universitat Oberta de Catalunya are used as data. Thus, the researchers can have information about the usefulness of Wikipedia in teaching and the intentions in use of it by academicians. In addition, Wikipedia users and non-users are classified according to their age, gender, academic title, department, teaching experience, and their effect on Wikipedia usage with this decision tree.

BACKGROUND

Data mining recognized as a sub-process of Knowledge Discovery in Databases (KDD) is a process to extract information from big data. It is an interdisciplinary field of finding correlations that enable us to make predictions about the future from large data sets to provide us information bringing algorithms and methods together from different areas such as artificial intelligence, machine learning, statistics, mathematics, and database systems.

The main goal of the data mining is to transform the extracted information into a comprehensible structure for further use.

Data mining functionalities are used to specify the kinds of patterns or knowledge to be found in data mining tasks. The functionalities include characterization and discrimination; the mining of frequent patterns, associations, and correlations; classification and regression; cluster analysis; and outlier detection (Han and Kamber, 2012).

Table 1 includes some of the historical developments of data mining and, in brief, the processes that the data mining has gone through from the 1960s to the present.

Data classification is an essential part of data mining. Classification is learning a function that maps (classifies) a data item into one of several predefined classes (Weiss and Kulikowski, 1991; Hand 1981; Fayyad et al., 1996). So, data classification is a two-step process, consisting of a *learning step* where a classification model is constructed and a *classification step* where the model is used to predict class labels for given data (Han and Kamber, 2012). Classification method makes use of mathematical techniques such as decision trees, linear programming, neural network and statistics (Fakhimi, 2015).

At present, decision tree model is one of the most effective and widely used methods for data mining. They are used as a convenient method for classification and

Figure 1. The data mining process
Source: (Bigus, 1996)

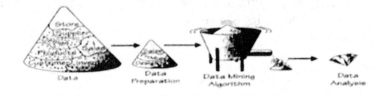

Table 1. Historical process of data mining

Developmental Steps	Answered Decision Problem	Usable Technologies	Product Providers	Characteristics
Data Collection (1960s)	" What was my total revenue in the last 5 years?"	Computers, Tape, Discs	IBM, CDC	Backward, Static Data Distribution
Data Access (1980s)	" What were unit sales in New England last March? "	Relational Databases, SQL, ODBC	Oracle, Sybase, Informix, IBM, Microsoft	Backward Dynamic Data Distribution at Record Level
Data Warehouses and Decision Support Systems (1990s)	" What were unit sales in New England last March? Drill down to Boston. "	OLAP, Multidimensional Database Systems, Data Warehouses	Pilot, Comshare, Arbor, Cognos, MicroStrategy	Backward Dynamic Data Distribution at Multiple Levels
Data Mining (Today)	"What's likely to happen to Boston unit sales next month and why?"	Advanced Algorithms, Multiprocessor Computers, Large Databases	Pilot, Lockheed, IBM, SGI, SPSS, SAS, Microsoft, etc.	Proactive Information Distribution for Future

(Source: An Introduction to Data Mining, Pilot Software Whitepaper, Pilot Software, 1998)

estimation problem due to its simple and easy to understand structure. A decision tree is a classifier expressed as a recursive partition of the training instances. It is constructed in a top-down manner, in each iteration, the instance space is partitioned by choosing the best attribute to split them (Agrawal and Gupta, 2013; Patel and Singh 2015).

Compared to other classification methods, decision tree classifiers are popular because those are easier to configure and have good accuracy. The construction of decision tree classifiers does not require any domain knowledge or parameter setting, and therefore is appropriate for exploratory knowledge discovery. Decision trees can handle multidimensional data. The learning and classification steps of decision tree induction are simple and fast. Decision tree induction algorithms have been used for classification in many application areas such as medicine, manufacturing and production, financial analysis, astronomy, and molecular biology (Han and Kamber, 2012).

There are several decision tree algorithms. Some of them are Iterative Dichotomizer version 3 (ID3) (Quinlan, 1986) and C4.5 (an industrial version of ID3) (Quinlan, 1993) which are entropy-based algorithms. ID3 decision tree algorithm was first introduced by J. Ross Quinlan (1986), a researcher in machine learning, to minimize the computational cost of classifying a given dataset. It is based on an inductive learning and heuristic concept introduced by Hunt et al. (1966). ID3 decision trees apply the notion of entropy introduced by Shannon (1948) to select the most appropriate attributes as the nodes of a classification tree (Li and Claramunt, 2006).

Quinlan later presented an entropy-based discretization with the C4.5 algorithm (a successor of ID3) (Quinlan, 1993). One of the latest studies that compares decision trees and other learning algorithms shows that C4.5 has a very good combination of error rate and speed (Hssina et al., 2014; Lim et al., 2000). The algorithm has the ability to handle an incomplete training dataset (Laencina et al., 2015), and to prune the resulting decision tree in order to reduce its size and optimize the decision path (Cherfi et al., 2018).

METHODOLOGY

Decision Tree Method

Decision tree algorithm constructs a flowchart-like structure where each internal (non-leaf) node denotes a test on an attribute, each branch corresponds to an outcome of the test, and each external (leaf) node denotes a class prediction. The topmost node in a tree is the root node. At each node, the algorithm chooses the "best" attribute to partition the data into individual classes (Han and Kamber, 2012).

The steps of the construction of a decision tree algorithm are as follows:

1. Create the S learning set.
2. Identify the best splitting attribute in a S set.
3. Create a node of the tree with the selected attribute and create sub-nodes or sub-leaves of the tree from that node. Identify the sample of sub-data set belonging to sub-nodes.
4. For each sub-data set created at the 3rd step
   a. If all samples belong to the same class
   b. If there is no attribute to split samples
   c. If there is no sample held the value of remaining attributes, end the process.

In all other cases, to split sub-dataset continue from the 2nd step (http://mail.baskent.edu.tr/~20410964/DM_8.pdf).

Figure 2. An example of a decision tree

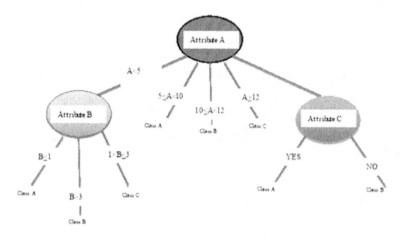

Figure 2 displays an example of a decision tree with 3 variables and 3 separate classes. The most important point in constructing decision trees is to determine which variable is the first node, that is, the root node.

The ID3 decision tree algorithm, first introduced by J. Ross Quinlan is a classification algorithm based on Information Entropy. It depends on the idea that all examples are mapped to different categories according to different values of the condition attribute set (Adhatrao et al., 2013).

C4.5, an extension of ID3, is a well-known decision tree algorithm to select the best attribute for classification. As a statistical classifier, C4.5 develops ID3 with the following changes: handling training data with missing values of attributes, handling differing cost attributes, pruning the decision tree after its creation and handling attributes with discrete and continuous values (Adhatrao, 2013).

For identifying the best splitting attribute of decision tree methods such as ID3, C4.5, the information gain is measured for each attribute. Entropy is used in the information gain measurement. The higher the information gain, the lower the entropy. Then, one can converge to the optimum classification.

Entropy is a measurement of uncertainty or randomness in a data set and it is a number between 0 and 1, independently of the size of the set. If all data in a set belong to a single class, then the entropy is zero (i.e., there is no uncertainty). The entropy would be maximum when the probabilities are all equal.

Given a database state D, H(D) finds the entropy in that state by using the following formula.

$$H(D) = \sum_{i=1}^{s} \left[p_i \log \left(\frac{1}{p_i} \right) \right]$$

When that state is split into s new states $S = \left\{ D_1, D_2, ..., D_s \right\}$, the entropy of those states can be looked at again. Each step chooses the state that orders splitting the most.

The algorithm C4.5 uses the Gain Ratio instead of information gain. The Gain Ratio is defined as

$$GainRatio\left(D, S\right) = \frac{Gain(D, S)}{H \left(\frac{|D_1|}{|D|}, ..., \frac{|D_s|}{|D|} \right)},$$

where $Gain(D, S) = H(D) - \sum_{i=1}^{s} P(D_i) H(D_i)$ and $H \left(\frac{|D_1|}{|D|}, ..., \frac{|D_s|}{|D|} \right)$ is splitting information. For splitting purposes, C4.5 uses the largest Gain Ratio that ensures a larger than average information gain (Dunham, 2012).

C4.5 maps the training set and uses the information gain ratio as a measurement to select splitting attributes and generates nodes from the root to the leaves (Cherfi, 2018). At each node of the tree, C4.5 chooses one attribute of the data that most effectively splits data set of samples S into subsets that can be one class or the other (Xiaoliang et. al., 2009). It is the normalized information gain (difference in entropy) that results from choosing an attribute for splitting the data. The attribute factor with the highest normalized information gain is considered to make the decision. The C4.5 algorithm then continues on the smaller sub-lists having next highest normalized information gain (Adhatrao, 2013).

Weka

Weka is the name of the software developed at the University of Waikato in New Zealand in 1993 for the purpose of machine learning and consists of the initials of the words "Waikato Environment for Knowledge Analysis". It includes most of the widely used data mining algorithms and methods. Basically, three data mining operations can be done with Weka: Classification, clustering and association. (https://tr.wikipedia.org/wiki/Weka)

Data

For the application of the study, the data used from the web site https://archieve.ics. uci.edu/ml/datasets/wiki4HE. It is an online survey delivered to all faculty members of the Universitat Oberta de Catalunya (UOC). Data were collected through this online survey sent to all full-time and part-time professors (2,128 people) at the university at the end of 2012 (Meseguer-Artol et. al., 2016).

Measurement

A 41-question questionnaire was held to measure effects of some aspects of the teaching use of Wikipedia in higher education. Some of the questions were scaled by 5-point Likert scale, ranging from "Strongly disagree (1)" to "Strongly agree (5)" (level of agreement) or from "Never (1)"to "Very often (5)" (frequency) (Aibar et al., 2013).

CLASSIFICATION OF THE USAGE OF WIKIPEDIA

Data in the dataset are classified by C4.5 algorithm with Weka programming. At the end of the classification the correct classification rate is calculated as 89,0323%. Since the correct classification rate is a high value, the classification made by C4.5 algorithm can be thought that it is successful. Related confusion matrix is formed as follows:

The decision tree algorithm and the decision tree table obtained by using C4.5 algorithm can be seen in Appendix 1 and Appendix 2, respectively. Since the information gain is the largest for the condition "I contribute to Wikipedia", this condition became the root node of the tree and the tree started to branch from here. As can be seen from the decision tree table, there are 46 leaves and 59 branches on the generated decision tree. In the decision tree, while each rectangular represents a class, each ellipse represents a condition.

Formed 46 classes in the decision tree are as follows:

Table 2. The confusion Matrix

Non-user	User	
236	6	Non-user
28	13	User

C1. Academicians who never contribute to Wikipedia.

C2. Female academicians who contribute to Wikipedia rarely.

C3. Male academicians who have no Ph.D. and contribute to Wikipedia rarely.

C4. Male academicians who have Ph.D. and contribute to Wikipedia rarely and who are strongly disagree with the thought that "Wikipedia improves visibility of students' work".

C5. Male academicians who have Ph.D. and contribute to Wikipedia rarely and who are disagree with the thought that "Wikipedia improves visibility of students' work".

C6. Male academicians who have Ph.D. and contribute to Wikipedia rarely and who are neutral with the thought that "Wikipedia improves visibility of students' work".

C7. Male academicians who have Ph.D. and contribute to Wikipedia rarely and who are agree with the thought that "Wikipedia improves visibility of students' work".

C8. Male academicians who have Ph.D. and contribute to Wikipedia rarely and who are strongly agree with the thought that "Wikipedia improves visibility of students' work".

C9. Academicians who contribute to Wikipedia once in a while, consult Wikipedia for other academic related issues never.

C10. Academicians who contribute to Wikipedia once in a while, consult Wikipedia for other academic related issues rarely.

C11. Academicians who contribute to Wikipedia once in a while, consult Wikipedia for other academic related issues once in a while.

C12. Academicians who contribute to Wikipedia once in a while, consult Wikipedia for other academic related issues very often and who are neutral about the thought that "It is easy to have a record of the contributions made in Wikipedia".

C13. Academicians who contribute to Wikipedia once in a while, consult Wikipedia for other academic related issues very often and who are strongly disagree with the thought that "It is easy to have a record of the contributions made in Wikipedia".

C14. Academicians who contribute to Wikipedia once in a while, consult Wikipedia for other academic related issues very often and who are disagree with the thought that "It is easy to have a record of the contributions made in Wikipedia".

C15. Academicians who contribute to Wikipedia once in a while, consult Wikipedia for other academic related issues very often and who are agree with the thought that "It is easy to have a record of the contributions made in Wikipedia".

C16. Academicians who contribute to Wikipedia once in a while, consult Wikipedia for other academic related issues very often and who are strongly agree with the thought that "It is easy to have a record of the contributions made in Wikipedia".

C17. Academicians who contribute to Wikipedia once in a while, consult Wikipedia for other academic related issues sometimes and who are strongly disagree with the thought that "Wikipedia is useful for teaching".

C18. Academicians who contribute to Wikipedia once in a while, consult Wikipedia for other academic related issues very often and who are disagree with the thought that "Wikipedia is useful for teaching".

C19. Academicians who contribute to Wikipedia once in a while, consult Wikipedia for other academic related issues very often and who are neutral about the thought that "Wikipedia is useful for teaching".

C20. Academicians who contribute to Wikipedia once in a while, consult Wikipedia for other academic related issues very often and who are strongly agree with the thought that "Wikipedia is useful for teaching".

C21. Academicians who contribute to Wikipedia once in a while, consult Wikipedia for other academic related issues sometimes and who are agree with the thought that "Wikipedia is useful for teaching" and who are strongly agree with the thought that "I agree my students use Wikipedia in my courses".

C22. Academicians who contribute to Wikipedia once in a while, consult Wikipedia for other academic related issues sometimes and who are agree with the thought that "Wikipedia is useful for teaching" and who are strongly disagree with the thought that "I agree my students use Wikipedia in my courses".

C23. Academicians who contribute to Wikipedia once in a while, consult Wikipedia for other academic related issues sometimes and who are agree with the thought that "Wikipedia is useful for teaching" and who are neutral about the thought that "I agree my students use Wikipedia in my courses".

C24. Academicians who contribute to Wikipedia once in a while, consult Wikipedia for other academic related issues sometimes and who are agree with the thought that "Wikipedia is useful for teaching" and who are disagree with the thought that "I agree my students use Wikipedia in my courses".

C25. Professors who contribute to Wikipedia once in a while, consult Wikipedia for other academic related issues sometimes and who are agree with the thought that "Wikipedia is useful for teaching" and "I agree my students use Wikipedia in my courses".

C26. Lecturers who contribute to Wikipedia once in a while, consult Wikipedia for other academic related issues sometimes and who are agree with the thought that "Wikipedia is useful for teaching" and "I agree my students use Wikipedia in my courses".

C27. Instructors who contribute to Wikipedia once in a while, consult Wikipedia for other academic related issues sometimes and who are agree with the thought that "Wikipedia is useful for teaching" and "I agree my students use Wikipedia in my courses".

C28. Adjunct professors who contribute to Wikipedia once in a while, consult Wikipedia for other academic related issues sometimes and who are agree with the thought that "Wikipedia is useful for teaching" and "I agree my students use Wikipedia in my courses".

C29. Associate professors who contribute to Wikipedia once in a while, consult Wikipedia for other academic related issues sometimes and who are agree with the thought that "Wikipedia is useful for teaching" and "I agree my students use Wikipedia in my courses".

C30. Assistant professors who contribute to Wikipedia once in a while, consult Wikipedia for other academic related issues sometimes and who are agree with the thought that "Wikipedia is useful for teaching" and "I agree my students use Wikipedia in my courses".

C31. Academicians who contribute to Wikipedia sometimes and who never recommend their students to use Wikipedia.

C32. Academicians who contribute to Wikipedia sometimes and who recommend their students to use Wikipedia once in a while.

C33. Academicians who contribute to Wikipedia sometimes and who recommend their students to use Wikipedia sometimes.

C34. Academicians from UOC who contribute to Wikipedia sometimes and who recommend their students to use Wikipedia very often.

C35. Academicians not from UOC who contribute to Wikipedia sometimes and who recommend their students to use Wikipedia very often.

C36. Academicians who contribute to Wikipedia sometimes and who recommend their students to use Wikipedia rarely and who are neutral about the thought that "To design educational activities using Wikipedia, it would be helpful: a best practices guide".

C37. Academicians who contribute to Wikipedia sometimes and who recommend their students to use Wikipedia rarely and who are strongly disagree with the thought that "To design educational activities using Wikipedia, it would be helpful: a best practices guide".

C38. Academicians who contribute to Wikipedia sometimes and who recommend their students to use Wikipedia rarely and who are disagree with the thought that "To design educational activities using Wikipedia, it would be helpful: a best practices guide".

C39. Academicians who contribute to Wikipedia sometimes and who recommend their students to use Wikipedia rarely and who are agree with the thought that "To design educational activities using Wikipedia, it would be helpful: a best practices guide".

C40. Academicians who contribute to Wikipedia sometimes and who recommend their students to use Wikipedia rarely and who are strongly agree with the thought that "To design educational activities using Wikipedia, it would be helpful: a best practices guide".

C41. Academicians who contribute to Wikipedia very often and who are agree with the thought that "In the future, I will recommend the use of Wikipedia to my colleagues and students".

C42. Academicians who contribute to Wikipedia very often and who are strongly disagree with the thought that "In the future, I will recommend the use of Wikipedia to my colleagues and students".

C43. Academicians who contribute to Wikipedia very often and who are disagree with the thought that "In the future, I will recommend the use of Wikipedia to my colleagues and students".

C44. Academicians who contribute to Wikipedia very often and who are strongly agree with the thought that "In the future, I will recommend the use of Wikipedia to my colleagues and students".

C45. Female academicians who contribute to Wikipedia very often and who are neutral about the thought that "In the future, I will recommend the use of Wikipedia to my colleagues and students".

C46. Male academicians who contribute to Wikipedia very often and who are neutral about the thought that "In the future, I will recommend the use of Wikipedia to my colleagues and students".

SOLUTIONS AND RECOMMENDATIONS

The study is structured as follows. First, the data were analyzed by the Weka program using 60 percent of data for training 40 percent of data for testing. Then an entropy-based decision tree algorithm was developed. With this decision tree, it can be understood that whether Wikipedia has been used as a teaching tool by academicians or not. Thus, the researchers can have information about the usefulness of Wikipedia in teaching and the intentions in use of it by academicians. In addition, Wikipedia users and non-users are classified according to some of their aspects and their effect on Wikipedia usage with this decision tree.

FUTURE RESEARCH DIRECTIONS

For the future studies, it can be investigated that when the type of entropy (calculated entropy for each node) has been changed, there would be found different decision trees. In addition, by using different decision tree algorithms instead of C4.5, it can be compared the success of different algorithms and classes generated by them. In this study, since some of the variables (such as age, teaching experience, etc.) are numerical, those cannot be observed in the classification. When those variables were categorized it would be tested whether those are in the classification or not.

CONCLUSION

In this study, the teaching use of Wikipedia in higher education was investigated by using decision trees. With Weka programming, 46 classes are obtained by using the algorithm C4.5 which has the correct classification rate 89,0323%. When the classes are examined, it is seen that academicians who are in the class of 21 from 46 classes in the decision tree are Wikipedia users and academicians in 25 classes are not Wikipedia users. Thus, it can be concluded that the researchers have had some idea about the usefulness of Wikipedia in teaching and the intentions in use of it by academicians.

It can be said that the condition "I contribute to Wikipedia once in a while" is an important condition in the classification, since, it has the most branching on the decision tree. With this in mind, the sub-branches of the condition "I consult Wikipedia for other academic related issues" and the condition "Wikipedia is useful for teaching" can be said to be important conditions in the classification.

After the classification, some profiles of academicians who are Wikipedia users and non-users are given in the following:

- Academicians who never contribute to Wikipedia are not users.
- Academicians who contribute to Wikipedia once in a while and consult Wikipedia for other academic related issues very often are users.
- Academicians who contribute to Wikipedia once in a while and consult Wikipedia for other academic related issues never or rarely are not users.
- Academicians who contribute to Wikipedia once in a while and consult Wikipedia for other academic related issues sometimes and strongly agree with the thought that "Wikipedia is useful for teaching" are users.
- Professors, lecturers, instructors and adjuncts who contribute to Wikipedia once in a while, consult Wikipedia for other academic related issues sometimes

and who are agree with the thought that "Wikipedia is useful for teaching" and "I agree my students use Wikipedia in my courses" are not users.

- Associate and assistant professors who contribute to Wikipedia once in a while, consult Wikipedia for other academic related issues sometimes and who are agree with the thought that "Wikipedia is useful for teaching" and "I agree my students use Wikipedia in my courses" are users.
- Academicians from UOC who contribute to Wikipedia sometimes and recommend their students to use Wikipedia very often are users.
- Academicians not from UOC who contribute to Wikipedia sometimes and recommend their students to use Wikipedia very often are not users.
- Academicians who contribute to Wikipedia sometimes and who recommend their students to use Wikipedia rarely and who are neutral about the thought that "To design educational activities using Wikipedia, it would be helpful: a best practices guide" are not users and in contrast who are not neutral about the thought that "To design educational activities using Wikipedia, it would be helpful: a best practices guide" are users.
- Academicians who contribute to Wikipedia very often and who are agree with the thought that "In the future, I will recommend the use of Wikipedia to my colleagues and students" are not users.
- Academicians who contribute to Wikipedia once in a while, consult Wikipedia for other academic related issues very often and who are neutral about the thought that "It is easy to have a record of the contributions made in Wikipedia" are not users, in contrast who are not neutral about the thought that "It is easy to have a record of the contributions made in Wikipedia" are users.
- Female academicians who contribute to Wikipedia rarely are not users, in contrast who contribute to Wikipedia very often and who are neutral about the thought that "In the future, I will recommend the use of Wikipedia to my colleagues and students" are users.
- Male academicians who contribute to Wikipedia very often and who are neutral about the thought that "In the future, I will recommend the use of Wikipedia to my colleagues and students" are not users.
- Male academicians who have no Ph.D. and contribute to Wikipedia rarely are not users.
- Male academicians who have Ph.D. and contribute to Wikipedia rarely and who are disagree or strongly agree with the thought that "Wikipedia improves visibility of students' work" are users.

REFERENCES

Adhatrao, K., Gaykar, A., Dhawan, A., Jha, R., & Honrao, V. (2013). Predicting students' performance using ID3 and C4.5 classification algorithms. *International Journal of Data Mining & Knowledge Management Process*, *3*(5), 39–52. doi:10.5121/ijdkp.2013.3504

Agrawal, G. L., & Gupta, H. (2013). Optimization of C4.5 decision tree algorithm for data mining application. *International Journal of Emerging Technology and Advanced Engineering*, *3*(3), 341–345.

Aibar, E., Lerga, M., Lladós-Masllorens, J., Meseguer-Artola, A., & Minguillón, J. (2013). Wikipedia in higher education: an empirical study on faculty perceptions and practices. In L. Gómez Chova, A. López Martínez, & I. Candel Torres (Eds.), *EDULEARN13 Proceedings, International Association for Technology, Education and Development, IATED* (pp. 4269-4275). Academic Press.

An Introduction to Data Mining. (1998). Pilot Software Whitepaper, Pilot Software. Retrieved from http://iproject.online.fr/intro1.htm

Bigus, P. J. (1996). *Data mining with neural networks: solving business problems from application development to decision support*. McGraw-Hill.

Cherfi, A., Nouira, K., & Ferchichi, A. (2018). Very fast C4.5 decision tree algorithm. *Applied Artificial Intelligence*, *32*(2), 119–137. doi:10.1080/08839514.2018.1447479

Dunham, M. H. (2002). *Data mining, introductory and advanced topics*. Prentice Hall.

Fakhimi, E. (2015). Data mining techniques for web mining: A review. *Applied Mathematics in Engineering. Management and Technology*, *3*(5), 81–90.

Fayyad, U., Piatetsky-Shapiro, G., & Smyth, P. (1996). From data mining to knowledge discovery in databases. *The Alumni Magazine*, *17*(3), 37–54.

Garca Laencina, P. J., Abreu, P. H., Abreu, M. H., & Afonoso, N. (2015). Missing data imputation on the 5-year survival prediction of breast cancer patients with unknown discrete values. *Computers in Biology and Medicine*, *59*, 125–133. doi:10.1016/j.compbiomed.2015.02.006 PMID:25725446

Han, J., Kamber, M., & Pei, J. (2012). *Data mining: concepts and techniques* (3rd ed.). Morgan Kaufmann.

Hand, D. J. (1981). *Discrimination and Classification*. Chichester, UK: Wiley.

Hssina, B., Merbouha, A., Ezzikouri, H. & Erritali, M. (2014). A comparative study of decision tree ID3 and C4.5. *International Journal of Advanced Computer Science and Applications,* 13-19.

Hunt, E., Martin, J., & Stone, P. (1966). *Experiments in induction.* Academic Press.

Karar ağacı (decison tree) nedir? (n.d.). Retrieved from http://mail.baskent. edu. tr/~20410964/DM_8.pdf

Li, X., & Claramount, C. (2006). A spatial entropy-based decision tree for classification of geographical information. *Transactions in GIS, 10*(3), 451–467. doi:10.1111/j.1467-9671.2006.01006.x

Lim, T. S., Loh, W. Y., & Shih, Y. S. (2000). A comparison of prediction accuracy, complexity,and training time of thirty-three old and new classification algorithms. *Machine Learning, 40*(3), 203–228. doi:10.1023/A:1007608224229

Meseguer-Artola, A., Aibar, E., Liadós, J., Minguillón, J., & Lerga, M. (2016). Factors That Influence the Teaching Use of Wikipedia in Higher Education. *Journal of the Association for Information Science and Technology, 67*(5), 1224–1232. doi:10.1002/asi.23488

Patel, N., & Singh, D. (2015). An algorithm to construct decision tree for machine learning based on similarity factor. *International Journal of Computers and Applications, 111*(10), 22–26. doi:10.5120/19575-1376

Quinlan, J. R. (1986). Induction of decision trees. *Machine Learning, 1*(1), 81–106. doi:10.1007/BF00116251

Quinlan, J. R. (1993). *C4.5: Programs for machine learning.* Morgan Kaufmann.

Shannon, C. E. (1948). A mathematical theory of communication. *The Bell System Technical Journal, 27*(3), 379–423, 623–656. doi:10.1002/j.1538-7305.1948. tb01338.x

Weiss, S. I., & Kulikowski, C. (1991). *Computer systems that learn: classification and prediction methods from statistics, neural networks, machine learning, and expert systems.* San Francisco, CA: Morgan Kaufmann.

Weka. (n.d.). Retrieved from https://tr.wikipedia.org/wiki/Weka

Xiaoliang, Z., Jian, W., Hongcan, Y., & Shangzhuo, W. (2009). Research and application of the improved algorithm C4.5 on decision tree. In *International Conference on Test and Measurement (ICTM)* (*vol. 2,* pp184-187). Academic Press. 10.1109/ICTM.2009.5413078

ADDITIONAL READING

Alan, M. A. (2014). Karar ağaçlarıyla öğrenci verilerinin sınıflandırılması. *Atatürk Üniversitesi İktisadi ve İdari Bilimler Dergisi, 28*(4), 101–112.

Dunham, M. H. (2002). *Data mining, introductory and advanced topics.* Prentice Hall.

Han, J., Kamber, M., & Pei, J. (2012). *Data mining: concepts and techniques* (3rd ed.). Morgan Kaufmann.

Meseguer-Artola, A., Aibar, E., Liadós, J., Minguillón, J., & Lerga, M. (2016). Factors That Influence the Teaching Use of Wikipedia in Higher Education. *Journal of the Association for Information Science and Technology, 67*(5), 1224–1232. doi:10.1002/asi.23488

Quinlan, J. R. (1986). Induction of decision trees. *Machine Learning, 1*(1), 81–106. doi:10.1007/BF00116251

Quinlan, J. R. (1993). *C4.5: Programs for machine learning.* Morgan Kaufmann.

Shannon, C. E. (1948). A mathematical theory of communication. *The Bell System Technical Journal, 27*(3), 379–423, 623–656. doi:10.1002/j.1538-7305.1948.tb01338.x

Weiss, S. I., & Kulikowski, C. (1991). *Computer systems that learn: classification and prediction methods from statistics, neural networks, machine learning, and expert systems.* San Francisco, CA: Morgan Kaufmann.

KEY TERMS AND DEFINITIONS

C4.5: A well-known decision tree algorithm to select the best attribute for classification.

Data Mining: A process to extract information from big data.

Decision Tree Model: A convenient method for classification and estimation problem.

Entropy: A measurement of uncertainty or randomness in a data set.

OpenCourseWare: (OCW): Course lessons created at universities and published for free via the internet.

Weka: A software program which includes most of the widely used data mining algorithms and methods.

Wikipedia: Is one of the world's most visited and used online encyclopedias.

APPENDIX

The classes generated by C4.5 algorithm

```
Exp4 = 1: 0 (580.0/26.0)
Exp4 = 2
|   GENDER = 0
|   |   PhD = 1
|   |   |   Vis1 = 3: 0 (17.0/6.0)
|   |   |   Vis1 = 2: 1 (5.0)
|   |   |   Vis1 = 4: 0 (9.0/2.0)
|   |   |   Vis1 = 5: 1 (3.0)
|   |   |   Vis1 = 1: 0 (0.0)
|   |   PhD = 0: 0 (68.0/13.0)
|   GENDER = 1: 0 (74.0/8.0)
Exp4 = 3
|   Exp2 = 4
|   |   PU3 = 3: 0 (5.0)
|   |   PU3 = 2: 0 (2.0)
|   |   PU3 = 4
|   |   |   Use5 = 4
|   |   |   |   UOC_POSITION = 2: 1 (2.0)
|   |   |   |   UOC_POSITION = 3: 1 (1.0)
|   |   |   |   UOC_POSITION = 4: 0 (0.0)
|   |   |   |   UOC_POSITION = 5: 0 (0.0)
|   |   |   |   UOC_POSITION = 1: 0 (0.0)
|   |   |   |   UOC_POSITION = 6: 0 (9.0/1.0)
|   |   |   Use5 = 2: 1 (1.0)
|   |   |   Use5 = 1: 0 (0.0)
|   |   |   Use5 = 3: 1 (6.0/1.0)
|   |   |   Use5 = 5: 0 (2.0)
|   |   PU3 = 5: 1 (4.0/1.0)
|   |   PU3 = 1: 0 (1.0)
|   Exp2 = 2: 0 (7.0)
|   Exp2 = 5
|   |   Vis2 = 3: 0 (10.0/2.0)
|   |   Vis2 = 4: 1 (6.0/1.0)
|   |   Vis2 = 2: 1 (3.0)
|   |   Vis2 = 5: 1 (3.0)
```

```
|    |    Vis2 = 1: 1 (2.0)
|    Exp2 = 3: 0 (40.0/3.0)
|    Exp2 = 1: 0 (1.0)
Exp4 - 4
|    Use3 = 1: 0 (2.0)
|    Use3 = 3: 0 (9.0/2.0)
|    Use3 = 5
|    |    UNIVERSITY = 1: 1 (6.0)
|    |    UNIVERSITY = 2: 0 (3.0/1.0)
|    Use3 = 4: 1 (11.0/2.0)
|    Use3 = 2
|    |    Inc1 = 5: 1 (0.0)
|    |    Inc1 = 4: 1 (3.0)
|    |    Inc1 = 3: 0 (2.0)
|    |    Inc1 = 1: 1 (1.0)
|    |    Inc1 = 2: 1 (0.0)
Exp4 = 5
|    BI1 = 2: 1 (0.0)
|    BI1 = 1: 1 (0.0)
|    BI1 = 3
|    |    GENDER = 0: 0 (3.0)
|    |    GENDER = 1: 1 (2.0)
|    BI1 = 5: 1 (7.0)
|    BI1 = 4: 0 (3.0)
```

Chapter 4
A Hybrid Pythagorean Group Decision Making Model for Website Selection

Himanshu Sharma
University of Delhi, India

Aakash Aakash
 https://orcid.org/0000-0002-3900-4215
University of Delhi, India

Anu G. Aggarwal
 https://orcid.org/0000-0001-5448-9540
University of Delhi, India

ABSTRACT

The digital revolution has transformed many offline retailers to perform their business activities online, resulting in tough competition in a dynamic marketing environment. A well-built, user friendly, and attractive e-commerce website will result in high traffic intensity and eventually impact the market position of the online vendor. Over the past few decades, a number of studies have been done to predict the key determinants of e-commerce system success. This chapter considers the criteria, namely system quality, content quality, use, trust, support, personalization, and electronic word-of-mouth. Evaluating objects based on a single criterion may pose to be subjective, which have shifted these decisions towards multiple criteria, and hence has popularized the concept of multi-criteria decision making (MCDM). This chapter combines Pythagorean fuzzy analytic hierarchy process (PFAHP) and complex proportional assessment of alternatives with grey relations (COPRAS-G), under multiple decision makers, to select the best e-commerce website from five alternatives.

DOI: 10.4018/978-1-5225-8238-0.ch004

INTRODUCTION

The unstoppable growth and rapid advancement in the internet technologies have given rise to electronic shopping (e-shopping) and selling through e-commerce websites. E-shopping is an activity of purchasing product/service using the internet. In the last ten years, the internet based technologies have continuously gained momentum and changed the way of marketing and selling the product/service by companies. In 2015, more than 12 billion devices were connected to the internet and it is expected to grow 8 billion within the period of 2015 – 2020, from 12 to 20 billion (Evans, 2015). This significant growth of technology has led to the enhancement in virtual shops, which become popular as e-shopping. E-shopping seems to be growing in all over the world including developing nations. A market research report published in 2015 on the growth of online shoppers across the globe indicates that online consumers will grow from 1.079 in 2013 to 1.623 billion in 2019(Evans, 2015). E-commerce provides various options such as payment alternatives, delivery options, convenience, and also allows flexibility regarding product/service. This saves cost, time, and creates an opportunity to generate high revenue from consumers' as well as retailers' prospective (Anu Gupta; Aggarwal & Aakash, 2018). It is an interactive medium which is not bound to any place, people, or time. Online shopping is a more convenient way to shop in comparison to brick and mortar stores, as it enables the customers to avoid travel related hassle to reach physical store for buying their desired products/services.

The technology revolution has changed the way of doing businesses online. In this digital world, there is a growing need of many offline retailers to do their business online due to sturdy competition in a dynamic market environment (Andam, 2003). One of the basic requirements of e-business is its website. Therefore, many companies are endowing huge finance in maintaining their website, through which customers can buy the required products/services. Indeed, customers are buying online more than offline, but the number of prospect customers does not actually transform into actual buyers (Hidayanto, Herbowo, Budi, & Sucahyo, 2014). This shows that customers might browse for product/service but do not make an actual purchase. From marketers', management's, and customers' prospective, there exists a number of factors that affect buying intention as well as website selection decision, which helps e-tailers to provide products/services accordingly. Due to availability of a number of e-commerce sites offers identical products/services, customers as well as marketers find it difficult to choose the best site for buying & selling goods. Thus, the main goal of this chapter is to provide the best solution for selecting the best e-commerce websites on the basis of various success factors with respect to customers. Over the last two decades, studies concerning the variables affecting information system (IS) success factors have been a topic of interest among the researchers (DeLone & McLean, 1992, 2003). Various combinations of these factors have been adopted by them to predict the key determinants of e-commerce system success. Though, much of the initial studies focused on the success with respect to the online system, recent studies have succeeded in adding the customer oriented measures that lead to success of these online platforms (Aggarwal; & Aakash, 2017; Molla & Licker, 2001). In the light of these studies, this chapter considers the criteria namely System Quality (SQ), Content Quality (CQ), Use (US), Trust (TR), Support (SUP), Personalization (PER), and Electronic word-of-mouth (EWOM).

There is more than one factor which affects the selection of e-commerce websites, which brings this problem comes under multiple criteria decision-making (MCDM). A large number of MCDM method have beings covered in the literature. But analytical hierarchy process (AHP) proposed by Saaty is one of the most famous and practical technique based on crisp values in the literature (Saaty, 1980). The crisp data cannot properly handle many real life problems related to MCDM as it is unable to handle subjectivity of human judgments and vagueness in decision making. To overcome this difficulty, Zadeh (1965) proposed a fuzzy set theory, which includes the degree of belongingness and non-belongingness (Zadeh, 1965). The fuzzy sets still have some drawbacks and there is growing need to develop new MCDM techniques. Moreover, fuzzy sets were extended by Atanassov to intuitionistic fuzzy sets (IFS) which includes 'hesitancy degree' in addition to the degree of belongingness and non-belongingness (Atanassov, 1986). A number of studies focus on the use of IFS in MCDM (Aggarwal, Sharma, & Tandon, 2017; H.-y. Zhang, Peng, Wang, & Wang, 2017). The IFS are proficient in the case of inexact data and imperative treatment (Ureña, Chiclana, Fujita, & Herrera-Viedma, 2015). On the other hand, the Pythagorean fuzzy sets (PFS) have grown as an active instrument to handle the vagueness in multiple criteria decision-making (MCDM) problems (Peng, Yuan, & Yang, 2017; Yager, 2014). The PFS is classified as sum of membership and non-membership degree whose additive squares should be maximum one. Hence, IFS fails to deal with this type of situation. For illustration, if a decision maker gives membership and non-membership measures as .7 and .4, respectively, then it can only be operative for PFS as all the IFS degree are subsets of PFS degree. Therefore, PFS are more efficient to handle vagueness than IFS. Additionally, there are many possible selection techniques namely PROMETHEE, ELECTRE, TOPSIS, VIKOR, MOORA, COPRAS, and many more.

In this study, we propose a model that combines Pythagorean fuzzy AHP (PFAHP) and COPRAS-G for selecting e-commerce websites under group decision making. Till now, PFAHP technique has few applications in the field of e-commerce. The distinguishing reason for taking COPRAS-G in comparison to other outranking approaches is that it uses significance and utility degree for systematic ranking of the alternatives. Using the extended e-commerce success model (A. Aggarwal &

Aakash, 2018), this paper explores SQ, CQ, US, TR, SUP, PER, and EWOM as main selection criteria. For calculating criteria weights, PFAHP technique is used and then COPRAS-G is used to select the best e-commerce website. A real-life case study considering top five e-commerce websites as alternatives is provided to validate the model. The research findingsmay help online retailers as well as marketers to form a clear picture of e-commerce website success criteria and then selecting the best e-commerce website for selling or promoting their offerings. Thus, proposed model presents an effective way for selecting best e-commerce website. Moreover, a group decision making technique is constructed for the selection of best e-commerce website. MCDM approaches are based on the information retrieved from a single expert, which may be a biased approach (Pérez, Alonso, Cabrerizo, Lu, & Herrera-Viedma, 2011). Thus, multi criteria group decision making (MCGDM) approaches were introduced to get the best solution based on inputs provided by multiple decision makers. Even though the decision makers may have same objective, their opinion towards the problem may vary. Earlier each decision maker was allocated equal weights, but later weighing them according to their expertise was found to be more reliable approach (Ureña et al., 2015).

The remaining chapter is structured as follows: the literature related to e-commerce success criteria and website selection using various combinations of MCDM techniques will be reviewed in the next section. Following that, the preliminaries and proposed PFAHP COPRAS-G methodology structure will be explained. After that, a real-life case study for XYZ Company will be presented. Then, PFAHP COPRAS-G steps and related calculation will be provided to implement the hybrid model. The results are discussed and interpreted in the penultimate section of this study, while the last section presents our conclusions and future scope.

LITERATURE REVIEW

E-Commerce Success Criteria

The early 90's witnessed the introduction of electronic commerce with the deployment of internet-based technologies and computer-to-computer communication. Ataburo, Muntaka, and Quansah (2017) defined e-commerce as "the sharing of business information, maintaining business relationships and conducting business transactions by means of telecommunications networks". According to them, the e-commerce system can be converted into a hierarchical form with three meta-levels: infrastructure, services/products, and structure; where all the lower levels operationally support to the higher ones. The e-commerce system provides many advantages over its offline counterpart such as: in-depth information, retailer-purchaser interaction, buying/

selling, distribution, delivery, and payment process among online vendors and purchasers. Also, the advent of e-commerce enabled the customers some amount of self-service by allowing them to perform activities such as affording credit cards, changing address, obtain customer feedbacks, and adding new products or services to their purchasing cart.

Table 1 gives the summary of the criterion used in e-commerce system success evaluation model in the literature. DeLone and McLean (D&M) have done a significant research in the area of IS success (DeLone & McLean, 1992, 2003, 2004). They identified six major dimensions namely: system quality, service quality, information quality, use, user satisfaction, and net benefits. As per these models, mainly first three criteria determine the level of IS success. A comprehensive list of past e–commerce success studies and their respective criteria is provided in Table 1.

Many researchers and practitioners analyzed the quality of e-commerce system on the basis of the customers. Some discussed the criteria of e-commerce website quality in detailed manner (Agarwal & Venkatesh, 2002; Andreou et al., 2005; Barnes & Vidgen, 2001; Barnes & Vidgen, 2006; Bauer et al., 2005; Guo & Shao, 2005; Jayawardhena, 2004; S. Kim & Lee, 2006; S. Kim & Stoel, 2004; Moustakis et al., 2006; Palmer, 2002; Y. A. Park & Gretzel, 2007; Ranganathan & Ganapathy, 2002; C.-C. Sun & Lin, 2009; Van Iwaarden et al., 2004; Yang et al., 2005) while other focused on the success criteria of customer satisfaction towards e-shopping (Bai et al., 2008; Choshin & Ghaffari, 2017; C. Kim et al., 2012; Koufaris, 2002; Loiacono et al., 2002; Rana et al., 2015; San Lim et al., 2016; Wu et al., 2003).

The pioneering work in the area of IS success measure, was done by DeLone and McLean (1992). They discussed a success model which concentrated on various variables impacting IS success. Their model stated an urgency to evaluate the success of e-commerce systems at three different levels: individual, system, and organizational. Moreover, the content quality, which is different from technical quality, affects the e-commerce systems (X. Zhang et al., 2000). E-commerce researchers also noticed the usability criterion by assessing the use level and satisfaction of users toward e-commerce systems (Jones & Kayworth, 1999). Though the topic has been researched and significant contributions have been made in this field, but less emphasis is put on integrating the dependent variable (customer satisfaction) and the independent variables. According to DeLone & McLean, *use* and *user satisfaction* were considered to be the dependent variables in the e-commerce system.

The Molla and Licker (2001) model of e-commerce revolutionized the previous studies by spanning all the online transaction processes and e-commerce systems' purposes. In order to capture the constructs ignored in previous model, few changes in the criteria were made in their model, by renaming the variables. The substitution of 'user satisfaction' by 'customer e-commerce satisfaction' warrants overcoming the association ambiguity between user satisfaction and organizational performance.

Table 1. E-commerce system success criteria (Compiled by Authors)

Authors	Criteria of e-commerce system success
(DeLone & McLean, 1992)	System Quality, Information quality, Use, User satisfaction, Individual Impact, Organizational Impact
(Bell & Tang, 1998)	Access, Content, Transactions, Usage, Structure, Navigation, Graphics, Usefulness, Features, User friendliness
(Jones & Kayworth, 1999)	Effectiveness, User needs, Performance, Usage
(Kardaras & Karakostas, 1999)	Effectiveness, Organizational impact, Use, Customer Support
(E. Kim, 1999)	Customization, Interactivity, Vividness, Understandability, Reliability, Relevance
(Nielsen, 1999)	Usability
(X. Zhang, Keeling, & Pavur, 2000)	Content Quality, Navigation, Presentation
(Liu & Arnett, 2000)	Information quality, Learning capability, Playfulness, System Quality, Use, Service quality
(Young & Benamati, 2000)	Information, Transaction, Frequently asked questions
(Smith, 2001)	Ease-of-use, Information content
(Molla & Licker, 2001)	System Quality, Content Quality, Use, Trust, Support, E-commerce customer satisfaction
(Schubert & Selz, 2001)	Ease-of-use, Navigation, Information quantity, Product quality, Global availability, Customization, Security, Tracking order status, Privacy
(Barnes & Vidgen, 2001)	Tangibles, Reliability, Responsiveness, Assurance, Empathy
(Palmer, 2002)	Navigation, Interactivity, Responsiveness, Content Quality, Use, Download speed
(Torkzadeh & Dhillon, 2002)	Electronic payment, Electronic product choice, Electronic vendor trust, Shopping travel
(Koufaris, 2002)	Ease-of-use, Usefulness, Shopping enjoyment, Perceived control, concentration
(Ranganathan & Ganapathy, 2002)	Information content, Design, Security, Privacy
(Loiacono, Chen, & Goodhue, 2002)	Usefulness, Ease-of-use, Entertainment, Complementary relationship
(Schmitz & Latzer, 2002)	Navigation, Information, Delivery services, Payment procedure, Consumer rights and data protection, Refund policy.
(Agarwal & Venkatesh, 2002)	Content, Ease-of-use, Promotion, Made-for-the-medium, Emotion
(Delone & McLean, 2003)	Information quality, System Quality, Service quality, Intention to use, user satisfaction, Net benefits
(Wu, Mahajan, & Balasubramanian, 2003)	Privacy, Technical support, Visual appearance, Information content, Enjoyment, Navigation, Cognitive outcomes
(S. Kim & Stoel, 2004)	Appearance, Entertainment, Informational fit-to-task, Transaction capability, Response time, Trust
(Van Iwaarden, Van Der Wiele, Ball, & Millen, 2004)	Assurance, Empathy, Responsiveness, Reliability, Tangibles

continued on following page

Table 1. Continued

Authors	Criteria of e-commerce system success
(Jayawardhena, 2004)	Website interface, Interaction, Reliability, Responsiveness, Assurance, Empathy
(Delone & Mclean, 2004)	System Quality, Information quality, Service quality, Usage, User satisfaction, Net benefits
(Bauer, Hammerschmidt, & Falk, 2005)	Service quality, Security, Trust, Payment transactions, Responsiveness
(Andreou et al., 2005)	Functionality, Reliability, Usability, Efficiency, Security, Ease-of-use
(Yang, Cai, Zhou, & Zhou, 2005)	Information quality, System Quality
(Guo & Shao, 2005)	Transaction, Navigability, System Quality, Useful links
(Moustakis, Tsironis, & Litos, 2006)	Content, Navigation, Design and structure, Appearance and multimedia, Uniqueness
(S. Kim & Lee, 2006)	Information fit-to-task, Trust, Response time, Design, Visual appeal, Innovativeness, Interactivity, Transaction
(Barnes & Vidgen, 2006)	Usability, Information quality, Website design, Trust, Empathy
(Y. A. Park & Gretzel, 2007)	Ease-of-use, Responsiveness, Security and privacy, Visual appearance, Information quality, Trust, Interactivity
(Bai, Law, & Wen, 2008)	Functionality, Usability, Customer satisfaction
(C.-C. Sun & Lin, 2009)	Service quality, Holdup cost, Technology acceptance factor
(Ramanathan, 2010)	Accessibility, Payment process, Privacy experience, Comparative prices, On-time delivery, Customer support, Ease-of-refunds, Satisfaction with claims, Customer loyalty
(Yu, Guo, Guo, & Huang, 2011)	Service quality, Product, Design, Technology, Logistics companies
(C. Kim, Galliers, Shin, Ryoo, & Kim, 2012)	System Quality, Information quality, Service quality
(Chen, Rungruengsamrit, Rajkumar, & Yen, 2013)	Information quality, System Quality, Service quality
(Ahmad, Abu Bakar, Faziharudean, & Mohamad Zaki, 2015)	Technological context, Organizational context, Environmental context
(Rana, Dwivedi, Williams, & Weerakkody, 2015)	System Quality, Information quality, Service quality, Perceived usefulness, Perceived ease-of-use, Perceived risk
(San Lim, Heng, Ng, & Cheah, 2016)	Usability, Credibility, Service quality, Transaction costs
(Choshin & Ghaffari, 2017)	Customer satisfaction, Awareness and knowledge, Costs, Infrastructures
(A. Aggarwal & Aakash, 2018)	System Quality, Content Quality, Usage, Trust, Customer support, Online customer feedback, Personalization

These changes were made to bring into the customer satisfaction agenda, which is centric to the modern marketing management policy. Also, two additional factors-trust and support captured the transactional and customer support components, and validate the association between use and CES. Though, the replacement of 'Use' with 'Usefulness' by many researchers has been proved to be an ambiguous concept. In their model, their key concept was Customer E-commerce Satisfaction (CES). The objective of retrieving information and conducting various activities convey the need for user's and customer's e-commerce satisfaction and extends beyond interpersonal dynamics of services and informational purpose.

After a decade, Delone and McLean (2003) extended their previous model by introducing a new construct 'net benefits' which mainly focused on the impact of service quality on the IS success. The updated D&M model is consistent with the latest changes in e-commerce system by enabling the customers and suppliers to make buying and selling decisions and do transactions using the internet. Later, another model was established byDelone and Mclean (2004), which further extended the success factors related to system success, but it was not consistent with literature related to the relationship between the website quality, customer satisfaction, and customer loyalty. It was observed that the net benefit introduced is a much diversified construct and needed a precise definition (Delone & Mclean, 2004). However, an attempt was made to extend the Molla and Licker model which concentrated on customer satisfaction influencing e-commerce system success by Wang (2008). In his study, some of the criteria introduced by Molla and Licker were replaced by System Quality, Information Quality, and User Satisfaction. Moreover, the Support and Trust criteria were incorporated into a single construct namely Service Quality. Thus, success of an online platform is found to be a multidimensional construct which over time has converged towards critical success factors and website service quality success factors. The extant studies have focused on website service by showing a structural relationship between user satisfaction, service quality, and e-commerce system success. Though, the objective here is to fill the gaps in previous literature based on customer oriented success factors.

Website Selection

An e-commerce website is a platform which enables the businesses to sell and promote their products/services as well as generate their market share. Regretfully, the consumer conversion rate is very low. Hence, developing an efficient website selection model has attracted researchers as well as practitioners. Many website selection studies has been reported in the literature, for example: the selection of airline websites (Apostolou & Economides, 2008; Chong & Law, 2018), travel websites (Law, 2007; P. Sun, Cárdenas, & Harrill, 2016), hotel websites (Ip, Law, &

Lee, 2012; Qi, Law, & Buhalis, 2017), apparel websites (E. J. Park, Kim, Funches, & Foxx, 2012), and destination websites (Qi, Law, & Buhalis, 2008; T. Zhang, Cheung, & Law, 2018).

Many researchers have utilized MCDM techniques to handle selection problems (Aghdaie, Zolfani, & Zavadskas, 2013; Kahraman et al., 2017; Zolfani, Chen, Rezaeiniya, & Tamošaitienė, 2012). Y. Lee and Kozar (2006) used AHP technique to select travel and electronics websites. Application of an integrated AHP-TOPSIS technique for selecting best B2C e-commerce website has been done (A. Aggarwal & Aakash, 2018). Bueyuekoezkan and Ruan (2007) applied FAHP and Fuzzy TOPSIS for prioritizing thirteen government websites on the basis of six criteria. Zolfani et al. (2012) applied AHP and COPRAS-G technique to select and rank suppliers. Aggarwal; and Aakash (2017) applied an integrated ME-OWA and FAHP approach for selecting best B2C e-commerce website. Aghdaie et al. (2013) presented a hybrid FAHP-COPRAS-G technique for selecting and evaluating marketing segments. Garg, Kumar, and Garg (2018) proposed an approach to select as well as rank e-learning websites using Fuzzy COPRAS method. Kaya and Kahraman (2011) utilized an integrated FAHP-ELECTRE method to rank bank websites. Aggarwal et al. (2017) proposed a hybrid IFAHP and IFMOORA method to rank OTA websites. Kahraman et al. (2017) represented an intuitionistic fuzzy (IF) technique for solid waste disposal website selection with the help of integrated IF-EDAS method.

AHP and Combination With Other MCDM Techniques for Website Selection

In the last two decades, AHP is widely used for selecting e-commerce websites. Table 2 gives a brief summary of e-commerce website selection using AHP as well as their combination with other MCDM techniques. These studies mainly focused into three categories, namely, e-commerce, e-learning, hotel and other websites. From these studies, out of eighteen selection experiments four uses solely AHP, one use solely FAHP, twelve uses a combination of AHP and FAHP, and only one use Single-Valued-Trapezoidal-Neutrosophic-Numbers (SVTNSs) with other theories and techniques.

More specifically, AHP has been used for selecting websites in e-commerce (Anu G Aggarwal & Aakash, 2018; N. Y. Lee & Choi, 2001; Moustakis et al., 2004; Ngai, 2003; Y. Zhu & Buchmann, 2002), fashion websites(N. Y. Lee & Choi, 2001), web sources (Y. Zhu & Buchmann, 2002), online advertising (Ngai, 2003), cell phone providers (Moustakis et al., 2004)and B2C-e-commerce websites (Anu G Aggarwal & Aakash, 2018). For example,N. Y. Lee and Choi (2001)have used AHP to evaluate 4fashion websites in Korea.

Table 2. E-commerce website selection using MCDM techniques (Compiled by Authors)

References	Market	Technique Used	Domain	No. of Websites	Criteria
(N. Y. Lee & Choi, 2001)	Korea	AHP	Fashion Websites	4	Price, Place, Product, Promotion
(Y. Zhu & Buchmann, 2002)	Germany	AHP	Web Sources	4	Source Stability, Data Quality, Application Specific
(Ngai, 2003)	Hong Kong	AHP	Online Advertising	5	Impression Rate, Monthly Cost, Audience Fit, Content, Look & Feel
(Moustakis, Litos, Dalivigas, & Tsironis, 2004)	Greece	AHP	Cell Phone Providers	3	Content, Navigation, Structure and Design, Appearance and Design, Uniqueness
(Bilsel, Büyüközkan, & Ruan, 2006)	Turkish	Fuzzy-AHP-PROMETHEE	Hospital Websites	9	Tangible, Reliability, Responsiveness, Assurance, Empathy, Quality of Information, Integration of Communication
(Bueyuekoezkan & Ruan, 2007)	Turkey	Fuzzy-VIKOR	E-learning Websites	13	Tangibles, Reliability, Responsiveness, Empathy, Quality of Information, Integration of Communication
(C.-C. Sun & Lin, 2009)	Taiwan	Fuzzy-AHP- TOPSIS	Online Shopping Websites	4	Specific holdup cost, Website service quality, Technology acceptance factor
(Büyüközkan, Arsenyan, & Ertek, 2010)	Turkish	Fuzzy-AHP- TOPSIS	E-learning Websites	12	Right and understandable content, Complete Content, Personalization, Security, Navigation, Interactivity, User interface
(Yu et al., 2011)	China	Fuzzy-AHP- TOPSIS	E-commerce Websites in E-alliance	5	Product, Design, Technology, Service Quality, Logistics Companies
(AYDIN & Kahraman, 2012)	Turkey	Fuzzy-AHP- VIKOR	E-commerce Websites	3	Ease of use, Product, Security, Customer relationship, Fulfillment
(Qi, Law, & Buhalis, 2013)	USA and Hong Kong	Fuzzy-AHP- TOPSIS	Hotel Websites	6	General Information, Reservation Information, Website Management, Surrounding Information, Accessibility, Navigation, Ease of use
(X. Zhu, Zhang, Zhang, & Yang, 2013)	China	Fuzzy-AHP- TOPSIS	B2C E-commerce Websites	10	Website design, Transmission Speed, Popularity, Information Quantity, Service
(Akincilar & Dagdeviren, 2014)	Turkey	AHP- PROMETHEE	Hotel Websites	15	Customer Oriented, Technology Oriented, Marketing Oriented, Security Oriented, Other Factors
(Panigrahi & Srivastava, 2015)	India	Fuzzy-AHP	Travel Websites	6	Response Time, Security, Reliability, Ease-of-use, Communication Facilities, Awareness

continued on following page

Table 2. Continued

References	Market	Technique Used	Domain	No. of Websites	Criteria
(Kang, Jang, & Park, 2016)	Korea	Fuzzy-AHP-TOPSIS, VIKOR, and GRA	B2C E-commerce Websites	6	Efficiency, System Availability, Fulfillment, Privacy
(Liang, Wang, & Zhang, 2017)	China	Single-Valued-Trapezoidal-Neutrosophic-Numbers(SVTNSs)-DEMATEL	B2C E-commerce Websites	6	Efficiency, System Availability, Fulfillment, Privacy
(Garg et al., 2018)	India	Fuzzy-AHP-COPRAS	E-learning Websites	8	Functionality, Maintainability, Portability, Reliability, Usability, Efficiency, Ease of Learning Community, Personalization, System Content, General Factors
(A. Aggarwal & Aakash, 2018)	India	AHP-TOPSIS	B2C E-commerce Websites	5	System Quality, Content Quality, Usage, Trust, Customer Support, Customer Feedback, Personalization

The conventional AHP assumes that expert's judgment is exact and using crisp values leading to inconsideration of uncertainty which comes through linguistic variables. In some cases the crisp value is not feasible for a particular problem, then fuzzy value is used. Fuzzy AHP has been used for selecting websites in e-commerce (AYDIN & Kahraman, 2012; Kang et al., 2016; C.-C. Sun & Lin, 2009; Yu et al., 2011; X. Zhu et al., 2013), e-learning (Bueyuekoezkan & Ruan, 2007; Büyüközkan et al., 2010; Garg et al., 2018), hotels (Qi et al., 2013), and other portals (Bilsel et al., 2006; Panigrahi & Srivastava, 2015).

The out ranking technique that is most commonly combined with FAHP is TOPSIS. This combination is mainly used in the selection of e-commerce websites. For example, Zhu et al. (2013) have used an integrated FAHP-TOPSIS technique to select B2C e-commerce websites (X. Zhu et al., 2013). Similarly, FAHP combined withTOPSIS for e-learning websites (Büyüközkan et al., 2010) and hotel websites (Qi et al., 2013). Similarly, the second most common combination of FAHP is with VIKOR for selecting e-commerce websites (AYDIN & Kahraman, 2012; Kang et al., 2016), and e-learning websites (Bueyuekoezkan & Ruan, 2007).

Furthermore, Table 2 gives the literature of last eighteen years related to the e-commerce website selection using the combination of AHP and FAHP with other various outranking techniques. For example, combination have been highlighted with other MCDM techniques such as AHP-PROMETHEE (Akincilar & Dagdeviren, 2014) and FAHP-PROMETHEE (Bilsel et al., 2006). Similarly, a combination of FAHP with the ranking technique COPRAS has been reported for the selection of e-learning websites (Garg et al., 2018). A single valued trapezoidal neutrosophic (SVTN) has also been combined with specialized out ranking technique such as DEMATEL for selecting B2C e-commerce website in Chinese market (Liang et al., 2017).

PRELIMINARIES

Customer Oriented Success Criteria

Here we discuss the various criteria considered in this study.

Content Quality (CQ)

It refers to the inner structure, layout, and format of the website design. It also conveys the customer's perception of public communication by an e-commerce system (Berger & Matt, 2016). Any e-commerce website in which information obtained and services are not available are considered valueless. The success of a website and its customer conversion and retention can be determined via its content quality. Various attributes taken up under this factor are: up-to-datedness, understandability, timeliness, and preciseness. By 'up-to-datedness' we mean the competence of the website to inform the customers about the product and their arrivals/departures of goods. 'Timeliness' implies the visitors obtain the information about the goods/ services in no time. 'Understandability' means how well is the data displayed on the website. Exact information regarding the products/services without any discrepancies is termed as 'preciseness'.

System Quality (SQ)

System quality refers to "structural characteristics of an e-commerce system and taps into its performance dynamics such as availability, adaptability, and response time" (Xu, Benbasat, & Cenfetelli, 2013). The design of the websites which explains how the content is available to the user and its ease of use makes the site more successful. The attributes considered under this are: online response time, 24-hour availability, page loading speed, and visual appearance. 'Online response time' means the effectiveness of the interface system of the website. By '24-hour availability' we mean that the e-commerce website is available the whole day and there are no off hours. The time taken by the website to reload or refresh and to migrate from various search results represents 'page loading speed'. By 'visual appearance' we mean the attractiveness of the website and also the readability of its content.

Trust (TR)

Trust is considered to be an important criterion for e-commerce success since customer is concerned about the privacy and security of his personal data including personal details and transaction details (Hidayanto et al., 2014). They stated that, "When providing online information, the level of security presents the major concern for customers". 'Security' represents the capability of an e-commerce system to assure the customers that there is no breach of customers' personal information while making a transaction. The capability of an e-commerce system to keep the customers' personal information confidential and protect the customers' data from being included into any database is termed as 'privacy'.

Use (US)

The usefulness of the website to the customers determines its success. For this, the number of 'hits' and 'visits' are used as an indicator of popularity of an e-commerce firm. Venkatesh, Morris, Davis, and Davis (2003) defined information and transaction as two components of 'use'. By 'information' we mean the significance of the content available on the website and the 'transaction' represents the how smoothly and effectively the payment process is carried out.

Support (SUP)

Another customer oriented criterion which helps in customer retention is support. The criterion includes tracking order status, payment alternatives, and Frequently Asked Question (FAQ) (Tarasewich & Warkentin, 2000). 'Tracking order status' represents the ability of the website to provide the customers to track the delivery status of their purchased product/service. Payment alternatives refer to the various payment options being provided by the e-commerce firm to its customers. 'Frequently asked questions' represents the potential of the firm's customer care to handle queries. Nowadays, online firms are providing 'price comparison' factor through which the customers can compare the online firm's product price with other competitor firms.

Personalization (PER)

Personalization is the process of customizing the goods and services as per customers' needs and wants. The importance of personalization lies in its dynamic nature in website structure or content (Bhati, Thu, Woon, Phuong, & Lynn, 2017). The attributes considered in the factor are: individual preferences, cross-selling, and up-selling. 'Individual preferences' means giving the customer an opportunity to build his own shopping cart and select the products/service by considering various filter searches based on their constraints. 'Up-selling' and 'Cross-selling' are two key variables for an online retailer to provide a supplementary or complementary product or service to potential buyers so as to convert him into a multiple product buyer instead of single.

Electronic Word-of-Mouth (EWOM)

The advancements in internet technology has enabled the purchasers to offer their consumption related experience to the potential customers (Baek, Oh, Yang, & Ahn, 2017), which in this study is termed as 'electronic word-of-mouth'. It refers to the feedback given by online customers regarding a product or service for others to see over the internet. Two major attributes considered under E-WOM are: online reviews and star ratings. 'Online reviews' mean the linguistic comments given by the previous purchasers on the e-commerce websites for the product/service purchased by them. Some of the applications provide the consumers the option to rate the offering by selecting stars, called the 'star ratings', which is consistent with the likert scale used by researchers (Ye, Law, & Gu, 2009).

Fuzzy Set Theory

The concept was introduced as a solution to the problem of uncertainty encountered by practitioners while using decision making models, whose judgments were based on crisp set (Zadeh, 1965). The fuzziness was incorporated into the set theory in such a way that it handled the human linguistic vagueness while making a decision or evaluation. Previous researchers have proved that these sets possess the characteristics of ordinary sets but have wider applicability in practical situations due to its generality (Bueyuekoezkan & Ruan, 2007). Fuzzy sets provide a mathematical framework to tackle problems which involve fuzzy criteria, relations, or phenomena. Next, we define these sets and the mathematical operations defined for them.

Definition 1: If Y is a collection of objects denoted by y then a fuzzy set F in Y is defined as $F = \{(y, \theta_F(y) \mid y \in Y$ where $\theta_F(y)$ is called a membership function which maps Y to the membership space (which is a crisp value). Its range is a subset of non-negative finite real numbers whose supremum is finite.

However, there exist some fuzzy sets which have fuzzy membership functions. They are defined as:

Definition 2: A type-m fuzzy set is a fuzzy set whose membership values are type $m-1, m > 1$ fuzzy sets on $\left[0,1\right]$.

Next we define the intersection and union operation with respect to fuzzy sets. Definition 3: The membership function for intersection of two fuzzy numbers F and G may be defined as

$$\theta_{F \cap G}(y) = Min\left(\theta_F(y), \theta_G(y)\right) \forall y \in Y \tag{1}$$

Definition 4: The membership function for union of two fuzzy numbers F and G may be defined as

$$\theta_{F \cup G}(y) = Max\left(\theta_F(y), \theta_G(y)\right) \forall y \in Y \tag{2}$$

In literature two types of fuzzy numbers namely triangular and trapezoidal have been discussed widely. However, much of the studies have adopted triangular numbers due to its ease in application (Garg et al., 2018).

Definition 5: A triangular fuzzy number (TFN) may be denoted as $\left(p, q, r\right)$ representing the smallest possible, most promising, and largest possible value, respectively. The membership function may be stated as:

$$\theta_F\left(y\right) = \begin{cases} 0 & y < p \\ \dfrac{y - p}{q - p} & p \le y < q \\ \dfrac{r - y}{r - q} & q \le y < r \\ 1 & y \ge r \end{cases} \tag{3}$$

Pythagorean Set Theory

Initially the fuzzy sets were extended to intuitionistic fuzzy sets (IFS) to provide a clearer picture of decision making under fuzziness which introduce a membership function as well as a non-membership function. They were able to handle the subjectivity in the input data by incorporating an additional 'hesitancy degree' apart from the degree of belongingness and non-belongingness (Atanassov, 1986). Nowadays, fuzzy sets have witnessed another extension under extant studies, namely Pythagorean fuzzy sets (PFS). One relaxation provided by these sets is that the sum of square of membership and non-membership degrees must be at most one, rather than the sum of membership and non-membership being at most one as in intuitionistic approaches (Yager, 2013). Below we define PFS and mathematical operations related to it.

Definition 6: Let Y be the universe of discourse. A PFS P in Y is defined as

$$P = \{\langle y, a_P\left(y\right), b_P\left(y\right)\rangle \mid y \in Y\} \tag{4}$$

where $a_P, b_P : Y \to \left[0,1\right]$ denote the degree of membership and degree of non-membership, respectively. The degree of indeterminacy is given by $c_P\left(y\right) = \sqrt{1 - a_P^2 - b_P^2}$. Here, $0 \le a_P + b_P \le 1$.

Definition 7: For any PFN p the score function and accuracy function may be defined as

$$s\left(p\right) = a_P^2 - b_P^2 \tag{5}$$

$$ac\left(p\right) = a_P^2 + b_P^2 \tag{6}$$

For any two PFNs p_1, p_2. If $s_{p_1} > s_{p_2}$ then $p_1 \succ p_2$.

1.   If $s_{p_1} = s_{p_2}$ then

    a.   If $ac_{p_1} > ac_{p_2}$ then $p_1 \succ p_2$. If $ac_{p_1} = ac_{p_2}$ then $p_1 \sim p_2$.

Definition 8: Let p. p_1. and p_2 .be three PFNs, and scalar $\alpha > 0$. then their operations are defined as

$$p_1 \oplus p_2 = \left(\sqrt{a_1^2 + a_2^2 - a_1^2 a_2^2}, b_1 b_2 \right) \tag{7}$$

$$p_1 \otimes p_2 = \left(a_1 a_2, \sqrt{b_1^2 + b_2^2 - b_1^2 b_2^2} \right) \tag{8}$$

$$\alpha p = \left(\sqrt{1 - \left(1 - a^2\right)^\alpha}, b^\alpha \right) \tag{9}$$

$$p^\alpha = \left(a^\alpha, \sqrt{1 - \left(1 - b^2\right)^\alpha} \right) \tag{10}$$

$$\frac{p_1}{p_2} = \left(\frac{a_1}{a_2}, \sqrt{\frac{b_1^2 - b_2^2}{1 - b_2^2}} \right) \tag{11}$$

$$p_1 \ominus p_2 = \left(\sqrt{\frac{a_1^2 - a_2^2}{1 - a_2^2}}, \frac{b_1}{b_2} \right) \tag{12}$$

Next we discuss the MCDM approaches used in this paper.

PFAHP COPRAS-G METHODOLOGY

Pythagorean Fuzzy Analytic Hierarchy Process (PFAHP)

AHP is used to handle both qualitative and quantitative data under multiple criteria. Overall, the technique is made up of three processes namely decomposition, comparative judgment, and priority synthesis (Zolfani et al., 2012). The key distinction of this method is that it makes possible to convert a complex problem into a hierarchical structure consisting of a goal, criteria, and various alternatives which are to be evaluated, which covers the decomposition part. Comparative judgment includes the pairwise comparison matrices constructed to measure the contribution of each criterion/alternative (at same level) to the overall objective fulfillment. Finally, the priority synthesis deals with the relative preference of the alternatives, based on the weights of the criteria. Thus, it is demarcated as an order preference technique, rather than an outranking approach. AHP has been extended by previous researchers over fuzzy and intuitionistic environment. This study attempts to further take it over Pythagorean framework, which is a less explored topic by extant scholars. The steps of the method are discussed below.

Step 1: Establish decision makers, criteria, and alternatives. Let $i = 1, 2, ..., l$ be alternatives; $j = 1, 2, ..., m$ be criteria; $K = 1, 2, ..., k$ be decision makers.

Step 2: Calculate weight for each decision maker

$$\sigma_k = \frac{a_k + c_k \left(\dfrac{a_k}{a_k + b_k} \right)}{\sum_k \left(a_k + c_k \left(\dfrac{a_k}{a_k + b_k} \right) \right)} k = 1, 2, ..., K \tag{13}$$

Step 3: Compute aggregated pair-wise matrix U using Interval Valued Pythagorean Fuzzy Weighted Averaging (IVPFWA) operator for group decision maker

$$IVPFWA = \left(\sqrt{1 - \Pi \left(1 - a_{gh}^2 \right)^{\sigma_k}}, \Pi b_{gh}{}^{\sigma_k} \right) g, h = 1, 2, ..., m \tag{14}$$

Step 4: Compute difference matrix $E = \left(e_{gh} \right)_{mXm} \cdot e^{L}_{gh} = a^{L^2}_{gh} - b^{U^2}_{gh}$ (15)

$$e^{U}_{gh} = a^{U^2}_{gh} - b^{L^2}_{gh} \tag{16}$$

Step 5: Compute interval multiplicative matrix $V = \left(v_{gh} \right)_{mXm}$.

$$v^{L}_{gh} = \sqrt{1000^{e^{L}_{gh}}} \tag{17}$$

$$v^{U}_{gh} = \sqrt{1000^{e^{U}_{gh}}} \tag{18}$$

Step 6: Calculate determinacy value $\beta = \left(\beta_{gh} \right)_{mXm}$

$$\beta_{gh} = 1 - \left(a^{U^2}_{gh} - a^{L^2}_{gh} \right) - \left(b^{U^2}_{gh} - b^{L^2}_{gh} \right) \tag{19}$$

Step 7: Calculate weight matrix $O = \left(o_{gh} \right)_{mXm}$

$$o_{gh} = \left(\frac{h^{L}_{gh} + h^{U}_{gh}}{2} \right) \beta_{gh} . \tag{20}$$

Step 8: Calculate normalized weights

$$w_j = \frac{\sum o_{gh}}{\sum \sum o_{gh}} \tag{21}$$

COPRAS-G

A decision making problem is concerned with the selection of the best alternative by the decision maker(s). Therefore, a robust method must be used for their evaluation. COPRAS is a preference ranking technique which tackles the maximization and minimization influences on the evaluation results separately. The whole selection process is based on the ideal and anti-ideal solutions obtained during its application

(Zavadskas, Kaklauskas, Turskis, & Tamošaitiene, 2008). Since most of the alternatives deal with uncertain future as the values of the criteria cannot be judged through crisp sets, researchers suggest to extend it over fuzzy sets or consider it in interval form. This motivates us to apply COPRAS-G for selection, whose steps are discussed below.

Step 1: Construct the decision matrix by each decision maker.

Step 2: Aggregate decision matrix $G = \left[\underline{y_{ij}}, \overline{y_{ij}} \right]$

$$FWA = \left(\prod \underline{y_{ij}}^{\sigma_k}, \prod \overline{y_{ij}}^{\sigma_k} \right) \tag{22}$$

Step 3: Obtain weights of the criteria.

Step 4: Construct the normalized decision matrix $\tilde{G} = \left[\overline{\tilde{y}_{ij}}, \underline{\tilde{y}_{ij}} \right]_{lXm}$ .using Fuzzy Weighted Averaging (FWA) operator

$$\overline{\tilde{y}_{ij}} = \frac{2\overline{y_{ij}}}{\sum_i \left[\overline{y_{ij}} + \underline{y_{ij}} \right]} \tag{23}$$

$$\underline{\tilde{y}_{ij}} = \frac{2\underline{y_{ij}}}{\sum_i \left[\overline{y_{ij}} + \underline{y_{ij}} \right]} \tag{24}$$

Step 5: Calculate weighted normalized decision matrix $\hat{G}$

$$\hat{G} = \tilde{G} \cdot w \tag{25}$$

Step 6: Calculate the criterion sums P_i and R_i whose larger and smaller values are preferred

$$P_i = \frac{1}{2} \sum_{j=1}^{t} (\widehat{y_{ij}} + \overline{\underline{\tilde{y}_{ij}}}) \tag{26}$$

$$R_i = \frac{1}{2} \sum_{j=t+1}^{m} (\widehat{y_{ij}} + \overline{y_{ij}}) \tag{27}$$

For $j = 1, 2, \ldots, t$ are the criteria which need to be maximized and remaining $(m - t)$ are the criteria which need to be minimized.

Step 7: Calculate the relative significance of each alternative

$$Q_i = P_i + \frac{\sum R_i}{R_i \sum \dfrac{1}{R_i}} \tag{28}$$

Step 8: Determine the priority order of the alternatives.

Proposed Computational Steps

In this subsection, we give the step by step method for the hybrid approach PFAHP and COPRAS-G under multiple decision makers. A pictorial representation of the proposed methodology is shown in Figure 1.

Step 1: State the number of alternatives, criteria, and the experts to be used in the model.

Step 2: Construct the pair-wise comparison matrix for comparing each criterion with the other using the linguistic scale provided in Table 3, for all the decision makers.

Step 3: Calculate weights for each decision maker using equation (13).

Step 4: Aggregate the ratings provided by each expert to form an aggregate decision matrix U using formula for IVPFWA given in equation (14).

Step 5: Compute difference matrix E using equations (15) and (16).

Step 6: Compute interval multiplicative matrix V using equations (17) and (18).

Step 7: Calculate determinacy value β using equation (19).

Step 8: Calculate weight matrix O using equation (20).

Step 9: Obtain the normalized global weights using equation (21).

Step 10: Obtain the decision matrix by each decision maker, by rating each alternative over every criterion, using the linguistic scale provided in Table 4.

Step 11: Considering the weight for each decision maker obtained from Step 3, formulate an aggregated decision matrix G using FWA operator given in equation (22).

Step 12: Construct the normalized decision matrix $\tilde{G}$ using equations (23) and (24).

Step 13: Calculate weighted normalized decision matrix $\hat{G}$ considering the weights obtained in Step 9, using equation (25).

Step 14: Calculate the criterion sums P_i and R_i for beneficial and non-beneficial criteria, respectively, using equations (26) and (27).

Step 15: Calculate the relative significance of each alternative Q_i using equation (28).

Step 16: Rank the alternatives in the decreasing values of Q_i.

CASE STUDY

Company Background

The proposed technique has been implemented for a retailer who wants to sell its products online. The identity of the company is not disclosed due to some privacy concerns. In this chapter, the firm is referred as XYZ Company. The XYZ Company was established in 1999 and deal with shoes and also with recognized offline

Figure 1. The proposed methodology

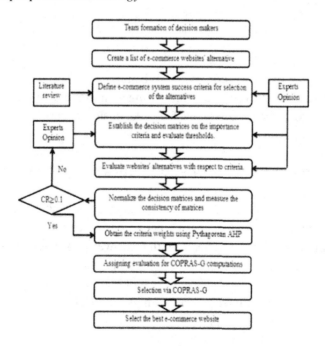

Table 4. Grey scale (Zavadskas et al., 2008)

Linguistic variables	Grey Numbers
Very Weak (VW)	[1,2]
Weak (W)	[2,4]
Medium (M)	[4,6]
Good (G)	[6,8]
Very Good (VG)	[8,9]

Table 3. Pythagorean linguistic scale (Pérez-Domínguez, Rodríguez-Picón, Alvarado-Iniesta, Luviano Cruz, & Xu, 2018)

Linguistic Scale				
Certainly low important (CLI)	.00	.00	.90	.00
Very low important (VLI)	.10	.20	.80	.90
Low important (LI)	.20	.35	.65	.80
Below average important (BAI)	.35	.45	.55	.65
Average important (AI)	.45	.55	.45	.55
Above average important (AAI)	.55	.65	.35	.45
High important (HI)	.65	.80	.20	.35
Very high important (VHI)	.80	.90	.10	.20
Certainly high important (CHI)	.90	.00	.00	.00
Exactly equal (EE)	.1965	.1965	.1965	.1965

suppliers. Selecting the best e-commerce website to sell its products online is a key concern for them. XYZ is well aware that selling their product online reduces set-up and operational cost. It will help to reach a wider customer base, thereby enhancing its sales opportunities.

Implementation of the Proposed Integrated MCDM Techniques

The XYZ's mission is to find out the best e-commerce website that can satisfy its needs. Five e-commerce websites have been considered as alternatives. At this stage, e-commerce experts' experience with these websites' alternatives is taken as reference. A description of these alternative e-commerce websites are provided below.

- **Snapdeal:** It is an online platform with its base Delhi. It provides wide range of products at reasonable prices.

- **ShopClues:** An online retail website, situated in Gurgaon, started in Silicon Valley. Among the most progressive online platforms in India, introduced in July 2011 in Silicon Valley.
- **Flipkart:** An e-commerce firmstarted in 2007, andfunctions only in India. It offers various product categories such as movies, music, games, mobiles, cameras, computers, healthcare and personal care.
- **Myntra:** Indian online shopping place based in Bangalore for shoes, clothing accessories for men and women.
- **Jabong:**The Indian lifestyle e-commerce site, selling apparel, footwear, accessories, beauty products, fragrances, home accessories for men, women & kids.

The criteria determined for the purpose of selecting and ranking e-commerce websites' alternatives are SQ, CQ, U, TR, SUP, PER, and EWOM. Two e-commerce experts are chosen for responses. These two experts are the quality assurance manager and sales coordination manager at XYZ firm. XYZ's quality assurance manager has been employed since 2007 and is one of the most experienced and oldest service staff of the firm. XYZ's sales coordination manager is working in the firm since 2011. In the past, he worked in various departments of company but currently working as a sales coordination manager. His role is to develop sales strategies and assessing the firm's progress. The conceptual framework in the form of a hierarchy is presented in Figure 2.

Moreover, the two decision makers DM1 and DM2 considered may be labeled as proficient and expert, respectively. This distinction is based on number of working years in the field of online marketing. Thus, to flout complexity we consider the preference weights of decision makers as $DM = \{DM1, DM2\} = \{0.7, 0.3\}$. The pair-wise comparison matrix for the criteria, as provided by each decision maker, is given in Table 5 and 6.

Next, we evaluate an aggregated pair-wise matrix using equation (14). After performing Steps 4 – 8, we obtain the normalized weight for each criterion, as shown in Table 7.

According to the above table, it may be noted that electronic word-of-mouth (.288), personalization (.232), and system quality (.180) are more important as compared to trust (.115), content quality (.100), support (.052), and use (.032), with respect to our overall objective. Now, we obtain the decision matrix based on the linguistic scale by each decision maker for different alternatives, which is presented in Table 8 and 9.

Aggregating the decision matrices using equation (22) and performing Steps 12-16, we obtain the ranking results as provided in Table 10.

Figure 2. Hierarchy of the problem

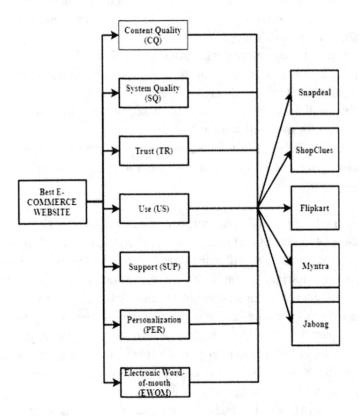

Table 5. Pair-wise comparison matrix by DM1(Compiled by Authors)

DM1	SQ	CQ	US	TR	SUP	PER	EWOM
SQ	EE	AI	AAI	AI	AAI	HI	VHI
CQ	AI	EE	AAI	AI	AAI	HI	VHI
US	BAI	BAI	EE	AAI	AI	AI	VHI
TR	AI	AI	BAI	EE	BAI	AI	HI
SUP	BAI	BAI	AI	AAI	EE	AI	AAI
PER	LI	LI	AI	AI	AI	EE	AI
EWOM	VLI	VLI	VLI	LI	BAI	AI	EE

Table 6. Pair-wise comparison matrix by DM2(Compiled by Authors)

DM2	SQ	CQ	US	TR	SUP	PER	EWOM
SQ	EE	HI	VHI	HI	AI	HI	VHI
CQ	LI	EE	AI	BAI	LI	VHI	HI
US	VLI	AI	EE	LI	VLI	HI	VHI
TR	LI	AAI	HI	EE	BAI	HI	AI
SUP	AI	HI	VHI	AAI	EE	AI	AAI
PER	LI	VLI	LI	LI	AI	EE	AI
EWOM	VLI	LI	VLI	AI	BAI	AI	EE

Table 7. PFAHP results(Compiled by Authors)

Criterion name	Global Weights
System Quality	.180
Content Quality	.100
Use	.032
Trust	.115
Support	.052
Personalization	.232
EWOM	.288

Table 8. Decision matrix by DM1(Compiled by Authors)

DM1	SQ	CQ	US	TR	SUP	PER	EWOM
Snapdeal	W	M	M	W	G	G	VW
ShopClues	G	M	W	M	M	G	G
Flipkart	G	G	W	W	G	M	M
Myntra	M	M	M	W	W	VW	VW
Jabong	M	W	W	VW	VW	G	G

According to the methodology adopted, higher value of relative significance (Q_i) or utility degree (N_i) implies better option. This implies that the website having the larger relative significance or a utility degree among all alternatives will be ranked at first, whereas the alterative with lowest relative significance or utility degree will be placed at the bottom of the list. The comparative selection of all five

Table 9. Decision matrix by DM2 (Compiled by Authors)

DM2	SQ	CQ	US	TR	SUP	PER	EWOM
Snapdeal	M	M	M	VW	W	W	G
ShopClues	W	W	M	G	M	W	VW
Flipkart	M	W	M	W	G	G	M
Myntra	G	G	W	M	M	W	M
Jabong	G	M	M	W	W	M	G

Table 10. COPRAS-G results (Compiled by Authors)

Alternative				N_i	Rank
Snapdeal	.172	.017	.199	19.92%	2
ShopClues	.173	.039	.185	18.52%	5
Flipkart	.204	.021	.226	22.62%	1
Myntra	.177	.024	.195	19.52%	3
Jabong	.159	.013	.194	19.42%	4

e-commerce websites on the basis of seven e-commerce success criteria is provided in Table 10 and Figure 3.

In Figure 3, we can see that e-commerce website Flipkart having the largest utility degree percentage as 22.62% is ranked one, trailed by Snapdeal at number 2, and Myntra at three. The e-commerce website ShopClues is ranked 5, i.e., having the lowest utility degree percentage. The results obtained in this case study depict that Flipkart should be preferred by XYZ Company, whereas ShopClues is least preferable. If XYZ Company will select Flipkart for selling their products online then they will get better results as compared to other alternatives. The hybrid approach based on PFAHP and COPRAS-G method can provide a simple, understandable and valid technique for practitioners as well as researchers. There are many reasons which make it preferable over other MCDM techniques such as simple formulations, less complexity, and better handling of vagueness in MCDM problems.

Figure 3. Comparative selection obtained from PFAHP and COPRAS-G method

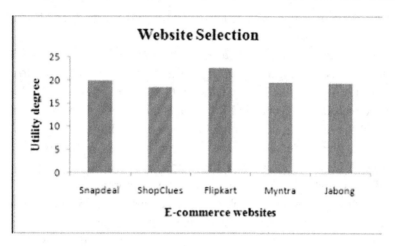

CONCLUSION AND FUTURE SCOPE

Today's marketing environment has become dynamic and firms need to implement right decisions about various marketing problems. Selection of e-commerce websites has become a significant marketing activity in the electronic era, which involves various e-commerce success criteria. Selection helps a company in various ways such as choosing its target segments, resources, competitive advantages, and satisfying customer's needs. E-commerce website selection can influence brand awareness, customer reach, accessibility, and monetary costs. Therefore, it is significant to select the best e-commerce website for every company. However, selecting best website is a challenging job since this problem involves complexity under the presence of multiple criteria. MCDM methods are used for evaluating, selecting, ranking, and comparing with multiple criteria and alternatives. If there are multiple alternatives available, then MCDM techniques can be used, since a decision needs to be taken that is favorable over others. The e-commerce website selection problem is usually influenced by uncertainty and vagueness in practice since the judgments of decision makers (DM) cannot be explained precisely in crisp values. Thus, DM's selection and preferences are usually expressed in terms of linguistic scale. Some previous studies extended the typical MCDM techniques to the fuzzy and Intuitionistic fuzzy (IF) environment. Many different MCDM, fuzzy MCDM, and IF MCDM techniques have been proposed in the literature (such as AHP, SWARA, PROMETHEE, CODAS, EDAS, TOPSIS, ELECTRE, etc.). Some unfavorable aspects of human statements are vagueness, ambiguity, and subjectivity that sometimes cannot be sufficiently handled in Fuzzy and IF fuzzy sets.

Pythagorean fuzzy sets (PFS) are useful tools to investigate vagueness in DM's judgments in terms of lack of information or data related to the problem. Therefore, this chapter proposed a hybrid model to select the best quality e-commerce website. This hybrid model integrates the Pythagorean fuzzy AHP (PFAHP) and the COPRAS-G with group decision making approach. First, the PFAHP technique used to calculate the success criteria weights. Then COPRAS-G method was used to rank different e-commerce website. Multiple decision makers are usually preferred than a single DM to avoid the biases in decision making process. Additionally, a real-life case study was presented to demonstrate the applicability of the hybrid model.

To the best of authors' knowledge, this chapter is the first to implement a PFAHP and COPRAS-G hybrid model to select the best e-commerce website. We have reported and discussed the results obtained in a case study involving an actual firm. In particular, this chapter showed that Flipkart was the best e-commerce website followed by Snapdeal and Myntra based on seven e-commerce success criteria. We also noted that EWOM was the most significant criterion followed by personalization in order to take e-commerce website selection decisions. Improving system quality in a highly competitive market and increasing consumer trust towards e-commerce website revealed to be two criteria of high importance. Use was ranked as the least important criterion as compared to other criteria. The results presented in this chapter may be beneficial to any firm who wants to construct their business online. These findings will also be helpful for e-commerce practitioners, in accordance to better understand their consumers' needs with respect to the success of e-commerce website. Even though the model application focuses e-commerce sector, this model may be adopted in other sectors in order to handle a selection problem. Moreover, this model made use of COPRAS-G technique to obtain alternatives' weights, which can also be obtained by other MCDM techniques in the future, such as TOPSIS, VIKOR, PROMTHEE, CODAS, EDAS, ELECTRE, etc. Only seven criteria are used for this research. More e-commerce success criteria can be used to enhance the effectiveness of the website selection process. Also, this study only considers Pythagorean fuzzy sets. Another promising future study would be to consider the hesitant Pythagorean fuzzy sets. These extensions give an idea for future research.

REFERENCES

Agarwal, R., & Venkatesh, V. (2002). Assessing a firm's web presence: A heuristic evaluation procedure for the measurement of usability. *Information Systems Research, 13*(2), 168–186. doi:10.1287/isre.13.2.168.84

Aggarwal, A., & Aakash, N. A. (2018). Multi-criteria based Prioritization of B2C E-Commerce Website. *International Journal of Society Systems Science, 10*(3), 201. doi:10.1504/IJSSS.2018.093940

Aggarwal, A. G., & Aakash. (2018). A Multi-attribute Online Advertising Budget Allocation Under Uncertain Preferences. *Journal of Engineering and Education, 14*(25), 10. doi:10.16925/.v14i0.2225

Aggarwal, A. G., & Aakash, N. A. (2018). Multi-criteria-based prioritisation of B2C e-commerce website. *International Journal of Society Systems Science, 10*(3), 201–222. doi:10.1504/IJSSS.2018.093940

Aggarwal, A. G., Sharma, H., & Tandon, A. (2017). *An Intuitionistic Approach for Ranking OTA Websites under Multi Criteria Group Decision Making Framework.* Paper presented at the Proceedings of the First International Conference on Information Technology and Knowledge Management, New Delhi, India.

Aggarwal, A. G., & Aakash. (2017). *An Innovative B2C E-commerce Websites Selection using the ME-OWA and Fuzzy AHP.* New Delhi, India: Academic Press.

Aghdaie, M. H., Zolfani, S. H., & Zavadskas, E. K. (2013). Market segment evaluation and selection based on application of fuzzy AHP and COPRAS-G methods. *Journal of Business Economics and Management, 14*(1), 213–233. doi:10.3846/16111699 .2012.721392

Ahmad, S. Z., Abu Bakar, A. R., Faziharudean, T. M., & Mohamad Zaki, K. A. (2015). An empirical study of factors affecting e-commerce adoption among small- and medium-sized enterprises in a developing country: Evidence from Malaysia. *Information Technology for Development, 21*(4), 555–572. doi:10.1080/0268110 2.2014.899961

Akincilar, A., & Dagdeviren, M. (2014). A hybrid multi-criteria decision making model to evaluate hotel websites. *International Journal of Hospitality Management, 36*, 263–271. doi:10.1016/j.ijhm.2013.10.002

Andam, Z. R. (2003). *E-commerce and e-business, e-primer for the information economy.* Society and Polity Series, UNDP-APDIP and e-ASEAN Task Force.

Andreou, A. S., Leonidou, C., Chrysostomou, C., Pitsillides, A., Samaras, G., Schizas, C., & Mavromous, S. M. (2005). Key issues for the design and development of mobile commerce services and applications. *International Journal of Mobile Communications, 3*(3), 303–323. doi:10.1504/IJMC.2005.006586

Apostolou, G., & Economides, A. A. (2008). *Airlines websites evaluation around the world.* Paper presented at the World Summit on Knowledge Society. 10.1007/978-3-540-87783-7_78

Ataburo, H., Muntaka, A. S., & Quansah, E. K. (2017). Linkages among E-Service Quality, Satisfaction, and Usage of E-Services within Higher Educational Environments. *International Journal of Business and Social Research, 7*(3), 10–26. doi:10.18533/ijbsr.v7i3.1040

Atanassov, K. T. (1986). Intuitionistic fuzzy sets. *Fuzzy Sets and Systems, 20*(1), 87–96. doi:10.1016/S0165-0114(86)80034-3

Aydin, S., & Kahraman, C. (2012). Evaluation of e-commerce website quality using fuzzy multi-criteria decision making approach. *IAENG International Journal of Computer Science, 39*(1).

Baek, H., Oh, S., Yang, H.-D., & Ahn, J. (2017). Electronic word-of-mouth, box office revenue and social media. *Electronic Commerce Research and Applications, 22*, 13–23. doi:10.1016/j.elerap.2017.02.001

Bai, B., Law, R., & Wen, I. (2008). The impact of website quality on customer satisfaction and purchase intentions: Evidence from Chinese online visitors. *International Journal of Hospitality Management, 27*(3), 391–402. doi:10.1016/j.ijhm.2007.10.008

Barnes, S. J., & Vidgen, R. (2001). An evaluation of cyber-bookshops: The WebQual method. *International Journal of Electronic Commerce, 6*(1), 11–30. doi:10.1080/10864415.2001.11044225

Barnes, S. J., & Vidgen, R. T. (2006). Data triangulation and web quality metrics: A case study in e-government. *Information & Management, 43*(6), 767–777. doi:10.1016/j.im.2006.06.001

Bauer, H. H., Hammerschmidt, M., & Falk, T. (2005). Measuring the quality of e-banking portals. *International Journal of Bank Marketing*, *23*(2), 153–175. doi:10.1108/02652320510584395

Bell, H., & Tang, N. K. (1998). The effectiveness of commercial Internet Web sites: A user's perspective. *Internet Research*, *8*(3), 219–228. doi:10.1108/10662249810217768

Berger, B., & Matt, C. (2016). *Media Meets Retail-Re-Evaluating Content Quality in the Context of B2C E-Commerce*. Paper presented at the ECIS.

Bhati, A., Thu, Y. T., Woon, S. K. H., Phuong, L. L., & Lynn, M. M. (2017). E-Commerce Usage and User Perspectives in Myanmar: An Exploratory Study. *Advanced Science Letters*, *23*(1), 519–523. doi:10.1166/asl.2017.7241

Bilsel, R. U., Büyüközkan, G., & Ruan, D. (2006). A fuzzy preference-ranking model for a quality evaluation of hospital web sites. *International Journal of Intelligent Systems*, *21*(11), 1181–1197. doi:10.1002/int.20177

Bueyuekoezkan, G., & Ruan, D. (2007). Evaluating government websites based on a fuzzy multiple criteria decision-making approach. *International Journal of Uncertainty, Fuzziness and Knowledge-based Systems*, *15*(03), 321–343. doi:10.1142/S0218488507004704

Büyüközkan, G., Arsenyan, J., & Ertek, G. (2010). Evaluation of e-learning web sites using fuzzy axiomatic design based approach. *International Journal of Computational Intelligence Systems*, *3*(1), 28–42. doi:10.1080/18756891.2010.9727675

Chen, J. V., Rungruengsamrit, D., Rajkumar, T., & Yen, D. C. (2013). Success of electronic commerce Web sites: A comparative study in two countries. *Information & Management*, *50*(6), 344–355. doi:10.1016/j.im.2013.02.007

Chong, S., & Law, R. (2018). Review of studies on airline website evaluation. *Journal of Travel & Tourism Marketing*, 1–16. doi:10.1080/10548408.2018.1494084

Choshin, M., & Ghaffari, A. (2017). An investigation of the impact of effective factors on the success of e-commerce in small-and medium-sized companies. *Computers in Human Behavior*, *66*, 67–74. doi:10.1016/j.chb.2016.09.026

DeLone, W. H., & McLean, E. R. (1992). Information systems success: The quest for the dependent variable. *Information Systems Research*, *3*(1), 60–95. doi:10.1287/isre.3.1.60

Delone, W. H., & McLean, E. R. (2003). The DeLone and McLean model of information systems success: A ten-year update. *Journal of Management Information Systems*, *19*(4), 9–30. doi:10.1080/07421222.2003.11045748

Delone, W. H., & Mclean, E. R. (2004). Measuring e-commerce success: Applying the DeLone & McLean information systems success model. *International Journal of Electronic Commerce*, *9*(1), 31–47. doi:10.1080/10864415.2004.11044317

Evans, K. (2015). *The number of global online shoppers will grow 50% by 2018*. Academic Press.

Garg, R., Kumar, R., & Garg, S. (2018). MADM-Based Parametric Selection and Ranking of E-Learning Websites Using Fuzzy COPRAS. *IEEE Transactions on Education*, (99): 1–8. doi:10.1109/TE.2018.2814611

Guo, S., & Shao, B. (2005). Quantitative evaluation of e-commercial Web sites of foreign trade enterprises in Chongqing. *Proceedings of ICSSSM*, *05*, 2005.

Hidayanto, A. N., Herbowo, A., Budi, N. F. A., & Sucahyo, Y. G. (2014). Determinant of customer trust on e-commerce and its impact to purchase and word of mouth intention: A case of Indonesia. *Journal of Computational Science*, *10*(12), 2395–2407. doi:10.3844/jcssp.2014.2395.2407

Ip, C., Law, R., & Lee, H. A. (2012). The evaluation of hotel website functionality by fuzzy analytic hierarchy process. *Journal of Travel & Tourism Marketing*, *29*(3), 263–278. doi:10.1080/10548408.2012.666173

Jayawardhena, C. (2004). Measurement of service quality in internet banking: The development of an instrument. *Journal of Marketing Management*, *20*(1-2), 185–207. doi:10.1362/0267257041773041177

Jones, M., & Kayworth, T. (1999). Corporate web performance evaluation: An exploratory assessment. *AMCIS 1999 Proceedings*, 88.

Kahraman, C., Keshavarz Ghorabaee, M., Zavadskas, E. K., Cevik Onar, S., Yazdani, M., & Oztaysi, B. (2017). Intuitionistic fuzzy EDAS method: An application to solid waste disposal site selection. *Journal of Environmental Engineering and Landscape Management*, *25*(1), 1–12. doi:10.3846/16486897.2017.1281139

Kang, D., Jang, W., & Park, Y. (2016). Evaluation of e-commerce websites using fuzzy hierarchical TOPSIS based on ES-QUAL. *Applied Soft Computing, 42,* 53–65. doi:10.1016/j.asoc.2016.01.017

Kardaras, D., & Karakostas, V. (1999). Measuring the Electronic Commerce Impact on Customer Satisfaction: Experiences, Problems and expectations of the banking sector in the UK. *Proceeding of the International conference of the Measurement of Electronic Commerce.*

Kaya, T., & Kahraman, C. (2011). A fuzzy approach to e-banking website quality assessment based on an integrated AHP-ELECTRE method. *Technological and Economic Development of Economy, 17*(2), 313–334. doi:10.3846/20294913.20 11.583727

Kim, C., Galliers, R. D., Shin, N., Ryoo, J.-H., & Kim, J. (2012). Factors influencing Internet shopping value and customer repurchase intention. *Electronic Commerce Research and Applications, 11*(4), 374–387. doi:10.1016/j.elerap.2012.04.002

Kim, E. (1999). A model of an effective web. *AMCIS 1999 Proceedings,* 181.

Kim, S., & Lee, Y. (2006). Global online marketplace: A cross-cultural comparison of website quality. *International Journal of Consumer Studies, 30*(6), 533–543. doi:10.1111/j.1470-6431.2006.00522.x

Kim, S., & Stoel, L. (2004). Apparel retailers: Website quality dimensions and satisfaction. *Journal of Retailing and Consumer Services, 11*(2), 109–117. doi:10.1016/S0969-6989(03)00010-9

Koufaris, M. (2002). Applying the technology acceptance model and flow theory to online consumer behavior. *Information Systems Research, 13*(2), 205–223. doi:10.1287/isre.13.2.205.83

Law, R. (2007). A fuzzy multiple criteria decision-making model for evaluating travel websites. *Asia Pacific Journal of Tourism Research, 12*(2), 147–159. doi:10.1080/10941660701243372

Lee, N. Y., & Choi, E. H. (2001). *Appling the AHP techniques to electronic commerce in a special attention to Fashion website selection.* Paper presented at the International Conference Human Society@ Internet.

Lee, Y., & Kozar, K. A. (2006). Investigating the effect of website quality on e-business success: An analytic hierarchy process (AHP) approach. *Decision Support Systems, 42*(3), 1383–1401. doi:10.1016/j.dss.2005.11.005

Liang, R., Wang, J., & Zhang, H. (2017). Evaluation of e-commerce websites: An integrated approach under a single-valued trapezoidal neutrosophic environment. *Knowledge-Based Systems, 135*, 44–59. doi:10.1016/j.knosys.2017.08.002

Liu, C., & Arnett, K. P. (2000). Exploring the factors associated with Web site success in the context of electronic commerce. *Information & Management, 38*(1), 23–33. doi:10.1016/S0378-7206(00)00049-5

Loiacono, E., Chen, D., & Goodhue, D. (2002). WebQual TM revisited: Predicting the intent to reuse a web site. *AMCIS 2002 Proceedings*, 46.

Molla, A., & Licker, P. S. (2001). E-commerce systems success: An attempt to extend and respecify the Delone and MacLean model of IS success. *Journal of Electronic Commerce Research, 2*(4), 131–141.

Moustakis, V., Litos, C., Dalivigas, A., & Tsironis, L. (2004). *Website Quality Assessment Criteria. IQ, 5*, 59–73.

Moustakis, V., Tsironis, L., & Litos, C. (2006). A model of web site quality assessment. *The Quality Management Journal, 13*(2), 22–37. doi:10.1080/106869 67.2006.11918547

Ngai, E. (2003). Selection of web sites for online advertising using the AHP. *Information & Management, 40*(4), 233–242. doi:10.1016/S0378-7206(02)00004-6

Nielsen, J. (1999). *Designing web usability: The practice of simplicity*. New Riders Publishing.

Palmer, J. W. (2002). Web site usability, design, and performance metrics. *Information Systems Research, 13*(2), 151–167. doi:10.1287/isre.13.2.151.88

Panigrahi, R., & Srivastava, P. R. (2015). *Evaluation of travel websites: A fuzzy analytical hierarchy process approach*. Paper presented at the Electrical Computer and Electronics (UPCON), 2015 IEEE UP Section Conference on. 10.1109/UPCON.2015.7456743

Park, E. J., Kim, E. Y., Funches, V. M., & Foxx, W. (2012). Apparel product attributes, web browsing, and e-impulse buying on shopping websites. *Journal of Business Research, 65*(11), 1583–1589. doi:10.1016/j.jbusres.2011.02.043

Park, Y. A., & Gretzel, U. (2007). Success factors for destination marketing web sites: A qualitative meta-analysis. *Journal of Travel Research, 46*(1), 46–63. doi:10.1177/0047287507302381

Peng, X., Yuan, H., & Yang, Y. (2017). Pythagorean fuzzy information measures and their applications. *International Journal of Intelligent Systems, 32*(10), 991–1029. doi:10.1002/int.21880

Pérez, I. J., Alonso, S., Cabrerizo, F. J., Lu, J., & Herrera-Viedma, E. (2011). *Modelling heterogeneity among experts in multi-criteria group decision making problems.* Paper presented at the International Conference on Modeling Decisions for Artificial Intelligence. 10.1007/978-3-642-22589-5_7

Pérez-Domínguez, L., Rodríguez-Picón, L. A., Alvarado-Iniesta, A., Luviano Cruz, D., & Xu, Z. (2018). MOORA under Pythagorean Fuzzy Set for Multiple Criteria Decision Making. *Complexity.*

Qi, S., Law, R., & Buhalis, D. (2008). Usability of Chinese destination management organization websites. *Journal of Travel & Tourism Marketing, 25*(2), 182–198. doi:10.1080/10548400802402933

Qi, S., Law, R., & Buhalis, D. (2013). A modified fuzzy hierarchical TOPSIS model for hotel website evaluation. *International Journal of Fuzzy System Applications, 3*(3), 82–101. doi:10.4018/ijfsa.2013070105

Qi, S., Law, R., & Buhalis, D. (2017). Comparative evaluation study of the websites of China-based and international luxury hotels. *Journal of China Tourism Research, 13*(1), 1–25. doi:10.1080/19388160.2017.1289135

Ramanathan, R. (2010). E-commerce success criteria: Determining which criteria count most. *Electronic Commerce Research, 10*(2), 191–208. doi:10.100710660-010-9051-3

Rana, N. P., Dwivedi, Y. K., Williams, M. D., & Weerakkody, V. (2015). Investigating success of an e-government initiative: Validation of an integrated IS success model. *Information Systems Frontiers, 17*(1), 127–142. doi:10.100710796-014-9504-7

Ranganathan, C., & Ganapathy, S. (2002). Key dimensions of business-to-consumer web sites. *Information & Management*, *39*(6), 457–465. doi:10.1016/S0378-7206(01)00112-4

Saaty, A. (1980). *The analytic hierarchy process*. Mc Graw Hill, Inc.

San Lim, Y., Heng, P. C., Ng, T. H., & Cheah, C. S. (2016). Customers' online website satisfaction in online apparel purchase: A study of Generation Y in Malaysia. *Asia Pacific Management Review*, *21*(2), 74–78. doi:10.1016/j.apmrv.2015.10.002

Schmitz, S. W., & Latzer, M. (2002). Competition in B2C e-Commerce: Analytical issues and empirical evidence. *Electronic Markets*, *12*(3), 163–174. doi:10.1080/101967802320245938

Schubert, P., & Selz, D. (2001). Measuring the effectiveness of e-commerce Web sites. In E-commerce and V-Business. Oxford, UK: Butterworth Heinemann.

Smith, A. G. (2001). Applying evaluation criteria to New Zealand government websites. *International Journal of Information Management*, *21*(2), 137–149. doi:10.1016/S0268-4012(01)00006-8

Sun, C.-C., & Lin, G. T. (2009). Using fuzzy TOPSIS method for evaluating the competitive advantages of shopping websites. *Expert Systems with Applications*, *36*(9), 11764–11771. doi:10.1016/j.eswa.2009.04.017

Sun, P., Cárdenas, D. A., & Harrill, R. (2016). Chinese customers' evaluation of travel website quality: A decision-tree analysis. *Journal of Hospitality Marketing & Management*, *25*(4), 476–497. doi:10.1080/19368623.2015.1037977

Tarasewich, P., & Warkentin, M. (2000). Issues in wireless E-commerce. *ACM SIGEcom Exchanges*, *1*(1), 21–25. doi:10.1145/844302.844307

Torkzadeh, G., & Dhillon, G. (2002). Measuring factors that influence the success of Internet commerce. *Information Systems Research*, *13*(2), 187–204. doi:10.1287/isre.13.2.187.87

Ureña, R., Chiclana, F., Fujita, H., & Herrera-Viedma, E. (2015). Confidence-consistency driven group decision making approach with incomplete reciprocal intuitionistic preference relations. *Knowledge-Based Systems*, *89*, 86–96. doi:10.1016/j.knosys.2015.06.020

Van Iwaarden, J., Van Der Wiele, T., Ball, L., & Millen, R. (2004). Perceptions about the quality of web sites: A survey amongst students at Northeastern University and Erasmus University. *Information & Management*, *41*(8), 947–959. doi:10.1016/j.im.2003.10.002

Venkatesh, V., Morris, M. G., Davis, G. B., & Davis, F. D. (2003). User acceptance of information technology: Toward a unified view. *Management Information Systems Quarterly*, *27*(3), 425–478. doi:10.2307/30036540

Wang, Y. S. (2008). Assessing e-commerce systems success: A respecification and validation of the DeLone and McLean model of IS success. *Information Systems Journal*, *18*(5), 529–557. doi:10.1111/j.1365-2575.2007.00268.x

Wu, F., Mahajan, V., & Balasubramanian, S. (2003). An analysis of e-business adoption and its impact on business performance. *Journal of the Academy of Marketing Science*, *31*(4), 425–447. doi:10.1177/0092070303255379

Xu, J. D., Benbasat, I., & Cenfetelli, R. T. (2013). Integrating service quality with system and information quality: An empirical test in the e-service context. *Management Information Systems Quarterly*, *37*(3), 777–794. doi:10.25300/MISQ/2013/37.3.05

Yager, R. R. (2013). *Pythagorean fuzzy subsets.* Paper presented at the IFSA World Congress and NAFIPS Annual Meeting (IFSA/NAFIPS), 2013 Joint. 10.1109/IFSA-NAFIPS.2013.6608375

Yager, R. R. (2014). Pythagorean membership grades in multicriteria decision making. *IEEE Transactions on Fuzzy Systems*, *22*(4), 958–965. doi:10.1109/TFUZZ.2013.2278989

Yang, Z., Cai, S., Zhou, Z., & Zhou, N. (2005). Development and validation of an instrument to measure user perceived service quality of information presenting web portals. *Information & Management*, *42*(4), 575–589. doi:10.1016/S0378-7206(04)00073-4

Ye, Q., Law, R., & Gu, B. (2009). The impact of online user reviews on hotel room sales. *International Journal of Hospitality Management*, *28*(1), 180–182. doi:10.1016/j.ijhm.2008.06.011

Young, D., & Benamati, J. (2000). Differences in public web sites: The current state of large US firms. *Journal of Electronic Commerce Research*, *1*(3), 94–105.

Yu, X., Guo, S., Guo, J., & Huang, X. (2011). Rank B2C e-commerce websites in e-alliance based on AHP and fuzzy TOPSIS. *Expert Systems with Applications*, *38*(4), 3550–3557. doi:10.1016/j.eswa.2010.08.143

Zadeh, L. A. (1965). Fuzzy sets. *Information and Control*, *8*(3), 338–353. doi:10.1016/S0019-9958(65)90241-X

Zavadskas, E. K., Kaklauskas, A., Turskis, Z., & Tamošaitiene, J. (2008). Selection of the effective dwelling house walls by applying attributes values determined at intervals. *Journal of Civil Engineering and Management*, *14*(2), 85–93. doi:10.3846/1392-3730.2008.14.3

Zhang, H.-y., Peng, H., Wang, J., & Wang, J. (2017). An extended outranking approach for multi-criteria decision-making problems with linguistic intuitionistic fuzzy numbers. *Applied Soft Computing*, *59*, 462–474. doi:10.1016/j.asoc.2017.06.013

Zhang, T., Cheung, C., & Law, R. (2018). Functionality Evaluation for Destination Marketing Websites in Smart Tourism Cities. *Journal of China Tourism Research*, 1–16.

Zhang, X., Keeling, K. B., & Pavur, R. J. (2000). Information quality of commericial web site home pages: an explorative analysis. *Proceedings of the twenty first international conference on Information systems*.

Zhu, X., Zhang, Q., Zhang, L., & Yang, J. (2013). Online Promotion of the E-Commerce Websites in Retail Market in China: An Empirical Study. *Journal of Electronic Commerce in Organizations*, *11*(2), 23–40. doi:10.4018/jeco.2013040103

Zhu, Y., & Buchmann, A. (2002). Evaluating and selecting web sources as external information resources of a data warehouse. *Web Information Systems Engineering, 2002. WISE 2002. Proceedings of the Third International Conference on*.

Zolfani, S. H., Chen, I.-S., Rezaeiniya, N., & Tamošaitienė, J. (2012). A hybrid MCDM model encompassing AHP and COPRAS-G methods for selecting company supplier in Iran. *Technological and Economic Development of Economy*, *18*(3), 529–543. doi:10.3846/20294913.2012.709472

Chapter 5

Comparison of Private Shopping Sites With User Data From Entropy-Based Moosra Method

Günay Kılıç
https://orcid.org/0000-0003-2236-7535
Pamukkale University, Turkey

Arzu Organ
Pamukkale University, Turkey

ABSTRACT

The share of electronic commerce (e-commerce) in total trade is increasing. There are many kinds of services and products within the scope of e-commerce. These products and services are subdivided according to their sales forms and product groups. In this chapter, only the private shopping websites in the online sales group were examined. Private shopping sites are the sites where the members buy certain products with limited stock in limited time. In this chapter, six leading sites are defined as alternatives for the purpose of comparison. When the studies in the literature are examined, it is seen that multi-criteria decision making methods are used in order to sort the special shopping sites by taking into consideration the criteria. Entropy method was used to determine the weights of the criteria under each main topic determined in the study. Moosra method was chosen from multi-criteria decision making methods in order to rank alternative websites. As a result, alternative sites were listed separately and then examined as to whether there was a relationship between these groups.

DOI: 10.4018/978-1-5225-8238-0.ch005

INTRODUCTION

The medium where information is most available in today's age is the Internet and websites, which are the most important part of the Internet. Websites are one of the most effective tools used to establish and maintain relations with organizations and individuals worldwide (Özsarı, et al., 2016:210).

With the increase in shopping through websites, the manufacturers of goods and services have begun to develop various competitive instruments to reach a wide range of customers. Opportunity sites strategy is one of the methods whose popularity has been increasing in recent years. Every day, dozens of businesses publicize their discount campaigns or benefits through opportunity sites (Yalçın and BAŞ., 2012:3).

Websites offer major opportunities for both businesses and consumers. Their benefits to businesses include savings in costs, effectiveness in sales and marketing activities, better customer relationships, customer continuity and loyalty, access to global markets, time-saving, equal opportunities, access to new markets and competitive advantage, efficiency and rich information. Their benefits to consumers, on the other hand, include easy shopping, time-saving, rich information, and comparison of products and services, and a controllable purchasing process. In addition, due to the fact that all stages of the sales from order to payment take place in a virtual environment, most of the costs in traditional sales are eliminated, providing a reduction in the costs, which is another important benefit of the Internet (Dündar, et al., 2007:289).

Consumers may be satisfied with their shopping experience from websites; however, the fact that there are many similar shopping sites may also cause them to be indecisive. Furthermore, consumers may be dissatisfied with the products they buy from websites. They may even be dissatisfied with or make complaints about the shopping websites. For this reason, managers of shopping websites should learn the reasons of these dissatisfactions and design consumer-oriented activities in order to satisfy consumers (Yılmaz, et al.,2016:103)). In addition, shopping websites should be designed so as to provide the best user experience (Genç, 2010:485).

Due to this increase in the websites, consumers, on the other hand, may have difficulties in making a decision on which shopping site to use. In this decision-making process, the properties of the websites play an important role. Decision-making is a part of daily life. People, big companies and even countries constantly need to make decisions. Even if the decision-making unit is a human or a machine, the decision maker must perform the following functions. A decision-maker receives information, collects information in itself, processes it in intelligence and makes a decision (Chankong & Haimes, 2008:3). Although people sometimes make decisions based on only one criterion, real life is much more complex. The decision-making problem is usually a complex process that requires multiple parameters to be evaluated together. The selection of the best alternative among a number of alternatives and a series of decision criteria is a Multi-Criteria Decision Making (MCDM) problem. Many MCDM methods have been developed to solve this problem. There is no clear evidence as to which is the best one of these methods (Evangelos, 2000:5). Examples of these methods include AHP, TOPSIS, PROMETHEE, VIKOR, and MOOSRA.

These methods have also been used in the selection of private shopping websites with multiple alternatives and criteria. in this study, six leading private shopping websites operating in Turkey have been compared with the Entropy-Based MOOSRA a method. MOOSRA method has been used to sort the websites. Entropy method, which is frequently used in the literature, has been used in the use of weights. These websites were compared in 3 different dimensions and the results were presented methodology. In this study, Entropy method, which is frequently used in weighting the criteria of MCDM problems, was used. the steps of the method are explained in detail and some studies conducted with this method in the literature are mentioned. after the weights were determined, MOOSRA method was used to sort the alternatives. The steps of the method and some studies with this method were mentioned.

ENTROPY METHOD

Entropy used to measure the disorder of a system in the natural sciences is adapted to measure the degree of uncertainty of a system in the social sciences (Han et, all., 2015: 218). By using Entropy, the uncertainty between the criteria in multi-criteria decision-making methods can be eliminated and weights can be assigned to criteria without the need for the personal opinion of the experts (Perçin & Sönmez, 2018: 570). Entropy is a very good scale in different decision making and evaluation processes and can be used to evaluate decision making units (Wu, 2011: 5163). Entropy method is used in the literature with many multi-criteria decision making methods for the performance evaluation of automotive companies, the Entropy-based MAUT method was used (Ömürbek et al., 2016). Performance measurement of insurance companies using entropy method combined with TOPSIS method (Wu, 2011). Entropy was used in the geographical market selection by using PROMETHEE method (Yavuz, 2016). The method was used to evaluate EU countries in terms of quality of life in combination with ARAS and MOOSRA methods (Ömürbek et al., 2017). ARAS, MOOSRA and COPRAS methods were used in the evaluation of the sustainability performance of banks and the weight of these methods were determined by Entropy method (Ömürbek et al., 2017).

The Entropy method consists of the following steps (Karami & Johansson, 2014: 524).

Step 1: Normalization of Decision Matrix P_{ij}

$$P_{ij} = \frac{a_{ij}}{\sum_{i=1}^{m} a_{ij}} \; ; \forall j, \; (i=1,..,m; \; j=1,..,n) \tag{2.1}$$

Step 2: Calculation of Entropy Values E_j.

$$E_j = \frac{-1}{\ln m} \sum_{i=1}^{m} [P_{ij} In P_{ij}] \; ; \forall j, \; (i=1,..,m; \; j=1,2..,n) \tag{2.2}$$

Step 3: Calculation of the Degree of Uncertainty d_j.

$$d_j = 1 - E_j \; ; \; \forall j, (j=1,2,\ldots,n) \tag{2.3}$$

Step 4: Calculation of Weights Wj.

$$W_j = \frac{d_j}{\sum_{j=1}^{n} d_j} \; ; \forall j, . \; (j=1,2,\ldots,n) \tag{2.4}$$

MSRA METHOD

This method helps the decision-makers to eliminate inappropriate alternatives after selecting the most appropriate alternatives to strengthen existing selection procedures. It is seen that the method is very robust, understandable and easy to calculate. MOORA and MOOSRA methods Compared to other alternative MCDM methods, the calculation time is low, the calculation is simple, transparent and flexible methods. With these methods, the relative importance of all criteria are taken into consideration and the alternatives can be ordered more accurately (Sarkar, 2015: 340). To some extent, the MOOSRA method is parallel to the MOORA method, but is more robust compared to MOORA (Ray, 2014: 560). The MOOSRA method was first introduced in 2012. The method used in the selection of cutting fluid for green production in 2014 was compared with AHP (Ray, 2014). Also, in the literature, MOORA and MOOSRA method were used in machine selection (Sarkar, 2015).

The MOOSRA method has been used in the selection of materials compared to PROMETHEE II, ORESTE and OCRA methods (Kumar & Ray, 2015). Considering the studies, it is seen that MULTIMOORA and MOOSRA methods are used for laptop selection (Adalı & Işık, 2017). The Entropy Based MOOSRA method was used in the selection of the logistics center (Ulutaş, 2018). MULTIMOORA, TPOP and MOOSRA method were used to select the critical path for the project (Dorfeshan, 2018). For the selection of UPS, the MOOSRA method was used which's weights was calculated by the CRITIC method (Demircioğlu & Coşkun: 2018).

The MOOSRA method consists of the following steps (Ray, 2014: 561-562):

Step 1: Creation of decision matrix with n criteria and m alternative X_{ij}.

$$X_{ij} = \begin{bmatrix} X_{11} & X_{12} & \cdots & X_{1n} \\ X_{21} & X_{22} & \cdots & X_{2n} \\ \cdots & \cdots & \cdots & \cdots \\ X_{m1} & X_{m2} & \cdots & X_{mn} \end{bmatrix} \tag{2.5}$$

Step 2: The values are normalized in the range of formula (2.6) to 0-1. Normalized data is shown as $X_{ij}*$ $X_{ij}.*$ shows that i. alternative normalized value on j.

$$X_{ij}* = \frac{x_{ij}}{\sqrt{\sum_{i=1}^{n} X_{ij}2}} \tag{2.6}$$

Step 3: The determination of alternative values according to the benefit and cost criteria can be calculated by the equation (2.7) Y_i.

$$Y_i = \frac{\sum_{j=1}^{g} w_j X_{ij}*}{\sum_{j=g+1}^{n} w_j X_{ij}*} \tag{2.7}$$

where g is the maximum value, w_j is the weight value.

Step 4: The alternatives can be listed in formula (2.8).

$$Y_i = \frac{\sum_{j=1}^{g} w_j X_{ij}{}^*}{\sum_{j=g+1}^{n} w_j X_{ij}{}^*} \tag{2.8}$$

APPLICATION

There are many private shopping site in Turkey. In this study six leading website in the sector in Turkey were selected as alternatives. The alternatives in the study are trendyol.com (Trendyol), markafoni.com (Markafoni), morhipo.com (Morhipo), 1v1y. com (1v1y), tozlu.com, lidyana.com (Lidyana). The alternatives were evaluated in terms of search engines statistics, website usage statistics, user evaluations, social media interactions and three dimensions were determined. These dimensions can be called web statistics, user reviews and feedback, and social media performance. Each dimension consists o5 sub-criteria. Three dimensions and criteria are shown in table 1.

Alternatives according to determined dimensions and criteria are listed by Entropy based MOOSRA method. The hierarchical model is given in figure 1.

Table 1. The details of dimensions and criteria

Dimensions	Criteria
Web Statistics (D1)	Google Trend (C1)
	Daily Page Views per Visitor (C2)
	Daily Time on Site (C3)
	Bounce Rate (C4)
	% of Traffic From Search (C5)
User Evaluations and Feedback (D2)	Satisfaction Level (C1)
	Total Interaction (C2)
	Thanks Rate (C3)
	Response Rate (C4)
	Response Time (C5)
Social Media Performance (D3)	Number of Facebook Followers (C1)
	Number of Twitter Followers (C2)
	Number of Tweets (C3)
	Number of Instagram Followers (C4)
	Number of Instagram Posts (C5)

Figure 1.

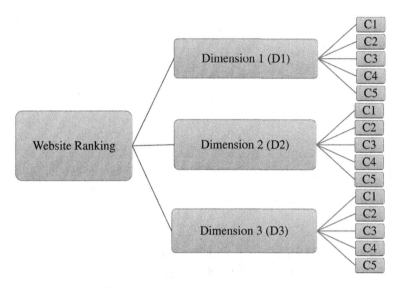

In the next part of the study, the criteria for each dimension are explained. Ranking according to each dimension.

Ranking According to Dimension: Web Statistics

The first dimension is the web statistics generated by the users on the websites reviewed. The first criterion used in this dimension was taken from trends.google.com

- **Google Trend (C1):** Trends.google.com consists of statistics on Google. com, the world's largest search engine. The interest shown over time in a search by regional or subject is ranked as 0-100. The higher the score shows the more searched website. Therefore, c1 criterion is taken as benefit criteria. As an example of other criteria, the data of the alternatives for the last 3 months as of 18.09.2018 are shown in Figure 2.
- **Daily Page Views per Visitor (C2):** The number of web pages that users view on the website daily. The number of pages displayed on similar websites may be indicative that the site is richer in content. Therefore, this criterion is taken as the criterion of benefit.
- **Daily Time on Site (C3):** Users' time spent on the web site is taken as seconds. The high duration of this site may be indicative of its rich and popular content. Therefore, these criterion is taken as the criterion of benefit.

Figure 2.

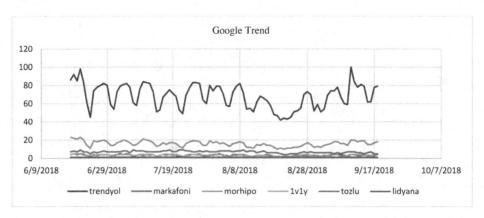

- **Bounce Rate (C4):** The bounce rate are indications that users are not standing on the site. This criterion, which was kept as a percentage, was taken as the cost criterion.
- **% of Traffic from Search (C5):** This is the criterion and the rate of coming to the site through the search engine. This is a cost criterion because it is considered that popular websites are not searched through the search engine.

The decision matrix according to the first dimension criteria is formed as in Table 2.

The weights determined by Entropy and criteria are given in table 3.

The criterion C1 in table 3 is more important than the other criteria.

Table 2. The decision matrix according to dimension: web statistics

	Google Trend (C1)	Daily Page Views per Visitor (C2)	Daily Time on Site (C3)	Bounce Rate (C4)	% of Traffic From Search (C5)
Trendyol	68,43	8,21	540	32,3	34,4
Markafoni	3,32	4,57	314	33,5	42,7
Morhipo	15,99	5,85	401	33,6	34,3
1v1y	3,26	5,45	371	32,1	29,3
Tozlu	6,87	7,55	502	25,4	38
Lidyana	1	3	151	51	46

Table 3. Determined weights by entropy

	Google Trend (C1)	Daily Page Views per Visitor (C2)	Daily Time on Site (C3)	Bounce Rate (C4)	% of Traffic From Search (C5)
w	0,85	0,05	0,07	0,02	0,01

The steps of the MOOSRA method are performed in sequence. In step 4, Y_i values are calculated from equality 2.8. The rankings with Y_i values are given in table 4.

Table 4 shows that Trendyol, the leading company in the sector, is the first in the ranking. Lidyana is the last one.

Ranking According to Dimension: User Evaluations and Feedback

www.sikayetvar.com is the world's first and biggest complaint platform operating since 2001. Ctomers can complain about the company and their opinions on this platform. The data used for rking in the second dimension consist of the evaluation of the websites of the users on this platform and feedbacks. Under this dimension, 5 criteria determined are as follows.

- **Sfaction Level (C1):** The first criterion is the percentage of satisfaction from the websites of the users. The criterion was taken as the criterion of benefit

Table 4. Ranking according to dimension: web statistics

Web Site	$\sum_{j=1}^{g} w_j X_{ij}*$	$\sum_{j=g+1}^{n} w_j X_{ij}*$	Y_i	Ranking
Trendyol	0,886	0,012	73,425	1
Markafoni	0,078	0,013	5,783	5
Morhipo	0,240	0,012	19,411	2
1v1y	0,084	0,011	7,389	4
Tozlu	0,144	0,011	13,167	3
Lidyana	0,033	0,018	1,836	6

because it was positive for the company that the urs were satisfied with the companies.

- **Total Interaction (C2):** The second criterion, the total interaction, is expressed as the sum of the complaint and thanks about the site. If the total interaction is over, it may be an indication of the size of the firm. Therefore, this criterion has been taken as a benefit criterion.
- **Thanks Rate (C3):** The rate of thanks in the total interaction is the third criterion. The Thanks rate, which is an indicator of the satisfaction of the company's services, has been taken as a benefit criterion.
- **Response Rate (C4):** The rate of responding to customer requests indicates the rate of respecting the user satisfaction of the website. Sites with high response rates may be considered interested in users' requests and complaints. And these sites can be considered as having provided better quality services. Therefore, this criterion has been taken as a benefit criterion.
- **Response Time (C5):** The company's response time to the complaints in minutes is the last criterion. It can be said that the sites that have returned to their customers in a short time provide good service. The short duration of this period is better for the company. This criterion was taken as the cost criterion.

The decision matrix according to the second dimension criteria is formed as in Table 5.

The weights determined by Entropy and criteria are given in table 6.

Table 6 shows that the weight of C3 and C5 is high and C4 is low.

The steps of the MOOSRA method are performed in sequence. In step 4, Y_i values are calculated from equality 2.8. The rankings with Y_i values are given in table 7.

Table 5. The decision matrix according to dimension: user evaluations and feedback

	Satisfaction Level (C1)	Total Interaction (C2)	Thanks Rate (C3)	Response Rate (C4)	Response Time (C5)
Trendyol	51	10363	0,14	99	56
Markafoni	48	194	0,11	98	120
Morhipo	53	4200	0,18	100	8
1vly	52	1218	0,23	100	60
Tozlu	91	588	0,37	96	300
Lidyana	22	267	0,05	70	2880

Table 6. Determined weights by entropy

	Satisfaction Level (C1)	Total Interaction (C2)	Thanks Rate (C3)	Response Rate (C4)	Response Time (C5)
w	0,040	0,084	0,397	0,004	0,475

Table 7. Ranking according to dimension: user evaluations and feedback

Web Site	$\sum_{j=1}^{g} w_j X_{ij}$ *	$\sum_{j=g+1}^{n} w_j X_{ij}$ *	Y_i	Ranking
Trendyol	0,406	0,009	44,255	2
Markafoni	0,040	0,020	2,055	5
Morhipo	0,195	0,001	148,515	1
1v1y	0,099	0,010	10,035	3
Tozlu	0,110	0,049	2,235	4
Lidyana	0,026	0,471	0,054	6

It is seen that Morhipo was the first company in Table 7. Trendyol, the leading company in the sector, follows the Morhipo as the second. Finally, Lidyana has worst ranking as in Table 2.

Ranking According to Dimension: Social Media Performance

Social media is used for double-sided media sharing and especially for websites to reach and inform customers. Social media networks, the most popular in social media, were used in this dimension. These social networks are as follows: www.facebook.com, www.instagram.com, and www.twitter.com.In this dimension, 5 criteria were formed with the data from social networks. These 5 criteria are explained as follows.

- **Number of Facebook Followers (C1):** The first criterion is the number of Facebook followers. The number of followers on Facebook, the largest social media platform in the world, indicates the popularity of the company. The criterion was taken as the benefit criterion.
- **Number of Twitter Followers (C2):** The second is the number of followers on twitter, another popular social media platform similar to the first criterion. This criterion is a benefit criterion, such as the previous criterion.

- **Number of Tweets (C3):** The third criterion is the number of tweets tweeted from the official twitter account of the web site. This criterion is taken as a criterion of benefit that shows the activity of social media departments.
- **Number of Instagram Followers (C4):** The number of followers on Instagram, which is another popular social media platform, is the fourth criterion. Similarly to the C1 and C2 criteria, it was taken as a benefit criterion.
- **Number of Instagram Posts (C5):** The number of posts on the Instagram account of the website. This criterion has been taken as a benefit criterion as the other criteria.

The decision matrix according to the third dimension criteria is formed as in Table 8.

The weights determined by Entropy and criteria are given in table 9.

When Table 9 is examined, it is seen that the number of followers on social media platforms is more important than the number of shares. It is noteworthy that the number of Instagram followers is more important than other criteria.

The steps of the MOOSRA method are performed in sequence. In step 4, Y_i values are calculated from equality 2.8. The rankings with Y_i values are given in table 10.

Table 8. The decision matrix according to dimension: social media performance

	Number of Facebook Followers (C1)	Number of Twitter Followers (C2)	Number of Tweets (C3)	Number of Instagram Followers (C4)	Number of Instagram Posts (C5)
Trendyol	2202910	147000	50700	1052641	5447
Markafoni	1341437	141000	36000	187468	6279
Morhipo	1074175	99300	25100	305745	5859
1vly	151047	36800	11700	51206	4592
Tozlu	2128719	12000	14100	879368	9805
Lidyana	192279	29600	9616	287554	6561

Table 9. Determined weights by entropy

	Satisfaction Level (C1)	Total Interaction (C2)	Thanks Rate (C3)	Response Rate (C4)	Response Time (C5)
w	0,265	0,246	0,161	0,3	0,028

Table 10. Ranking according to dimension: social media performance

Web Site	$\sum_{j=1}^{g} w_j X_{ij}*$	Y_i	Ranking
Trendyol	0,666	0,666	1
Markafoni	0,383	0,383	3
Morhipo	0,317	0,317	4
1v1y	0,096	0,096	6
Tozlu	0,404	0,404	2
Lidyana	0,139	0,139	5

In Table 10 Trendyol is first web site. Unlike other dimensions, 1v1y was the last in this dimension.

In the literature, there are studies in which web site content is evaluated by users opinion. In this study, real numerical data were used. The Internet is used as a source of information, the data of the internet search engines, web page statistics, users' web evaluations and data of social media platforms have been used in the rankings. The rankings in the three dimension previously determined are given together in Table 11.

When Table 11 is analyzed, it is seen that there is a positive relationship between Web Statistics and User Evaluations and Feedback (correlation =0,88). The correlation between Web Statistics and Social Media Performance is 0.54. The correlation between User Evaluations and Feedback and Social Media Performance is 0.31. It can be assumed from this point of view that only User Evaluations and Feedback can be used to get a great idea about Web Statistics. Likewise, it can be said that Web Statistics can explain User Evaluations and Feedback. Social Media Performance in not effective for explaining other two dimensions.

Table 11. Ranking according to three dimensions

Web Site	Web Statistics	User Evaluations and Feedback	Social Media Performance
Trendyol	1	2	1
Markafoni	5	5	3
Morhipo	2	1	4
1v1y	4	3	6
Tozlu	3	4	2
Lidyana	6	6	5

CONCLUSION

Businesses with special shopping sites within the website, first of all the number of online visitors to do is to increase as much as possible. Thus, they will have the opportunity to sell their products more. Businesses in order to build relationships with customers, clients need to understand that they have established preferences and how they interact with websites. The focus is on designing a website that can appeal to consumers to re-visit their website and identify the content of the website. Website owners should be able to determine the advantages and weaknesses of their websites, the opportunities offered by their sites and the threats they receive from other sites, in other words, SWOT analysis.

Businesses should evaluate their own websites and compare them with other sites in order to gain competitive advantage. Multi-criteria decision-making methods may be preferred in the evaluation of websites. Entropy-based MOOSRA method was used in this study. In this article study, the websites were examined in 3 dimensions. In the first dimension evaluation, the search statistics of the websites, the daily web pages, the time spent on the customers' website and the site being recognized, theTrendyol website became the first.

In the second dimension, the percentages of satisfaction from the websites, the total number of grievances and gratitude about the site, the rate of gratitude, the rate of responding to the customer requests, and the time to answer the complaints were taken into consideration. When we listed the websites, the first place was the Morhipo website, the 2nd Trendyol website.

In the evaluation in the third dimension, it is also important to follow the websites in social media. The first leading website is Trendyol, which is the leading firm in the sector. In the last row, 1v1y is seen as different from other dimensions. In the last row of other dimensions, Lidyana is seen as the second.

The Trendyol which is first ranked in dimension D1 and D3, should further develop itself according to the D2 dimension. This means that Trendyol must to pay more attention to customer needs and their complaints. Websites can improve themselves by taking a look at the rankings based on the top ranked web sites. By using social media departments more actively, they can carry higher D3 rankings.

In the future, our recommendation to work on the evaluation of websites is to compare websites that do business around the world. In addition, different criteria and different multi-criteria decision making methods can be done with this type of studies. working with different methods and comparing the results.

REFERENCES

Adalı, E. A., & Işık, A. T. (2017). The Multi-Objective Decision Making Methods Based on MULTIMOORA and MOOSRA for the Laptop Selection Problem. *Journal of Industrial Engineering International*, *13*(2), 229–237. doi:10.100740092-016-0175-5

Chankong, V., & Haimes, Y. Y. (2008). *Multiobjective Decision Making: Theory And Methodology*. Courier Dover Publications.

Demircioğlu, M., & Coşkun, İ. T. (2018). CRITIC-MOOSRA Yöntemi ve UPS Seçimi Üzerine Bir Uygulama. *Çukurova Üniversitesi Sosyal Bilimler Enstitüsü Dergisi, 27*(1), 183-195.

Dorfeshan, Y., Mousavi, S. M., Mohagheghi, V., & Vahdani, B. (2018). Selecting Project-Critical Path by a New Interval Type-2 Fuzzy Decision Methodology Based on MULTIMOORA, MOOSRA and TPOP methods. *Computers & Industrial Engineering*, *120*, 160–178. doi:10.1016/j.cie.2018.04.015

Dündar, S., Ecer, F., & Özdemir, Ş. (2007). Fuzzy Topsis Yöntemi İle Sanal Mağazalarin Web Sitelerinin Değerlendirilmesi. *Atatürk Üniversitesi İktisadi ve İdari Bilimler Dergisi, 21*(1).

Elibol, H., & Kesici, B. (2004). Çağdaş İşletmecilik Açisindan Elektronik Ticaret. *Selçuk Üniversitesi Sosyal Bilimler Enstitüsü Dergisi*, (11), 303-329.

Evangelos, T. (2000). Multi-Criteria Decision Making Methods: a Comparative Study. Kluwer Academic Publication.

Genç, H. (2010). İnternetteki etkileşim merkezi sosyal ağlar ve e-iş 2.0 uygulamaları. *Akademik Bilişim*, 481-487.

Han, B., Liu, H., & Wang, R. (2015). Urban Ecological Security Assessment for Cities in the Beijing–Tianjin–Hebei Metropolitan Region Based on Fuzzy And Entropy Methods. *Ecological Modelling*, *318*, 217–225. doi:10.1016/j.ecolmodel.2014.12.015

Karami, A., & Johansson, R. (2014). Utilization of Multi Attribute Decision Making Techniques to Integrate Automatic and Manual Ranking of Options. *Journal of Information Science and Engineering*, *30*, 519–534.

Kumar, R., & Ray, A. (2015). Optimal Selection of Material: an Eclectic Decision. *Journal of The Institution of Engineers (India): Series C, 96*(1), 29-33.

Ömürbek, N., Eren, H & Dağ, O. (2017). Entropi-ARAS ve Entropi-MOOSRA Yöntemleri İle Yaşam Kalitesi Açısından AB Ülkelerinin Değerlendirilmesi. *Ömer Halisdemir Üniversitesi, İktisadi Ve İdari Bilimler Fakültesi Dergisi, 10*(2), 29-48.

Ömürbek, N., Karaatlı, M., & Balcı, H. F. (2016). Entropi Temelli MAUT ve SAW Yöntemleri ile Otomotiv Firmalarının Performans Değerlemesi. *Dokuz Eylül Üniversitesi İktisadi ve İdari Bilimler Fakültesi Dergisi, 31*(1).

Ömürbek, V., Aksoy, E., & Akçakanat, Ö. (2017). Bankaların Sürdürülebilirlik Performanslarının ARAS, MOOSRA ve COPRAS Yöntemleri İle Değerlendirilmesi. *Visionary E-Journal/Vizyoner Dergisi, 8*(19).

Özsarı, S. H., & Hoşgör, H. (2016). ve Gündüz Hoşgör, D., (2016). Hastane Web Site Performanslarının Halkla İlişkiler ve Tanıtım Açısından İncelenmesi: Türkiye, Hindistan ve Irlanda Örnekleri. *ACU Sağlık Bil. Dergisi, 4*, 209–217.

Perçin, S., & Sönmez, Ö. (2018). Bütünleşik Entropi Ağırlık ve TOPSIS Yöntemleri Kullanılarak Türk Sigorta Şirketlerinin Performansının Ölçülmesi. *Uluslararası İktisadi ve İdari İncelemeler Dergisi*, 565-582.

Ray, A. (2014). Green Cutting Fluid Selection Using MOOSRA Method. *International Journal of Research in Engineering and Technology, 3*(3), 559–563.

Sarkar, A., Panja, S. C., Das, D., & Sarkar, B. (2015). Developing An Efficient Decision Support System for Non-Traditional Machine Selection: An Application of MOORA and MOOSRA. *Production & Manufacturing Research, 3*(1), 324–342. doi:10.1080/21693277.2014.895688

Ulutaş, A., Karaköy, Ç., Arıç, K.H., & Cengiz, E. (2018). Çok Kriterli Karar Verme Yöntemleri ile Lojistik Merkezi Yeri Seçimi. *İktisadi Yenilik Dergisi, 5*(2), 45-53.

Wu, J., Sun, J., Liang, L., & Zha, Y. (2011). Determination of Weights for Ultimate Cross Efficiency Using Shannon Entropy. *Expert Systems with Applications, 38*(5), 5162–5165. doi:10.1016/j.eswa.2010.10.046

Yalçın, F. & Mehmet, B. A. Ş. (2012). Elektronik Ticarette Müşteri Memnuniyeti: Fırsat Siteleri Üzerine Bir Araştırma. *İktisadi ve İdari Bilimler Fakültesi Dergisi, 14*(3), 1-16.

Yavuz, V. A. (2016). Coğrafi Pazar Seçiminde PROMETHEE ve Entropi Yöntemlerine Dayalı Çok Kriterli Bir Analiz: Mobilya Sektöründe Bir Uygulama. *Ömer Halisdemir Üniversitesi İktisadi ve İdari Bilimler Fakültesi Dergisi, 9*(2), 163-177.

Yılmaz, V., Arı, E., & Doğan, R. (2016). Online alışverişte müşteri şikayet niyetleri ve davranışlarının yapısal eşitlik modeli ile incelenmesi. *Journal of Yaşar University, 11*(42), 102–112.

KEY TERMS AND DEFINITIONS

MCDM: Multi-criteria decision making.

TOPSIS: It is an acronym for "technique for order preference by similarity to ideal solution."

UPS: Universal power supply.

Chapter 6
ERP Software Selection Based on Intuitionistic Fuzzy VIKOR Method

Burak Efe
Necmettin Erbakan University, Turkey

ABSTRACT

This chapter uses intuitionistic fuzzy VIKOR (IFVIKOR) for the application of ERP software selection. First, priority values of criteria in ERP software selection problem have been determined by using the judgments of the experts. IFWA operator is utilized to integrate the judgments of the experts about the weights of criteria. Then, the result of the IFVIKOR can be employed to define the most appropriate ERP alternative in uncertain environment. Intuitionistic fuzzy numbers are presented in all phases in order to overcome any vagueness in the decision-making process. The final decision depends on the degree of importance of each decision so that wrong degree of importance causes the mistaken result. The researchers generally determine the degrees of importance of each decision makers according to special characteristics of each decision maker as subjectivity. In order to overcome this subjectivity in this chapter, the judgments of decision makers are degraded to unique decision by using the importance degree of each expert. There is no study about ERP software selection using IFVIKOR.

DOI: 10.4018/978-1-5225-8238-0.ch006

INTRODUCTION

An enterprise resource planning (ERP) system is a business process management software that combines a number of modular software implementations to meet all the needs of a firm. An ERP system is the knowledge framework of a firm that automates and combines whole business tasks like purchase, sales, inventory control, human resource, production planning and finance. Applications of ERP systems are one of the most important investment projects due to the difficulty, high cost and adaptation risks. Firms have spent billions of dollars and utilized many amounts of man-hours for installing detail ERP software systems (Yusuf et al., 2004). Unprecedented market competition has impressed whole facets of business environment with the conclusion that firms need to decrease total costs, be more sensitive to customer requirements and reduce lead times. To overcome these challenges, novel software systems known in the business environment as ERP systems have surfaced in the market targeting primarily large scale organizations (Karsak and Ozogul, 2009). Any ERP software in market cannot fully meet the needs and expectations of companies, because every company runs its business with different strategies and goals. Thus, to increase the chance of success, management must choose appropriate software that most closely suits its requirements (Ayağ and Özdemir, 2007). Therefore, ERP software selection is an extremely serious and difficult decision making problem for managers. Many firms apply their ERP software hastily without exactly understanding the inclusions for requirements of their business strategies and goals. The conclusion of this hurry approach is the failure in ERP software selection that leads to the failure of project or firm performance will get weakened (Liao et al., 2007).

This chapter consists of five sections. The second presents the related literature review. The third section consists of methods that used IFWA operator and IFVIKOR in ERP software selection. Section four is related with ERP software selection application of the developed decision making approach. The conclusion of this chapter is presented in Section five.

BACKGROUND

Lee et al. (2004) studied on SWOT based ERP software selection. Wei et al. (2005) defined AHP model which enables a firm to determine the factors of ERP software selection. Liao et al. (2007) introduced a similarity degree based algorithm about ERP systems, which may be defined by various linguistic statements. A linear programming model is set up for deciding the most convenient ERP software. Ayağ and Ozdemir (2007) adopted the fuzzy extension of the analytic network process (ANP) based intelligent approach to select the most convenient ERP software alternative. Karsak and Ozogul (2009) suggested a comprehensive framework for the proper ERP selection among possible choices based on quality function deployment (QFD), fuzzy linear regression and zero-one goal programming. Sen and Baracli (2010) adopted fuzzy QFD approach to select the best ERP software. Méxas et al. (2012) proposed AHP approach to investigate the opinions of information technology experts about the importance of ERP software evaluation criteria and sub-criteria in the construction industry. Asl et al. (2012) proposed an integrated approach, which defines the most important criteria of ERP software using Delphi method and ranks these criteria using Shannon Entropy method. Gürbüz et al. (2012) suggested an assessment framework using an integration approach that utilizes ANP, Choquet integral and Measuring Attractiveness by a Categorical Based Evaluation Technique for the evaluation of four ERP software alternatives. Oztaysi (2015) used interval type-2 fuzzy number based AHP approach to evaluate ERP selection problem. Khan and Faisal (2015) examined grey theory based approach for ERP vendor selection. Efe (2016) presented fuzzy AHP method to determine the weights of ERP selection criteria and fuzzy TOPSIS method to rank four ERP alternatives. Borissova et al. (2016) focused on ERP selection by using SMART and combinatorial optimization. Çakır (2016) introduced fuzzy linguistic preference relations to define the weights of ERP selection criteria and fuzzy TOPSIS method to rank ERP alternatives. López and Ishizaka (2017) proposed group AHP sorting method for cloud based ERP solutions. Peng and Wang (2017) suggested hesitant uncertain linguistic Z-numbers based aggregation operators and VIKOR (VIsekriterijumska optimizacija i KOmpromisno Resenje) approach to evaluate ERP options. Gupta and Naqvi (2017) applied fuzzy TOPSIS approach for critical success factors based ERP selection. Temur and Bolat (2018) used the cloud-based design optimization approach for ERP selection under uncertain environment. İbrahim et al. (2018) presented AHP and support vector machine approach to increase user satisfaction level in ERP.

ERP selection process includes defining of expert decision makers to make selection, determining suitable alternatives, determining ERP selection criteria, weighting the criteria and evaluation of alternatives phases. A real life application is presented in order to provide the better understanding of the proposed approach. The firm wants to select the most suitable ERP software so the managers assign the five experts committee comprising of experts in ERP software domain. After initial elimination, ten alternatives have been remained for further assessment. An expert team of five decision makers E1, E2, E3, E4 and E5 were asked to fill a questionnaire in order to define the most proper alternative. E1, E2 and E3 are a software engineering, a computer engineering and an electronic engineering, respectively while E4 and E5 are academicians. They worked in website area for least 5 years so that they have enough knowledge and experience about ERP evaluation. The importance degree of decision makers are assigned in order to show their differences in the group decision making problem so that the importance degrees of E1, E2, E3, E4 and E5 decision makers can be defined as (0.20, 0.25, 0.15, 0.15, 0.25), respectively.

This study proposes intuitionistic fuzzy number based VIKOR (IFVIKOR) for ERP selection problem. Priorities of ERP evaluation criteria have been defined by utilizing IFWA (intuitionistic fuzzy weighted averaging) operator. The selection rankings of ERP alternatives are defined by using IFVIKOR. There is no study about ERP selection using IFVIKOR approach.

Firstly, this chapter defined purchasing fee (C1), updating fee (C2), product quality (C3), quick response to customer demands (C4), online customer service support and help (C5), easy to find needs (C6), easy to get different pages in website (C7), completing a transaction quickly (C8), on-time delivery (C9), accurate delivery of products (C10), accurate billing (C11).

Secondly, the priorities of criteria in software selection will be determined by IFWA operator. The specialists' opinions are used to obtain the priorities of criteria by employing the linguistic scale, which is demonstrated in Table 1. Eleven criteria based ten ERP software alternatives are evaluated according to five experts' judgments. Group opinion of five experts are acquired after opinions are degraded to only one value by using IFWA operator so it is used for the ERP selection in IFVIKOR stage. Finally, the ranking of ERP alternatives will be identified by using IFVIKOR. The ranking evaluations of alternatives will be defined by using the scale in Table 1. Figure 1. presents a systematic approach for ERP software selection.

MAIN FOCUS OF THE CHAPTER

IFWA Operator

IFWA operator, which is called an intuitionistic fuzzy weighted averaging, can be utilized to aggregate the opinions of experts based on intuitionistic fuzzy decision

Table 1. Linguistic values for criteria of software selection

Linguistic variables	IFNs
Very high (VH)	(0.95,0.05,0.00)
High (H)	(0.75,0.15,0.10)
Medium (M)	(0.50,0.40,0.10)
Equal (E)	(0.50,0.50,0.00)
Low (L)	(0.25,0.65,0.10)
Very low (VL)	(0.05,0.95,0.00)

Figure 1. A systematic approach for ERP selection

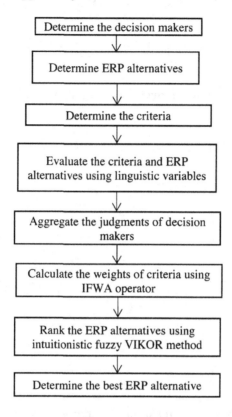

matter. In the group decision-making process, the judgments of all decision makers must be aggregated to obtain the aggregated decision matrix as a group judgment without loss of knowledge. Thus, this chapter used IFWA operator in Eq 1. IFWA operator handles the weights of the decision makers λ_k, the membership degree of the IFN of preference relation on j of i according to k^{th} decision maker $\mu_{ij}^{(k)}$, the non-membership degree of the IFN of preference relation on j of i according to k^{th} decision maker $\left(v_{ij}^{(k)}\right)$. $R^{(k)} = \left(r_{ij}^{(k)}\right)_{m \times n}$ be an intuitionistic fuzzy decision matrix of the kth expert. Let $\lambda = \left\{\lambda_1, \lambda_2, ..., \lambda_t\right\}$ be the importance degree of all experts where $\sum_{k=1}^{t} \lambda_k = 1$, $\lambda_k \in \left[0,1\right]$. IFWA operator, which is presented by Xu (2007), is used in order to aggregate the opinions of all experts. IFWA operator is presented in Eq 1.

$$r_{ij} = IFWA_{\lambda}\left(r_{ij}^{(1)}, r_{ij}^{(2)}, ..., r_{ij}^{(t)}\right) = \lambda_1 r_{ij}^{(1)} \oplus \lambda_2 r_{ij}^{(2)} \oplus ... \oplus \lambda_t r_{ij}^{(t)} =$$

$$\left(1 - \prod_{k=1}^{t}\left(1 - \mu_{ij}^{(k)}\right)^{\lambda_k}, \prod_{k=1}^{t}\left(\left(v_{ij}^{(k)}\right)^{\lambda_k}\right), \prod_{k=1}^{t}\left(1 - \mu_{ij}^{(k)}\right)^{\lambda_k} - \prod_{k=1}^{t}\left(\left(v_{ij}^{(k)}\right)^{\lambda_k}\right)\right) \qquad (1)$$

The aggregated intuitionistic fuzzy decision matrix (R) is indicated in Eq 2:

$$R = \begin{bmatrix} r_{11} & r_{12} & \cdots & r_{1n} \\ r_{21} & r_{22} & \cdots & r_{2n} \\ \vdots & \vdots & & \vdots \\ r_{m1} & r_{m2} & \cdots & r_{mn} \end{bmatrix} \qquad (2)$$

where

$$r_{ij} = \left(\mu_{ij}, v_{ij}, \pi_{ij}\right), \mu_{ij} = 1 - \prod_{k=1}^{t}\left(1 - \mu_{ij}^{(k)}\right)^{\lambda_k}, v_{ij} = \prod_{k=1}^{t}\left(\left(v_{ij}^{(k)}\right)^{\lambda_k}\right),$$

$$\pi_{ij} = \prod_{k=1}^{t}\left(1 - \mu_{ij}^{(k)}\right)^{\lambda_k} - \prod_{k=1}^{t}\left(\left(v_{ij}^{(k)}\right)^{\lambda_k}\right), i \in M, j \in N.$$

r_{ij} shows the preference relation on j of i. R shows the group judgment in decision making process. Each decision maker has a judgment about the preference relation on j of i. The judgment of each decision maker must be aggregated for a general evaluation. R is acquired by aggregating the judgments of the decision makers (Efe et al., 2015).

Intuitionistic Fuzzy VIKOR Method

The VIKOR method was developed by Opricovic (1998) and Opricovic and Tzeng (2004) for multi-criteria decision making problems. VIKOR method focuses to rank and to select a set of alternatives. It also defines a compromise solution, which is the closest to the ideal solution, for a complex problem so that the decision makers obtain a final decision. VIKOR method calculates positive and negative ideal solutions as ratio. Nevertheless, VIKOR method provides a compromise solution in an advantageous ratio. The compromise solution means reaching agreement with a common consensus in a decision making problem involving conflicting criteria. The IFVIKOR method, which integrates VIKOR method and IFS, is employed to rank the alternatives for a risk evaluation in an uncertain environment in this chapter. The IFVIKOR method can be presented in Eq. 3-10 (Chatterjee et al., 2013):

Step 1: Define the intuitionistic fuzzy positive ideal solution $f_j^* = \left(\mu_j^*, v_j^* \right)$ and the intuitionistic fuzzy negative ideal solution $f_j^- = \left(\mu_j^-, v_j^- \right)$ values of all criteria ratings, $j=1,2,...,n$. This step is realized by using Eqs 3-4:

$$f_j^* = \begin{cases} \max_i r_{ij} & \textit{for benefit criteria} \\ \min_i r_{ij} & \textit{for cos t criteria} \end{cases} \quad i = 1,2,...,m \tag{3}$$

$$f_j^- = \begin{cases} \min_i r_{ij} & \textit{for benefit criteria} \\ \max_i r_{ij} & \textit{for cos t criteria} \end{cases} \quad i = 1,2,...,m \tag{4}$$

Step 2: Calculate the normalized intuitionistic fuzzy difference $\bar{d}_{ij}$ using Euclidean distance in Eqs 5-7

$$\bar{d}_{ij} = \frac{d\left(f_j^*, r_{ij} \right)}{d\left(f_j^*, f_j^- \right)} \tag{5}$$

$$d\left(f_j^*, r_{ij} \right) = \sqrt{\frac{1}{2}\left[\left(\mu_j^* - \mu_{ij} \right)^2 + \left(v_j^* - v_{ij} \right)^2 + \left(\pi_j^* - \pi_{ij} \right)^2 \right]} \tag{6}$$

$$d\left(f_j^*, f_j^- \right) = \sqrt{\frac{1}{2}\left[\left(\mu_j^* - \mu_j^- \right)^2 + \left(v_j^* - v_j^- \right)^2 + \left(\pi_j^* - \pi_j^- \right)^2 \right]} \tag{7}$$

Step 3: Calculate the values S_i and R_i and Q_i, i=1,2,...,m. This step is realized by using Eqs 8-10:

127

$$S_i = \sum_{j=1}^{n} w_j \times \overline{d}_{ij} \tag{8}$$

$$R_i = \max_j \left(w_j \times \overline{d}_{ij} \right) \tag{9}$$

$$Q_i = v \frac{S_i - S^*}{S^- - S^*} + (1-v) \frac{R_i - R^*}{R^- - R^*} \tag{10}$$

where $S^* = \min_i S_i$, $S^- = \max_i S_i$, $R^* = \min_i R_i$, $R^- = \max_i R_i$, w_j is the weight of jth criterion and v is presented as a weight for the strategy of maximum group utility, whereas $1-v$ is the weight of the minimum individual regret. The value of v is handled to 0.5 in this chapter. The first part maximum group utility and the second part minimum individual regret of Eq 10 are calculated by using Eqs 5-7.

Step 4: Rank the alternatives sorting by the values S, R and Q. The final result can be presented by three ranking lists.

Step 5: Propose a compromise solution of the alternative *(a¹)*, which is the best ranked by the measure Q (minimum), if the following two conditions are satisfied (Opricovic and Tzeng; 2007):

1. **Acceptable Advantage:** $Q(a^2) - Q(a^1) \geq DQ$, where (a^2) is the alternative with the second position in the ranking list by Q; DQ=1/(m-1); m is the number of alternative.
2. **Acceptable Stability in Decision Making:** Alternative (a^1) must also be the best ranked by S or/and R. The best alternative, ranked by Q, is the one with minimum value of Q.

SOLUTIONS AND RECOMMENDATIONS

A ERP evaluation process includes defining of expert decision makers to make selection, determining suitable ERP alternatives, determining criteria that examined in evaluation phases, weighting the criteria and evaluation of alternatives phases. A real life application is presented in order to provide the better understanding of the proposed approach.

A questionnaire study was presented to fill to five decision makers E1, E2, E3, E4 and E5 in order to determine the most appropriate ERP alternative. E1, E2 and E3 are a software engineering, a computer engineering and an electronic engineering, respectively while E4 and E5 are academicians. They worked in website area for least 5 years so that they have enough knowledge and experience about ERP evaluation. The importance degree of decision makers are assigned in order to show their differences in the group decision making problem so that the importance degrees of E1, E2, E3, E4 and E5 decision makers can be defined as (0.20,0.25,0.15,0.15,0.25), respectively. Table 2 introduces the importance degree of each criteria according to five experts. IFWA operator can be utilized to aggregate the judgments of experts based on importance degree of experts. The group opinion of five experts is shown in Table 3.

IFVIKOR method is proposed to evaluate the ERP alternatives under an intuitionistic fuzzy environment. Five experts utilize the linguistic rating variables indicated in Table 1 to determine the rating of ERP alternatives based on each criteria. Five experts presented their judgments about five ERP alternatives based on the eleven criteria. They are shown in Table 4.

Table 2. The importance degree of each criteria according to each expert

	C1	C2	C3	C4	C5	C6	C7	C8	C9	C10	C11
E1	VH	M	M	M	L	M	L	M	H	L	M
E2	H	M	H	L	M	L	VL	L	M	M	M
E3	H	H	M	H	L	L	L	M	L	H	L
E4	H	H	M	M	L	H	L	L	M	L	H
E5	M	M	M	M	VL	M	M	L	L	M	M

Table 3. The group opinion of five experts

	C1	C2	C3	C4
Weight	(0.785,0.154,0.062)	(0.594,0.298,0.108)	(0.580,0.313,0.107)	(0.501,0.390,0.109)
	C5	**C6**	**C7**	**C8**
Weight	(0.281,0.633,0.086)	(0.470,0.419,0.111)	(0.281,0.633,0.086)	(0.349,0.548,0.102)
	C9	**C10**	**C11**	
Weight	(0.488,0.399,0.113)	(0.481,0.409,0.110)	(0.521,0.371,0.108)	

Table 4. Evaluation data for alternatives

E1

	A1	A2	A3	A4	A5	A6	A7	A8	A9	A10
C1	H	L	M	H	M	H	H	L	M	H
C2	L	M	L	H	H	H	M	VL	M	M
C3	L	H	M	H	VL	H	H	L	H	M
C4	M	M	M	M	VH	H	H	H	VH	VH
C5	M	M	L	VH	M	L	L	M	M	H
C6	L	M	L	L	M	M	L	H	M	M
C7	VH	M	L	M	VH	H	L	H	H	M
C8	M	M	L	H	H	H	VL	M	VH	VH
C9	M	H	M	VL	M	M	M	VH	VH	H
C10	VH	H	M	M	H	M	H	H	VH	M
C11	L	M	L	VH	M	L	L	M	M	M

E3

	A1	A2	A3	A4	A5	A6	A7	A8	A9	A10
C1	H	H	M	M	L	H	VH	M	H	M
C2	M	L	M	M	VH	VH	VH	M	H	M
C3	M	M	H	M	M	H	H	H	M	H
C4	M	H	L	M	VH	H	M	H	VH	H
C5	M	M	M	H	M	H	VL	VL	M	M
C6	H	H	H	VL	M	M	H	VH	VH	M
C7	M	L	L	M	VH	L	H	M	H	H

E2

	A1	A2	A3	A4	A5	A6	A7	A8	A9	A10
C1	H	H	L	H	M	VH	H	L	VH	H
C2	M	H	L	H	VH	VH	H	M	M	M
C3	H	H	H	M	M	H	H	H	H	H
C4	M	M	L	M	VH	M	H	M	H	VH
C5	M	M	L	VL	M	H	VL	L	M	M
C6	L	M	L	VH	M	M	M	VH	M	M
C7	VH	L	L	VL	VH	L	L	H	H	H
C8	M	M	M	H	M	H	L	VL	H	VH
C9	M	M	L	VL	H	L	L	VH	M	M
C10	H	H	M	M	VH	H	L	VH	VH	H
C11	L	M	M	VH	H	M	VL	L	H	VH

E4

	A1	A2	A3	A4	A5	A6	A7	A8	A9	A10
C1	M	H	M	L	H	H	H	M	H	M
C2	M	L	M	L	L	L	L	VL	M	H
C3	VH	M	H	VL	H	VH	VH	H	M	H
C4	M	M	L	M	H	M	L	H	M	H
C5	H	H	H	H	M	L	VL	M	VH	M
C6	M	M	M	VL	M	H	H	VH	VH	M
C7	M	L	L	M	VH	L	H	H	VH	VH

continued on following page

Table 4. Continued

E2

	A1	A2	A3	A4	A5	A6	A7	A8	A9	A10
C8	M	M	L	VH	M	M	VL	M	M	VH
C9	M	M	M	VL	M	H	L	H	M	M
C10	H	L	M	M	VH	H	H	M	H	M
C11	M	H	M	H	M	M	VL	M	H	M

E1

	A1	A2	A3	A4	A5	A6	A7	A8	A9	A10
C8	H	H	L	H	M	M	L	L	H	M
C9	M	M	L	VL	M	H	H	VH	VH	H
C10	VH	L	L	H	VH	H	H	H	VH	M
C11	M	H	M	H	M	M	L	L	M	H

E5

	A1	A2	A3	A4	A5	A6	A7	A8	A9	A10
C1	H	H	M	L	L	M	M	L	M	H
C2	M	M	M	H	M	H	VH	L	M	M
C3	H	L	M	VH	H	VH	H	VH	H	H
C4	H	M	M	L	VH	M	L	H	VH	M
C5	M	H	L	VL	H	H	VL	VL	M	H
C6	L	H	L	VH	H	L	M	H	VH	M
C7	H	M	L	VH	H	M	L	VH	VH	VH
C8	M	M	H	H	M	H	H	VL	M	VH
C9	VH	H	M	L	M	L	H	VH	VH	M
C10	H	M	M	M	M	M	H	H	H	VH
C11	L	M	M	VH	H	H	VL	M	M	M

131

The group decision of five experts based on their importance is obtained with using IFWA operator and the aggregated intuitionistic fuzzy rating of each alternative under eleven criteria is shown in Table 5. This chapter used IFWA operator to aggregate the judgments of the decision makers.

The values of S, R, and Q are computed by using Eqs 8-10 for the ten alternatives and are presented in Table 6. The rankings of the ten alternatives by values of S, R, and Q are indicated in Table 7. Alternative 8 is the most appropriate ERP software according to the results of S, R, Q.

CONCLUSION

This study has examined the intuitionistic fuzzy VIKOR in ERP software selection problem that includes ten alternatives. The initial five experts' opinions and the literature review investigated the framework, which performed as the fundamental for modeling the suggested eleven criteria (purchasing fee, updating fee, product quality, quick response to customer demands, online customer service support and help, easy to find needs, easy to get different pages in website, completing a transaction quickly, on-time delivery, accurate delivery of products, accurate billing) to assist ERP software selection. All judgments of experts are characterized based on linguistic values by intuitionistic fuzzy numbers, which deals with uncertainty. IFWA operator is used to integrate the judgments of the experts. IFWA operator is utilized to obtain the weights of criteria that considers in software selection. Intuitionistic fuzzy VIKOR approach is used to rank the ERP alternatives in uncertain environment. IFVIKOR approach is preferred instead of the classical VIKOR approach when the decision makers evaluate the alternative/criteria as linguistic variables. Crisp numbers cause information loss in uncertain environment. This chapter presents the intuitionistic fuzzy VIKOR approach in order to overcome this limitation in uncertain environment. The weights acquired from the judgments of experts are incorporated in IFVIKOR calculations and the ten alternatives priorities are defined for selecting the most suitable ERP software. In future studies, the proposed method can be utilized for dealing with vagueness under IT2TrF set environment for ERP software selection.

Table 5. The group opinion of five experts for alternatives

	A1	A2	A3	A4	A5
C1	(0.720,0.174,0.104)	(0.689,0.201,0.110)	(0.447,0.452,0.102)	(0.570,0.312,0.118)	(0.470,0.419,0.111)
C2	(0.458,0.441,0.101)	(0.525,0.362,0.113)	(0.400,0.498,0.102)	(0.673,0.217,0.111)	(0.816,0.154,0.030)
C3	(0.729,0.198,0.074)	(0.595,0.290,0.115)	(0.597,0.291,0.112)	(0.730,0.223,0.047)	(0.569,0.321,0.110)
C4	(0.580,0.313,0.107)	(0.549,0.345,0.105)	(0.375,0.522,0.102)	(0.447,0.452,0.102)	(0.936,0.059,0.005)
C5	(0.549,0.345,0.105)	(0.621,0.270,0.109)	(0.401,0.485,0.113)	(0.919,0.070,0.012)	(0.580,0.313,0.107)
C6	(0.401,0.485,0.113)	(0.621,0.270,0.109)	(0.401,0.485,0.113)	(0.094,0.881,0.026)	(0.580,0.313,0.107)
C7	(0.866,0.106,0.028)	(0.375,0.522,0.102)	(0.294,0.604,0.101)	(0.888,0.104,0.008)	(0.925,0.066,0.009)
C8	(0.549,0.345,0.105)	(0.549,0.345,0.105)	(0.485,0.399,0.116)	(0.804,0.127,0.069)	(0.565,0.329,0.107)
C9	(0.719,0.238,0.043)	(0.634,0.257,0.109)	(0.412,0.486,0.102)	(0.105,0.864,0.031)	(0.580,0.313,0.107)
C10	(0.858,0.102,0.040)	(0.587,0.298,0.116)	(0.469,0.430,0.101)	(0.549,0.345,0.105)	(0.877,0.105,0.018)
C11	(0.336,0.562,0.102)	(0.594,0.298,0.108)	(0.458,0.441,0.101)	(0.919,0.070,0.012)	(0.646,0.245,0.109)

	A6	A7	A8	A9	A10
C1	(0.801,0.146,0.053)	(0.766,0.163,0.071)	(0.336,0.562,0.102)	(0.772,0.177,0.051)	(0.692,0.201,0.106)
C2	(0.845,0.120,0.034)	(0.822,0.147,0.031)	(0.307,0.611,0.081)	(0.549,0.345,0.105)	(0.549,0.345,0.105)
C3	(0.869,0.097,0.035)	(0.804,0.127,0.069)	(0.792,0.153,0.055)	(0.692,0.201,0.106)	(0.713,0.183,0.105)
C4	(0.608,0.284,0.109)	(0.570,0.312,0.118)	(0.703,0.192,0.106)	(0.925,0.066,0.009)	(0.840,0.135,0.024)
C5	(0.633,0.251,0.117)	(0.094,0.881,0.026)	(0.285,0.638,0.077)	(0.646,0.293,0.061)	(0.634,0.257,0.109)
C6	(0.501,0.390,0.109)	(0.560,0.328,0.112)	(0.897,0.082,0.021)	(0.859,0.127,0.013)	(0.549,0.345,0.105)
C7	(0.456,0.429,0.115)	(0.461,0.419,0.121)	(0.814,0.132,0.053)	(0.869,0.097,0.035)	(0.849,0.118,0.033)
C8	(0.692,0.201,0.106)	(0.136,0.816,0.048)	(0.268,0.663,0.069)	(0.761,0.178,0.061)	(0.929,0.068,0.002)
C9	(0.503,0.380,0.117)	(0.554,0.328,0.118)	(0.936,0.059,0.005)	(0.874,0.115,0.011)	(0.608,0.284,0.109)
C10	(0.658,0.233,0.108)	(0.671,0.216,0.113)	(0.723,0.174,0.104)	(0.905,0.078,0.018)	(0.764,0.186,0.050)
C11	(0.544,0.345,0.111)	(0.125,0.832,0.043)	(0.412,0.486,0.102)	(0.621,0.270,0.109)	(0.747,0.205,0.048)

Table 6. The values of S, R and Q for alternatives

	S	R	Q
A1	(0.9759,0.0077,0.0165)	(0.7389,0.1945,0.0666)	0.9170
A2	(0.9841,0.0043,0.0116)	(0.7097,0.2213,0.0690)	0.9046
A3	(0.9765,0.0052,0.0183)	(0.5403,0.3528,0.1069)	0.7146
A4	(0.9805,0.0054,0.0142)	(0.5677,0.3596,0.0727)	0.7351
A5	(0.9579,0.0147,0.0274)	(0.5796,0.3130,0.1074)	0.7142
A6	(0.9842,0.0044,0.0114)	(0.7845,0.1539,0.0616)	0.9869
A7	(0.9896,0.0023,0.0081)	(0.7634,0.1725,0.0641)	0.9771
A8	(0.7887,0.1198,0.0916)	(0.3366,0.5757,0.0877)	0.0000
A9	(0.9438,0.0247,0.0315)	(0.7607,0.1748,0.0644)	0.8615
A10	(0.9523,0.0192,0.0285)	(0.7114,0.2198,0.0689)	0.8286

Table 7. The ranking of alternatives by S, R and Q

	A1	A2	A3	A4	A5	A6	A7	A8	A9	A10
S	5	8	6	7	4	9	10	1	2	3
R	7	5	2	3	4	10	9	1	8	6
Q	8	7	3	4	2	10	9	1	6	5

REFERENCES

Asl, M. B., Khalilzadeh, A., Youshanlouei, H. R., & Mood, M. M. (2012). Identifying and ranking the effective factors on selecting Enterprise Resource Planning (ERP) system using the combined Delphi and Shannon Entropy approach. *Procedia: Social and Behavioral Sciences*, *41*, 513–520. doi:10.1016/j.sbspro.2012.04.063

Ayağ, Z., & Özdemİr, R. G. (2007). An intelligent approach to ERP software selection through fuzzy ANP. *International Journal of Production Research*, *45*(10), 2169–2194. doi:10.1080/00207540600724849

Borissova, D., Mustakerov, I., Korsemov, D., & Dimitrova, V. (2016). Evaluation and selection of ERP software by SMART and combinatorial optimization. *Int. Journal Advanced Modeling and Optimization*, *18*(1), 145–152.

Çakır, S. (2016). Selecting appropriate ERP software using integrated fuzzy linguistic preference relations–fuzzy TOPSIS method. *International Journal of Computational Intelligence Systems*, *9*(3), 433–449. doi:10.1080/18756891.2016.1175810

Chatterjee, K., Kar, M. B., & Kar, S. (2013). Strategic Decisions Using Intuitionistic Fuzzy Vikor Method for Information System (IS) Outsourcing. *2013 International Symposium on Computational and Business Intelligence*, 123-126. 10.1109/ISCBI.2013.33

Efe, B. (2016). An integrated fuzzy multi criteria group decision making approach for ERP system selection. *Applied Soft Computing*, *38*, 106–117. doi:10.1016/j.asoc.2015.09.037

Efe, B., Boran, F. E., & Kurt, M. (2015). Sezgisel Bulanik Topsis Yöntemi Kullanilarak Ergonomik Ürün Konsept Seçimi. *Mühendislik Bilimleri ve Tasarım Dergisi*, *3*(3), 433–440.

Gupta, R., & Naqvi, S. K. (2017). A Framework for Applying CSFs to ERP Software Selection: An Extension of Fuzzy TOPSIS Approach. *International Journal of Intelligent Information Technologies*, *13*(2), 41–62. doi:10.4018/IJIIT.2017040103

Gürbüz, T., Alptekin, S. E., & Alptekin, G. I. (2012). A hybrid MCDM methodology for ERP selection problem with interacting criteria. *Decision Support Systems*, *54*(1), 206–214. doi:10.1016/j.dss.2012.05.006

İbrahim, S. H., Duraisamy, S., & Sridevi, U. K. (2018). Flexible and reliable ERP project customization framework to improve user satisfaction level. *Cluster Computing*, 1–7.

Karsak, E. E., & Ozogul, C. O. (2009). An integrated decision making approach for ERP system selection. *Expert Systems with Applications, 36*(1), 660–667. doi:10.1016/j.eswa.2007.09.016

Khan, H., & Faisal, M. N. (2015). A Grey-based approach for ERP vendor selection in small and medium enterprises in Qatar. *International Journal of Business Information Systems, 19*(4), 465–487. doi:10.1504/IJBIS.2015.070205

Lee, H. S., Shen, P. D., & Chih, W. L. (2004). A Fuzzy Multiple Criteria Decision Making Model for Software Selection. *Fuzz- IEEE, 3*, 1709-1713.

Liao, X., Li, Y., & Lu, B. (2007). A model for selecting an ERP system based on linguistic information processing. *Information Systems, 32*(7), 1005–1017. doi:10.1016/j.is.2006.10.005

López, C., & Ishizaka, A. (2017). GAHPSort: A new group multi-criteria decision method for sorting a large number of the cloud-based ERP solutions. *Computers in Industry, 92*, 12–24. doi:10.1016/j.compind.2017.06.007

Méxas, M. P., Quelhas, O. L. G., & Costa, H. G. (2012). Prioritization of enterprise resource planning systems criteria: Focusing on construction industry. *International Journal of Production Economics, 139*(1), 340–350. doi:10.1016/j.ijpe.2012.05.025

Opricovic, S. (1998). *Multi-criteria optimization of civil engineering systems.* Belgrade: Faculty of Civil Engineering.

Opricovic, S., & Tzeng, G. (2007). Extended VIKOR method in comparison with outranking methods. *European Journal of Operational Research, 178*(2), 514–529. doi:10.1016/j.ejor.2006.01.020

Oztaysi, B. (2015). A Group Decision Making Approach Using Interval Type-2 Fuzzy AHP for Enterprise Information Systems Project Selection. *Journal of Multiple-Valued Logic & Soft Computing, 24*(5).

Peng, H. G., & Wang, J. Q. (2017). Hesitant uncertain linguistic Z-numbers and their application in multi-criteria group decision-making problems. *International Journal of Fuzzy Systems, 19*(5), 1300–1316. doi:10.100740815-016-0257-y

Sen, C. G., & Baraçlı, H. (2010). Fuzzy quality function deployment based methodology for acquiring enterprise software selection requirements. *Expert Systems with Applications*, *37*(4), 3415–3426. doi:10.1016/j.eswa.2009.10.006

Temur, G. T., & Bolat, B. (2018). A robust MCDM approach for ERP system selection under uncertain environment based on worst case scenario. *Journal of Enterprise Information Management*, *31*(3), 405–425. doi:10.1108/JEIM-12-2017-0175

Wei, C. C., Chien, C. F., & Wang, M. J. J. (2005). An AHP-based approach to ERP system selection. *International Journal of Production Economics*, *96*(1), 47–62. doi:10.1016/j.ijpe.2004.03.004

Xu, Z. S. (2007). Intuitionistic fuzzy aggregation operators. *IEEE Transactions on Fuzzy Systems*, *15*(6), 1179–1187. doi:10.1109/TFUZZ.2006.890678

Yusuf, Y., Gunasekaran, A., & Abthorpe, M. S. (2004). Enterprise information Systems Project implementation: A case study of ERP in Rolls-Royce. *International Journal of Production Economics*, *87*(3), 251–266. doi:10.1016/j.ijpe.2003.10.004

Chapter 7
Process of Placing Advertisements on Website Homepage

Gitanjali Kalia
Chitkara University, India

ABSTRACT

We cannot find any website without advertisements on it. As the number of websites has increased enormously, marketers are trying every niche to target the consumers. While designing a website, a lot of elements are kept in mind. Type of website, ad layout opted, type of internet ad, duration, and position of the ad on the website will be discussed. As the research is based on Harold Laswell model of communication (i.e., who says what, to whom, which channel, and with what effect), the role of the marketers and the way the message is communicated to the online consumers will be discussed. Earlier researches done under this topic will be discussed so as to understand the scope of the research conducted and model suggested. The chapter will include the model suggested at the end of the research and how the basic model of communication by Harold Laswell has diversified over a period of time.

DOI: 10.4018/978-1-5225-8238-0.ch007

INTRODUCTION

India within a span of last 10 years has been the apple eye of the Global market with context to not just the ratio of population but also the relevance of free capital market. Advertising has been the nervous system of today's business and what has added to its addiction is its amalgamation with Information, Communication and Technologies resulting into ecommerce business. Nowadays, we cannot find any website without advertisements on it. As the numbers of websites have increased enormously, marketers are trying every niche to target the Consumers through various social platforms. Therefore, the demand exists to understand the scope of online advertisements on various websites especially the homepages.

Essential Requirements of Posting Online Advertisements on Homepage

Digital media has shrunken the whole world in a form of global village where every minute detail regarding any corner of the world is available on the click of the mouse. Being an audio-visual-textual medium, all the marketers and advertisers try their level best to attain the attention of the netizen towards their websites. He tries to upturn every stone that forms the base of developing an informative and aesthetic website. A successful website is an amalgamation of many elements such as graphics, colors, text, headlines, etc. Therefore the researcher tends to study the following aspects of websites and online advertisements on it:

Different Formats of Website

These days we notice that online market is flooded with number of websites that can be categorised under various formats. Though the whole journey was triggered off with social media as key indicator, the formats have expanded over period of time. From informational web portals to social networking sites, news portals to classified websites, company website to retailer website, every business is available on the internet. Whether it is product promotion, company popularity, social awareness or dissemination of information, websites are designed in the way of their objectivity. Thus the type of website decides the category of the product to be advertised on it.

Formats of Internet Ad

With the change of era from traditional advertising to web advertising, advertisers have gone smarter in reaching out to their customers. While surfing, the advertisers adopts various advertising formats like banner ads, interstitials, pop up, pop under, floating ads and many more to target the netizen and enhance their visibility and usage of the product. It is very essential to choose and adapt right kind of format as all are not successful among the netizens as some ads are completely ignored and treated as irritating element.

Design Layout of Advertisement

A layout refers to rough designing of the advertisement and portrays the placement of the print ad elements in the advertisement. Though designing is a part of creative aspect but there are specific categories of layouts like Big picture layout, Copy Heavy Layout, Multipanel Layout, Mondrain Layout, etc. that designer can opt for designing the advertisement and getting the maximum click is also important criteria for the marketers.

Longevity of the Ad

Being the medium with media convergence where advertisements are designed in different audio, visual and graphical formats, the advertisers uses every method to attract the consumers in which the longevity of the ad on homepage makes a lot of difference.

As we all notice that many times the ads appearing on the webpage are either flickering or appear permanently on the home page. There is also a category when other options or buttons on the homepage are clicked the ad displayed on the homepage gets changed while some ads remain unchanged.

Placement of the Ad

The advertisement should be designed in such an aesthetic way that it creates maximum attraction among netizen. Opportunity to Read (OTR) & Opportunity to See (OTS) are quintessential concepts used in OOH advertising but with context to digital media placement of advertisements on homepages makes an impact on the visibility of the ad among consumers.

Therefore, it becomes crucial to place and position the online advertisements at a place that is easily noticeable and catches the eye of the netizen.

Persuasive Technique

Persuasion is regarded as major function of advertising and words used for persuading the buyer makes a lot of impact. We generally notice the action oriented words like buy now, 50% discount freebies, etc. being used on advertisements to pull netizen towards making a purchase. All the ads uses persuasion words as per their objective to sell, brand recall, creating awareness, etc.

Depending on the category of the website, it is also essential to decide whether the site should carry purchase option with the advertisements or not. As in context to e-commerce and classified portal, providing purchasing option to the consumer is mandatory but not for other type of websites such as Rediff that has created a separate ecommerce page titled Rediff shopping. Also, advertising doesn't work on sales building nowadays rather than brand building through interactive marketing is there aim.

Homepage Layout

The type of page layout of the website also decides the online advertisement to be uploaded on the homepage and the placement of the ad as well. Depending upon different type of layouts few advertisements are placed above the mast head, whereas few are placed on the both sides of the webpage.

STATEMENT OF PROBLEM

Online advertising is the new marketing trend that includes persuading the consumer through online display of goods, ideas and services that have flooded the market with brands and has given a lucrative platform to the marketers and retailers. Therefore, this subject has led to a lot of research studies that have been conducted on various aspects of online advertising from websites to particular homepages, types of internet advertisements, factors affecting advertisements, etc. Homepages are the first point of contact among consumers that decide whether to further surf the site or not (Singh & Dalal, 1999). It is also researched that lot of connection exists between website reputation & website content (Shamdasani, Stanaland & Tan, 2001).

On one hand where majority of studies have been conducted on the political, business and library websites, there exist contradiction between usage of internet advertisements because of their popularity and irritating properties. Communication of correct information in context to products and offers on the front page of local websites was found to be top priority (Vihonen, 2013).

Though lot of aspects of online advertising are studied but there are various gaps that need to be filled and further researched on. The reviewed studies show that informational category of websites has not been studied to the extent; therefore a lot of scope prevails for further research in this aspect. Most of the studies are on aesthetics of homepages but its layout aspect is yet to be examined which leads to the proposed study. The creative aspect and creative parameters in context to online advertisements are also the area which has been not studied at a length so the proposed study aims for that angles so that a new dimension may be carved out.

As most of the studies have been conducted in context to customer's preference with the website layout and its content on them. Hence, it is also essential to study the customer's preference with the aesthetics of the homepage and layouts of the advertisements, their placement and information displayed on them.

OBJECTIVES OF THE STUDY

The study was undertaken to achieve the following objectives:

- To analyse the content of online advertisements appearing on the homepage of the websites on various parameters like layouts of website, types of internet advertisements, product category, placement of websites, etc.
- To understand how consumers respond towards advertisements on those websites.
- To analyse the layout designs used for the advertisements and homepage of the website.

RESEARCH METHODOLOGY

In order to achieve the objectives of the research, it is very important to conduct the research in a systematic order by forming a methodology and following it step by step.

Therefore for conducting the research on the selected topic, the researcher adopted two research methodologies for data collection and its analysis i.e.

1. Content Analysis
2. Survey

Content Analysis

The researcher selected and analysed the homepages of four websites based on their popularity on different parameters selected through literature review.

1. **Survey:** An online survey was conducted among netizens as it was study on online ads.
    a. **Sample Size:** The study was conducted through an online survey among 500 respondents as sample size.
    b. **Sampling Technique:** The questionnaire used for collecting data was designed through Google form and later Chi-square was applied through SPSS was applied on data collected for further calculations.

THEORETICAL FRAMEWORK OF THE STUDY

Harold Lasswell's model of communicaion also known as action model is the best model for stuyding the basic commuication process and components used in it. He is accredated for providing invaluable inputs to study propoganda in context to media context which was later used and applied by other media fields. Therefore in order to study the communication process being used bt advertisrs for online media, this theory was selected to be apt.

Figure 1. Components of Harold Laswell Model (Sneha, 2017)

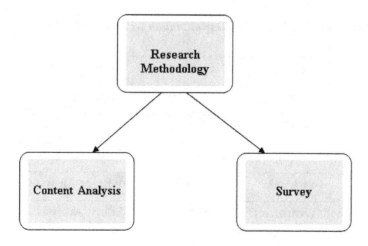

In his model, he explained the questions asked during the process of communication that is made up of statement like who is saying? What is being said? Who is being affected?, where content i.e. 'What is being said' is analysed as content (Macnamara, 2003).

So, lets study the components of Laswell model that forms the basic model of communication. The communication process kick starts with the communicator 'Who' is the sender or source of the message and has full control over the message. He could be an advertiser or marketer who designs the message i.e. 'Says What'. The messages refer to the content posted on homepages of the website in form of online advertisement. Then these messages are carried through a medium i.e 'Channel' which is internet in context to this study. Later this channel carries the message to the receiver i.e. netizen in this study and stands for component 'To Whom' and the last component studies the effect of the message in form of feedback given by the consumers.

REVIEW OF LITERATURE

The researcher declared that people engage 90 percent more with modern looking sites than the traditional looking sites. Consumers are able to engage and recall more than 50% content of the news sites that are image heavy and modular looking in design as compared to sites with more staid, newspaper-inspired designs (Lichterman, 2015). Another researcher found that webpages displaying clean structure, easy

Table 1. Components of Harold Lasswell model with analysis

Question	Element	Analysis
Who	Communicator	Control Analysis
Says What?	Message	Content Analysis
In which channel?	Medium	Media Analysis
To whom?	Audience	Audience Analysis
With What effect?	Effect	Effects Analysis

usability and wide options are the strength of webpage and local pages were found to be boring by customers. Hence, the potential of local store web pages still remains unexplored. It was found that only 10% of the visitors leave the page after entering the front page (Vihonen, 2013).

Creativity was found to be the most influential variable considered by the advertising agencies whereas the other core variables affecting the activities of advertising agencies includes internal variables like relationship management, account manager, creativity, uncluttered homepage and external variables like direct email and sponsored ads (Behboudi, 2012). Another research concluded that clean webpages have high preference for advertisers and consumers. Consumers prefer sites that less cluttered with ads as they have recall value and empower brands. It was also found that consumers spend twice the time on clean webpages that carry one or two ads of particular brand Mitchel (2012).

CONCLUSION

After conducting the research, it was found that most internet ads appearing on the homepage of the websites fall under the category of banner advertisements and appear in formats of Skyscraper, Rectangular and Square formats followed by Pop-up ads. 970*250 and 300*250 pixels are the standardised banner sizes used by advertisements displayed on the homepage of the website. It was also found that most of the homepages were designed in different layouts out of which Headline & Gallery, Power Grid and Fixed Sidebar are the most commonly applied *website layouts* used by the web designers. The researcher also concluded that the advertisements related to products like ecommerce, clothing, etc. were designed in big picture layout whereas advertisements of service oriented products like banks were designed in copy heavy layouts. With context to the usage of persuasive words, *services ads* contain persuasive words like apply now; know more while following the copy heavy advertisement layout whereas *product advertisements* contain words like discount offers, and shop now, schemes and prices. Additional information like address panel, offers and images of the product is also carried in some of the online advertisements.

The result concluded that most of the online advertisements appearing on homepage where that of banking and insurance i.e. service oriented products whereas advertisements of product categories like E-commerce and mobile phone dominated in terms of number of advertisements on homepages. It was found that rich ads i.e.

visual or movable advertisements are more liked by the netizens especially the ones displaying the functionality of the product. It was found that advertisements placed above the mast head and on the right side of the homepage is the most preferred areas for the placement and also attracts the consumer and is more visible. It is concluded that though consumers get attracted to motion or visual ads but bright colors also appeal them. It was also found that persuasive information is equally important for them such as discount or promotional offers.

Suggestive Model for the Process Posting Advertisements on the Homepage of the Website

Taking Harold Lasswell model as the base for the study, five basic elements of communication process have been studied i.e. who, says what, through which channel, to whom and with what effects in context to the online advertising. In it, the content and consumer's perception regarding online advertisements appearing on the homepage of the website were studied and the researcher has proposed the above model that demonstrates the process whose explanation is mentioned below:

- **Who:** In this model 'who' i.e. sender refers to the online marketing strategist or the advertiser who selects the particular website for their product, idea or service campaign and design the content to be inserted in the advertisement. As the controller of the message they can design to what extend the message needs to be effectively communicated to the consumers.
- **Says What:** In the next step i.e. 'says what' the content present on the website is analysed. The research finds that the website content should be in relation to the content of the online advertisement uploaded on the website. There are few factors which should be kept in mind while designing the website and designing the online advertisement that attracts the viewers and increases its visibility and clicks.
- **Part I:** While selecting the website for campaign, the advertiser should check the website layout, website reputation and also the elements of uncluttered website are important for effective display.
- **Part II:** Whereas while designing the online advertisements, the advertisers should make it sure that advertisement is designed as per the suitable layout as per product, idea or service oriented ad. Also other factors like color, placement, functionality, information displayed are aptly highlighted.

- **Which channel:** Channel here stands for the medium which is used to carry the messages from one place to another i.e. internet through which the internet advertising runs.
- **Whom:** The next element of who stands for the consumers who can also be referred as viewers and netizens for whom the online advertisement are designed.
- **What Effect:** Last but the most essential element of this process is the feedback i.e. what is the effect of the whole process of displaying the online advertisements on the homepage of the website.

In this model, feedback is attained by the sender at two levels. First is the *immediate feedback* where the viewer rejects (close) or clicks the advertisements and other another is *an indirect feedback* to the sender where he needs to understand the consumer perception about the website and online advertisement preference and strategise his online campaign as per their needs.

Figure 2. Process of posting advertisements on the homepage of the website (Kalia, 2018)

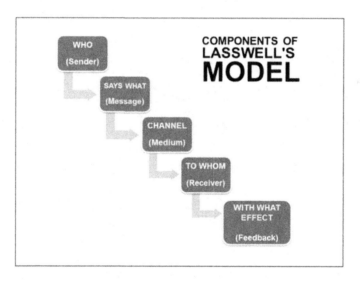

ACADEMIC AND MANAGERIAL IMPLICATIONS

As the maximum time is spent on the digital platform these days, researches are in continuous process of understanding the consumer psychology that makes him understand his behavioural patterns with context to online purchase. Therefore, this chapter will give researchers new dimensions for their academic research, as management and digital marketing course being structured in many universities across world.

As a netizen of the digital world, this research could be of great help to professionals of advertising industries, marketers, designers, online strategist and brand owners who are trying very hard to reach to the niche consumers when one is flooded with number of brands in the online market. The research will give then an insight as to how website should be selected for posting the advertisements so as to get the maximum clicks and what format should be used for designing those ads. This chapter will also propel them to understand which ad formats should be used and where the ads should be placed on the homepages, so that it has maximum visibility as per the consumers preference.

REFERENCES

Angelie, L. (2014). *Types of Ad Layout on Behance*. Retrieved from https://www.behance.net/gallery/14774035/Types-of-Ad-Layout

Behboudi, Hanzaee, K. H., Koshksaray, A. A., Tabar, M. J. S., & Taheri, Z. (2012). A Review of the Activities of Advertising Agencies in Online World. *International Journal of Marketing Studies*, *4*(1), 138–150. doi:10.5539/ijms.v4n1p138

Calitz M.G. (2009). *Pilot Study*. University of South Africa. doi:10.1097/IGC.0b013e3182842efa.End-of-Life

Chatterjee, P. (2008). Are Unclicked Ads Wasted? Enduring Effects of Banner and Pop-Up Ad Exposures on Brand Memory and Attitudes. *Journal of Electronic Commerce Research*, *9*(1), 51–61.

Kalia, G. (2018). *Effect of Online Advertising on Consumers: A Study*. Ph.D Thesis.

Macnamara, J. (2003). Media Content Analysis: Its Uses; Benefits and Best Practice Methodology. *Asia Pacific Public Relations Journal*, *6*(1), 1–23.

Mitchel, K. (2012). *Uncluttered Web Pages Make Ads Work Better*. SAY Media and IPG Media Lab _ Business Wire. Retrieved from http://www.businesswire.com/news/home/20120607005281/en/Uncluttered-Web-Pages-Ads-Work-Research-Media

Osgood, A., & Angela, D. (2010). *Intro to Google Adwords*. Retrieved from https://www.slideshare.net/BostonLogic/logic-classroom-google-adwordsv2

Priyanka, S. (2012). A Study on Impact of Online Advertising on Consumer Behavior (With Special Reference to E-mails). *International Journal of Engineering and Management Sciences*, *3*(4), 461–465.

Shamdasani, P. N., Stanaland, A. J. S., & Tan, J. (2001). Location, Location, Location: Insights for Advertising Placement on the Web. *Journal of Advertising Research, 41*(4), 7 LP-21. Retrieved from http://www.journalofadvertisingresearch.com/content/41/4/7.abstract

Singh, S. N., & Dalal, N. P. (1999). Web Home Pages as Home Page as Advertisments. *Magazine Communications of the ACM*, *42*(8), 91–98. doi:10.1145/310930.310978

Studio, D. (2017). *Banner Design final.pdf*. Retrieved from http://studiodejavu. photo/banner-design

Vihonen, J. (2013). *The Effects of Internet Pages and Online Advertising in Consumer behaviour Case IKEA Tampere. Department of Applied sciences*. Tampere University.

Chapter 8
University Website Performance Evaluation Using Fuzzy SWARA and WASPAS–F

Alptekin Ulutaş

(iD) https://orcid.org/0000-0002-8130-1301
Cumhuriyet University, Turkey

ABSTRACT

The internet has become an indispensable tool for humanity to access any knowledge. Many companies use the internet to provide their customers with information about their organizations. Website development is a tiring process that requires huge investments. If the performance of the website falls below the expected performance, it will have a negative impact on the website owner. Therefore, the measurement of website performance is an important task for companies. Since many factors or criteria affects the website performance, the use of multi-criteria decision-making methods will be helpful to the performance measurement. In this chapter, fuzzy SWARA and WASPAS-F methods are used to evaluate the performance of 10 state universities' websites located in Turkey. According to the results, the website of Erciyes University has been determined to have the best performance among the 10 universities evaluated. Future research may extend the sample size of the websites of universities.

DOI: 10.4018/978-1-5225-8238-0.ch008

INTRODUCTION

Nowadays, the internet has become undoubtedly the most important and indispensable part of our lives. In many areas, such as commercial activities, cultural activities, and educational activities etc., the internet has become an inevitable tool for accessing the information and communication. Many organizations that provide services to their customers present information about their enterprise on their websites using the internet. Website development has a complicated and exhausting process, requiring huge investments. Despite all this, if the website does not show the expected performance value, it will result in a negative effect on the website owner. Therefore, the evaluation of website performance has become a necessity for organizations.

There are many factors that affect the performance of the website. Factors vary with respect to the type of website to be evaluated, but some general criteria may be as follows; accessibility, content, and personalization etc. If the alternatives need to be evaluated with respect to the performance levels in the factors or the criteria and the number of factors or criteria is high, MCDM methods are used to solve these types of problems. In the literature, there are some single MCDM methods used to evaluate websites. For instance, Guo and Zhao (2010) proposed analytic hierarchy process (AHP) to assess the quality of information service of high-tech industry information centre located in China. Kumar and Zayaraz (2011) used AHP to choose the right web service based on QoS constraints. Additionally, there are also integrated model to evaluate the performance of websites. Büyüközkan and Ruan (2007) proposed fuzzy AHP and fuzzy TOPSIS (Technique for order preference by the similarity to ideal solution) to rank Turkish government websites. Kaya and Kahraman (2011) integrated fuzzy AHP and fuzzy ELECTRE to evaluate the quality level of the e-banking websites. Burmaoglu and Kazancoglu (2012) used fuzzy AHP and fuzzy VIKOR to evaluate e-government websites from a group of chosen European Union countries. Kabak and Burmaoğlu (2013) combined fuzzy DEMATEL (Decision Making Trial and Evaluation Laboratory) and fuzzy ANP (Analytic Network Process) to evaluate the performance of electronic public procurement websites. Ecer (2014) integrated AHP and COPRAS-G (grey complex proportional assessment) to evaluate and rank bank websites. Vatansever and Akgül (2014) proposed fuzzy AHP to assess the quality of private shopping websites in Turkey. Kang et al. (2016) developed fuzzy hierarchical TOPSIS based on E-S-QUAL to assess e-commerce websites. Büyüközkan et al. (2016) proposed intuitionistic fuzzy AHP and intuitionistic fuzzy VIKOR methods to assess hospital web services. Stanujkic et al. (2017) developed fuzzy MCDM model based on triangular intuitionistic fuzzy numbers to assess the quality of hotel websites. Vatansever and Akgül (2018) developed a model including Entropy method and grey relational analysis to measure the performance of the airline websites. Rouyendegh et al. (2018) combined AHP and Intuitionistic Fuzzy TOPSIS to assess the performance of E-commerce websites. Abdel-Basset et al. (2018) developed neutrosophic VIKOR (VlseKriterijumska Optimizacija I Kompromisno Resenje) method to assess e-government websites. In the literature, there are some studies to evaluate the quality of university websites. For instance, Stanujkic et al. (2012) used AHP and ARAS (Additive Ratio Assessment) method to assess the websites of some universities located in Serbia. Nagpal et al. (2015) integrated two fuzzy MCDM methods including fuzzy AHP and fuzzy TOPSIS to evaluate and rank university websites. In this study, the quality of four university websites were evaluated based on four criteria including response time, ease of use, ease of navigation, and informative. In another attempt, Nagpal et al. (2016) used fuzzy AHP and Entropy method to assess usability of academic institutes' websites. Authors divided criteria into two parts (subjective and objective) due to the containing of the data type. They were able to use ease of use and informative as objective criteria while taking ease of navigation and response time as objective criteria. To evaluate subjective criteria, they used fuzzy AHP and to evaluate objective criteria, they used entropy method. The one of the current research, Pamučar et al. (2018) integrated interval rough AHP and interval rough MABAC (Multi Attributive Border Approximation Area Comparison) methods to evaluate 15 faculties in the University of East Sarajevo (Bosnia and Herzegovina). The authors have obtained data related to the evaluation process from nine experts.

In this study, a fuzzy hybrid model including fuzzy SWARA (Step-wise Weight Assessment Ratio Analysis) and WASPAS-F (Fuzzy Weighted Aggregated Sum-Product Assessment) to evaluate the performance of university websites. The performances of Sivas Cumhuriyet University (SCU) and 9 state universities, which are İnönü University (IU), Erciyes University (EU), Tokat Gaziosmanpaşa University (TGU), Yozgat Bozok University (YBU), Kahramanmaraş Sütçü İmam University (KSU), Ordu University (OU), Giresun University (GU), Erzincan Binali Yıldırım University (EBYU), and Abdullah Gül University (AGU), in neighbouring provinces of Sivas city were measured by the proposed fuzzy model. The weights of these criteria were determined by the fuzzy SWARA method. After determining the weights of the criteria, the performances of ten universities' web sites were evaluated by the WASPAS-F method. This study presents one contribution to the literature. These two models consisting of fuzzy SWARA and WASPAS-F were first used together for the first time to evaluate the performance of university websites.

METHODOLOGY

Basic Operations in Fuzzy Numbers

Let us suppose that $\tilde{F} = \left(l_F, m_F, u_F \right)$ and $\tilde{G} = \left(l_G, m_G, u_G \right)$ are fuzzy triangular numbers. Basic operations are performed on these fuzzy numbers as follows (Gani and Assarudeen, 2012):

$$\tilde{F} + \tilde{G} = (l_F + l_G, m_F + m_G, u_F + u_G) \tag{1}$$

$$\tilde{F} - \tilde{G} = (l_F - u_G, m_F - m_G, u_F - l_G) \tag{2}$$

$$\tilde{F} \times \tilde{G} = (\min(l_F \times l_G, l_F \times u_G, u_F \times l_G, u_F \times u_G), m_F \times m_G, \max(l_F \times l_G, l_F \times u_G, u_F \times l_G, u_F \times u_G)) \tag{3}$$

$$\tilde{F} / \tilde{G} = (\min(l_F / l_G, l_F / u_G, u_F / l_G, u_F / u_G), m_F / m_G, \max(l_F / l_G, l_F / u_G, u_F / l_G, u_F / u_G)) \tag{4}$$

Additionally, the power of these fuzzy numbers can be calculated as follows (Turskis et al., 2015):

$$\tilde{F}^{\tilde{G}} = (l_F^{\,u_G}, m_F^{\,m_G}, u_F^{\,l_G}) \tag{5}$$

Fuzzy SWARA

In this study, fuzzy SWARA is utilised to identify the weights of criteria. Crisp SWARA was developed by Keršuliene et al. (2010). Crisp numbers are not sufficient to handle uncertainty; therefore, fuzzy numbers are used to do this. Fuzzy SWARA's steps are indicated as follows (Mavi et al., 2017; Zarbakhshnia et al., 2018):

Step 1: Criteria are sorted with respect to their importance level.
Step 2: After sorting of criteria by importance levels, commencing from the second criterion, each criterion is compared with the above criterion to obtain $\tilde{a}_j$ (the

comparative importance of average value). The comparison between criteria is made by using linguistic expressions indicated in Table 1. These expressions are converted into fuzzy numbers showed in Table 1.

Step 3: The $\tilde{c}_j$ (coefficient) is calculated as follows:

$$\tilde{c}_j = \begin{cases} \tilde{1} & j = 1 \\ \tilde{a}_j + 1 & j > 1 \end{cases} \tag{6}$$

Step 4: The $\tilde{t}_j$ (recalculated weight) is computed as follows:

$$\tilde{t}_j = \begin{cases} \tilde{1} & j = 1 \\ \dfrac{\tilde{t}_{j-1}}{\tilde{c}_j} & j > 1 \end{cases} \tag{7}$$

Step 5: By using Equation 8, the weight of each criterion ($\tilde{w}_j$) is obtained for each decision maker individually. Equation 9 is utilised to consolidate the weights of criteria and they are transferred into WASPAS-F:

$$\tilde{w}_j = \frac{\tilde{t}_j}{\sum\limits_{k=1}^{n} \tilde{t}_k} \tag{8}$$

Table 1. Linguistic expressions and fuzzy numbers for criteria comparison (Chang, 1996)

Linguistic Expressions	Fuzzy Numbers
Equally Important	(1,1,1)
Moderately Less Important	(2/3,1,3/2)
Less Important	(2/5,1/2,2/3)
Very Less Important	(2/7,1/3,2/5)
Much Less Important	(2/9,1/4,2/7)

WASPAS-F

To rank university websites with respect to their performance, WASPAS-F (Turskis et al., 2015) is utilised in this study. Crisp WASPAS was presented by Zavadskas et al. (2012). The steps of WASPAS-F are showed as follows. Step 1: Linguistic scores presented in Table 2 are assigned by decision makers to evaluate the performance of university websites under defined criteria. Then, these scores are transformed into fuzzy scores by utilising Table 2.

Step 1: Fuzzy scores gathered from decision makers are combined by using Equation 9 to develop fuzzy decision matrix showed in Equation 10:

$$l_{y_{ij}} = \frac{\sum_{r=1}^{R} l_{y_{ijr}}}{R}, \quad m_{y_{ij}} = \frac{\sum_{r=1}^{R} m_{y_{ijr}}}{R}, \quad u_{y_{ij}} = \frac{\sum_{r=1}^{R} u_{y_{ijr}}}{R} \quad ; \quad \tilde{y}_{ij} = (l_{y_{ij}}, m_{y_{ij}}, u_{y_{ij}}) \tag{9}$$

$$\tilde{Y} = (\tilde{y}_{ij})_{b \times n} \tag{10}$$

Step 2: In order to normalize fuzzy decision matrix, Equation 11 is used. $\tilde{y}'_{ij}$ is an element of $\tilde{Y}'$ (normalized fuzzy decision matrix):

$$\tilde{y}'_{ij} = \left(\frac{l_{y_{ij}}}{\max(l_{y_{ij}})}, \frac{m_{y_{ij}}}{\max(m_{y_{ij}})}, \frac{u_{y_{ij}}}{\max(u_{y_{ij}})} \right) \tag{11}$$

Table 2. Linguistic and fuzzy scores

Linguistic Scores	Fuzzy Scores
Very Good	(8,9,10)
Good	(6,7,8)
Medium	(4,5,6)
Bad	(2,3,4)
Very Bad	(0,1,2)

Step 3: Fuzzy weighted sum model (WSM) ($\tilde{Q}_i$) and fuzzy weighted product model (WPM) ($\tilde{P}_i$) are computed as:

$$\tilde{Q}_i = \sum_{j=1}^{n} \tilde{y}'_{ij} \times \tilde{w}_j \tag{12}$$

$$\tilde{P}_i = \prod_{j=1}^{n} \tilde{y}'^{\tilde{w}_j}_{ij} \tag{13}$$

Step 4: Fuzzy weighted sum model (WSM) ($\tilde{Q}_i = \left(l_{Q_i}, m_{Q_i}, u_{Q_i}\right)$) and fuzzy weighted product model (WPM) ($\tilde{P}_i = \left(l_{P_i}, m_{P_i}, u_{P_i}\right)$) are converted into crisp values (Q_i, P_i) by using Equations 14 and 15:

$$Q_i = \left(\frac{l_{Q_i} + m_{Q_i} + u_{Q_i}}{3}\right) \tag{14}$$

$$P_i = \left(\frac{l_{P_i} + m_{P_i} + u_{P_i}}{3}\right) \tag{15}$$

Step 5: In the final step, overall performance score (K_i) for each website is computed as:

$$K_i = 0,5 \times Q_i + 0,5 \times P_i \tag{16}$$

APPLICATION

In this study, fuzzy SWARA and WASPAS-F methods are proposed to measure the performance of 10 state universities' websites (Sivas Cumhuriyet University (SCU), İnönü University (IU), Erciyes University (EU), Tokat Gaziosmanpaşa University (TGU), Yozgat Bozok University (YBU), Kahramanmaraş Sütçü İmam University (KSU), Ordu University (OU), Giresun University (GU), Erzincan Binali Yıldırım University (EBYU), and Abdullah Gül University (AGU)). An expert team including two academicians and one informatics specialist was formed to assess the performance of the websites of universities. The list of criteria in the literature for evaluating the performance of the websites was shown to the expert team and the team is asked to choose criteria from this list, which they wish to use to evaluate the university websites. The team unanimously has set seven criteria for the evaluation process. These seven criteria are Ease Of Use (EOU), Security (S), Navigation (N), Content (C), Response Time (RT), Aesthetics (AS), and Accessibility (AY). First, fuzzy SWARA is implemented to the collected data from experts in order to determine criteria weights. Table 3 presents the results of fuzzy SWARA of data obtained from Expert 1.

The computation process of criteria weights will be similar for other experts. Equation 9 is used to combine the determined criteria weights for each expert. Combined weights are indicated in Table 4.

Table 3. The results of fuzzy SWARA (Expert 1)

Criteria	Ranking	Criteria	$\tilde{a}_j$	$\tilde{c}_j$	$\tilde{t}_j$	$\tilde{w}_j$
EOU	3	S		(1,1,1)	(1,1,1)	(0.372,0.434,0.514)
S	1	C	(0.667,1,1.5)	(1.667,2,2.5)	(0.4,0.5,0.6)	(0.149,0.217,0.308)
N	5	EOU	(0.667,1,1.5)	(1.667,2,2.5)	(0.16,0.25,0.36)	(0.059,0.109,0.185)
C	2	RT	(0.4,0.5,0.667)	(1.4,1.5,1.667)	(0.096,0.167,0.257)	(0.036,0.073,0.132)
RT	4	N	(0.667,1,1.5)	(1.667,2,2.5)	(0.038,0.084,0.154)	(0.014,0.036,0.079)
AS	7	AY	(0.667,1,1.5)	(1.667,2,2.5)	(0.015,0.042,0.092)	(0.006,0.018,0.047)
AY	6	AS	(1,1,1)	(2,2,2)	(0.008,0.021,0.046)	(0.003,0.009,0.024)

Table 4. Combined weights

Criteria	$\tilde{w}_j$
S	(0.372,0.434,0.514)
N	(0.138,0.203,0.289)
EOU	(0.099,0.157,0.238)
C	(0.044,0.082,0.141)
RT	(0.031,0.059,0.106)
AS	(0.010,0.023,0.048)
AY	(0.005,0.016,0.040)

The criteria according to the weights found with fuzzy SWARA indicated in Table 4 are listed as follows; Security (S), Navigation (N), Ease Of Use (EOU), Content (C), Response Time (RT), Aesthetics (AS), and Accessibility (AY). According to Table 4, the most important criterion is determined as Security (S). After using fuzzy SWARA to determine the weights of criteria, WASPAS-F will be used to evaluate the performance of websites of universities. Fuzzy decision matrix is presented in Table 5.

To normalize fuzzy decision matrix, Equation 11 is utilised. Normalized fuzzy decision matrix is presented in Table 6.

After structuring of fuzzy normalized matrix, Equations 12-16 are used to obtain overall performance scores of university websites. The results of WASPAS-F are presented in Table 7.

The order of the websites of universities according to Table 7 is as follows; EU > AGU > YBU > SCU > KSU > TGU > GU > EBYU > OU > IU. According to the results, the website of Erciyes University has been determined to have the best performance among the ten universities evaluated.

Table 5. Fuzzy decision matrix

Universities	Criteria			
	EOU	**S**	**RT**	**N**
SCU	(6,7,8)	(4.667,5.667,6.667)	(6.667,7.667,8.667)	(6,7,8)
IU	(4,5,6)	(4.667,5.667,6.667)	(6,7,8)	(1.333,2.333,3.333)
EU	(6.667,7.667,8.667)	(6,7,8)	(6,7,8)	(7.333,8.333,9.333)
TGU	(4.667,5.667,6.667)	(5.333,6.333,7.333)	(5.333,6.333,7.333)	(2.667,3.667,4.667)
YBU	(4.667,5.667,6.667)	(6,7,8)	(6,7,8)	(4.667,5.667,6.667)
KSU	(5.333,6.333,7.333)	(4.667,5.667,6.667)	(5.333,6.333,7.333)	(6,7,8)
OU	(6,7,8)	(4,5,6)	(3.333,4.333,5.333)	(4,5,6)
GU	(6,7,8)	(4,5,6)	(4.667,5.667,6.667)	(5.333,6.333,7.333)
EBYU	(4.667,5.667,6.667)	(4,5,6)	(4.667,5.667,6.667)	(4.667,5.667,6.667)
AGU	(6,7,8)	(4.667,5.667,6.667)	(6,7,8)	(7.333,8.333,9.333)

Universities	Criteria		
	C	**AS**	**AY**
SCU	(3.333,4.333,5.333)	(7.333,8.333,9.333)	(6,7,8)
IU	(1.333,2.333,3.333)	(2.667,3.667,4.667)	(4,5,6)
EU	(6.667,7.667,8.667)	(4,5,6)	(6,7,8)
TGU	(6,7,8)	(6.667,7.667,8.667)	(5.333,6.333,7.333)
YBU	(6,7,8)	(1.333,2.333,3.333)	(4,5,6)
KSU	(3.333,4.333,5.333)	(4,5,6)	(4,5,6)
OU	(5.333,6.333,7.333)	(4.667,5.667,6.667)	(3.333,4.333,5.333)
GU	(4.667,5.667,6.667)	(3.333,4.333,5.333)	(3.333,4.333,5.333)
EBYU	(6,7,8)	(2.667,3.667,4.667)	(4,5,6)
AGU	(6,7,8)	(4.667,5.667,6.667)	(4.667,5.667,6.667)

CONCLUSION

Many organizations serving customers offer information about their business through the website. Website development is a complex and tiring process that requires large investments. However, if the website does not indicate the expected performance value, it will have a negative impact on the website owner. Thus, evaluation of website performance has become a requirement for organizations. To measure the performance of websites, the use of MCDM methods can be helpful due to the performance measurement of websites containing many factors or criteria.

Table 6. Normalized fuzzy decision matrix

Universities	Criteria			
	EOU	**S**	**RT**	**N**
SCU	(0.900,0.913,0.923)	(0.778,0.810,0.833)	(1,1,1)	(0.818,0.840,0.857)
IU	(0.600,0.652,0.692)	(0.778,0.810,0.833)	(0.900,0.913,0.923)	(0.182,0.280,0.357)
EU	(1,1,1)	(1,1,1)	(0.900,0.913,0.923)	(1,1,1)
TGU	(0.700,0.739,0.769)	(0.889,0.905,0.917)	(0.800,0.826,0.846)	(0.364,0.440,0.500)
YBU	(0.700,0.739,0.769)	(1,1,1)	(0.900,0.913,0.923)	(0.636,0.680,0.714)
KSU	(0.800,0.826,0.846)	(0.778,0.810,0.833)	(0.800,0.826,0.846)	(0.818,0.840,0.857)
OU	(0.900,0.913,0.923)	(0.667,0.714,0.750)	(0.500,0.565,0.615)	(0.545,0.600,0.643)
GU	(0.900,0.913,0.923)	(0.667,0.714,0.750)	(0.700,0.739,0.769)	(0.727,0.760,0.786)
EBYU	(0.700,0.739,0.769)	(0.667,0.714,0.750)	(0.700,0.739,0.769)	(0.636,0.680,0.714)
AGU	(0.900,0.913,0.923)	(0.778,0.810,0.833)	(0.900,0.913,0.923)	(1,1,1)

Universities	Criteria		
	C	**AS**	**AY**
SCU	(0.500,0.565,0.615)	(1,1,1)	(1,1,1)
IU	(0.200,0.304,0.385)	(0.364,0.440,0.500)	(0.667,0.714,0.750)
EU	(1,1,1)	(0.545,0.600,0.643)	(1,1,1)
TGU	(0.900,0.913,0.923)	(0.909,0.920,0.929)	(0.889,0.905,0.917)
YBU	(0.900,0.913,0.923)	(0.182,0.280,0.357)	(0.667,0.714,0.750)
KSU	(0.500,0.565,0.615)	(0.545,0.600,0.643)	(0.667,0.714,0.750)
OU	(0.800,0.826,0.846)	(0.636,0.680,0.714)	(0.556,0.619,0.667)
GU	(0.700,0.739,0.769)	(0.455,0.520,0.571)	(0.556,0.619,0.667)
EBYU	(0.900,0.913,0.923)	(0.364,0.440,0.500)	(0.667,0.714,0.750)
AGU	(0.900,0.913,0.923)	(0.636,0.680,0.714)	(0.778,0.810,0.833)

Table 7. The results of WASPAS-F

Universities	Results					
	$\tilde{Q}_i$	$\tilde{P}_i$	Q_i	P_i	K_i	**Rankings**
SCU	(0.559,0.810,1.177)	(0.734,0.829,0.889)	0.849	0.817	0.833	4
IU	(0.417,0.611,0.902)	(0.351,0.581,0.741)	0.643	0.558	0.601	10
EU	(0.691,0.960,1.351)	(0.960,0.983,0.994)	1.001	0.979	0.990	1
TGU	(0.528,0.757,1.101)	(0.616,0.756,0.849)	0.795	0.740	0.768	6
YBU	(0.602,0.834,1.178)	(0.711,0.843,0.914)	0.871	0.823	0.847	3
KSU	(0.536,0.773,1.115)	(0.666,0.792,0.871)	0.808	0.776	0.792	5
OU	(0.472,0.702,1.037)	(0.573,0.717,0.817)	0.737	0.702	0.720	9
GU	(0.498,0.734,1.077)	(0.623,0.755,0.840)	0.770	0.739	0.755	7
EBYU	(0.474,0.704,1.041)	(0.583,0.725,0.820)	0.740	0.709	0.725	8
AGU	(0.594,0.856,1.232)	(0.809,0.879,0.917)	0.894	0.868	0.881	2

In this study, fuzzy SWARA and WASPAS-F methods are used to measure the performance of 10 universities' websites. The order of the websites of universities according to the results is as follows; EU > AGU > YBU > SCU > KSU > TGU > GU > EBYU > OU > IU. According to the results, the website of Erciyes University (EU) has been determined to have the best performance among the ten universities evaluated. This study presents one contribution to the literature. These two models consisting of fuzzy SWARA and WASPAS-F were first used together for the first time to evaluate the performance of university websites. Future research may implement these fuzzy methods so as to address another MCDM problem, such as third party logistics provider selection, warehouse selection and supplier performance evaluation. Additionally, future research may extend the sample size of the websites of universities.

REFERENCES

Abdel-Basset, M., Zhou, Y., Mohamed, M., & Chang, V. (2018). A group decision making framework based on neutrosophic VIKOR approach for e-government website evaluation. *Journal of Intelligent & Fuzzy Systems*, *34*(6), 4213–4224. doi:10.3233/JIFS-171952

Burmaoglu, S., & Kazancoglu, Y. (2012). E-government website evaluation with hybrid MCDM method in fuzzy environment. *International Journal of Applied Decision Sciences*, *5*(2), 163–181. doi:10.1504/IJADS.2012.046504

Büyüközkan, G., Feyzioğlu, O., & Gocer, F. (2016, December). Evaluation of hospital web services using intuitionistic fuzzy AHP and intuitionistic fuzzy VIKOR. In *Industrial Engineering and Engineering Management (IEEM), 2016 IEEE International Conference on* (pp. 607-611). IEEE. 10.1109/IEEM.2016.7797947

Büyüközkan, G., & Ruan, D. (2007). Evaluating government websites based on a fuzzy multiple criteria decision-making approach. *International Journal of Uncertainty, Fuzziness and Knowledge-based Systems*, *15*(03), 321–343. doi:10.1142/S0218488507004704

Chang, D. Y. (1996). Applications of the extent analysis method on fuzzy AHP. *European Journal of Operational Research*, *95*(3), 649–655. doi:10.1016/0377-2217(95)00300-2

Ecer, F. (2014). A hybrid banking websites quality evaluation model using AHP and COPRAS-G: A Turkey case. *Technological and Economic Development of Economy*, *20*(4), 758–782. doi:10.3846/20294913.2014.915596

Gani, A. N., & Assarudeen, S. M. (2012). A new operation on triangular fuzzy number for solving fuzzy linear programming problem. *Applied Mathematical Sciences*, *6*(11), 525–532.

Guo, M., & Zhao, Y. (2009). AHP-Based Evaluation of Information Service Quality of Information Center Web Portals in High-Tech Industry. In *Management and Service Science, 2009. MASS'09. International Conference on* (pp. 1-4). IEEE. 10.1109/ICMSS.2009.5301245

Kabak, M., & Burmaoğlu, S. (2013). A holistic evaluation of the e-procurement website by using a hybrid MCDM methodology. *Electronic Government, an International Journal*, *10*(2), 125-150.

Kang, D., Jang, W., & Park, Y. (2016). Evaluation of e-commerce websites using fuzzy hierarchical TOPSIS based on ES-QUAL. *Applied Soft Computing, 42*, 53–65. doi:10.1016/j.asoc.2016.01.017

Kaya, T., & Kahraman, C. (2011). A fuzzy approach to e-banking website quality assessment based on an integrated AHP-ELECTRE method. *Technological and Economic Development of Economy, 17*(2), 313–334. doi:10.3846/20294913.2011.583727

Keršuliene, V., Zavadskas, E. K., & Turskis, Z. (2010). Selection of rational dispute resolution method by applying new step-wise weight assessment ratio analysis (SWARA). *Journal of business economics and management, 11*(2), 243–258. doi:10.3846/jbem.2010.12

Kumar, R. D., & Zayaraz, G. (2011). A QoS aware quantitative web service selection model. *International Journal on Computer Science and Engineering, 3*(4), 1534–1538.

Mavi, R. K., Goh, M., & Zarbakhshnia, N. (2017). Sustainable third-party reverse logistic provider selection with fuzzy SWARA and fuzzy MOORA in plastic industry. *International Journal of Advanced Manufacturing Technology, 91*(5-8), 2401–2418. doi:10.100700170-016-9880-x

Nagpal, R., Mehrotra, D., & Bhatia, P. K. (2016). Usability evaluation of website using combined weighted method: Fuzzy AHP and entropy approach. *International Journal of System Assurance Engineering and Management, 7*(4), 408–417. doi:10.100713198-016-0462-y

Nagpal, R., Mehrotra, D., Bhatia, P. K., & Sharma, A. (2015). Rank university websites using fuzzy AHP and fuzzy TOPSIS approach on usability. *International Journal of Information Engineering and Electronic Business, 7*(1), 29.

Pamučar, D., Stević, Ž., & Zavadskas, E. K. (2018). Integration of interval rough AHP and interval rough MABAC methods for evaluating university web pages. *Applied Soft Computing, 67*, 141–163. doi:10.1016/j.asoc.2018.02.057

Rouyendegh, B. D., Topuz, K., Dag, A., & Oztekin, A. (2018). An AHP-IFT Integrated Model for Performance Evaluation of E-Commerce Web Sites. *Information Systems Frontiers*, 1–11.

Stanujkic, D., & Jovanovic, R. (2012). Measuring a quality of faculty website using ARAS method. In *Proceeding of the International Scientific Conference Contemporary Issues in Business, Management and Education* (pp. 545-554). Academic Press.

Stanujkic, D., Zavadskas, E. K., Karabasevic, D., Urosevic, S., & Maksimovic, M. (2017). An approach for evaluating website quality in hotel industry based on triangular intuitionistic fuzzy numbers. *Informatica, 28*(4), 725–748. doi:10.15388/Informatica.2017.153

Turskis, Z., Zavadskas, E. K., Antucheviciene, J., & Kosareva, N. (2015). A hybrid model based on fuzzy AHP and fuzzy WASPAS for construction site selection. *International Journal of Computers, Communications & Control, 10*(6), 113–128. doi:10.15837/ijccc.2015.6.2078

Vatansever, K., & Akgul, Y. (2014). Applying fuzzy analytic hierarchy process for evaluating service quality of private shopping website quality: A case study in Turkey. *Journal of Business Economics and Finance, 3*(3), 283–301.

Vatansever, K., & Akgűl, Y. (2018). Performance evaluation of websites using entropy and grey relational analysis methods: The case of airline companies. *Decision Science Letters, 7*(2), 119–130. doi:10.5267/j.dsl.2017.6.005

Zarbakhshnia, N., Soleimani, H., & Ghaderi, H. (2018). Sustainable third-party reverse logistics provider evaluation and selection using fuzzy SWARA and developed fuzzy COPRAS in the presence of risk criteria. *Applied Soft Computing, 65*, 307–319. doi:10.1016/j.asoc.2018.01.023

Zavadskas, E. K., Turskis, Z., Antucheviciene, J., & Zakarevicius, A. (2012). Optimization of weighted aggregated sum product assessment. *Elektronika ir Elektrotechnika, 122*(6), 3–6. doi:10.5755/j01.eee.122.6.1810

Chapter 9
Website Evaluation Using Interval Type-2 Fuzzy-Number-Based TOPSIS Approach

Burak Efe
Necmettin Erbakan University, Turkey

ABSTRACT

In recent years, with the development of the internet, there has been an increase in interest in the internet thanks to other technological developments. In the face of increased user demand, educational institution websites have to maintain high quality of service for a sustainable success. The authors present the possibility degree based TOPSIS method with IT2F numbers as an extension of TOPSIS method to evaluate the educational institution websites. In contrast to precise numbers in TOPSIS method, the merit of fuzzy TOPSIS method is to handle the fuzzy numbers to evaluate the alternatives. Type-1 fuzzy numbers consider crisp membership degrees to express fuzzy numbers but IT2F numbers handle more uncertainties than type-1 fuzzy numbers. The subjective judgments of the decision makers are aggregated by using the IT2F number operations to determine the weights of these criteria. IT2TrF numbers-based TOPSIS phase is employed to rank alternatives based on criteria so that assessment process is completed. The proposed method is applied to evaluate the educational institution websites.

DOI: 10.4018/978-1-5225-8238-0.ch009

INTRODUCTION

Information storage is one of the basic attributes of corporation performance. Internet, which is indispensable for our daily activities, ensures storing large datasets. Internet affects marketing methods as handling relationships between consumers and corporations. Websites of big corporations present interactive experience to the consumers to help deciding between buying alternatives. Similarly, educational institutions must develop their websites to increase the content and quality of information for users. The future and current students can reach the desired information more easily. The quality of the institution websites also help to the institution's own teaching personel looking for specific information related to the teaching process and scientific research (Pamučar et al., 2018).

Pamučar et al. (2018) considered the integration of interval rough AHP and interval rough MABAC methods for evaluating university web pages. Akıncılar and Dağdeviren (2014) presented the combination of AHP and PROMETHEE methods for evaluating hotel websites. Tzeng et al. (2005) handled fuzzy based Choquet integral model for evaluating enterprise intranet web sites. Stanujkic et al. (2015) used the intuitionistic fuzzy set for measuring website quality. Roy et al. (2017) presented AHP approach to consider the quality of academic websites. Hsu and Shih (2016) considered ANP, Kano model, DEMATEL and VIKOR methods the e-service quality of house rental websites. Bilsel et al. (2006) presented AHP and fuzzy PROMETHEE methods for measuring performance of hospital websites. Yu et al. (2011) utilized AHP and fuzzy TOPSIS methods for e-commerce websites. Lee and Kozar (2006) investigated the effect of website quality on e-business success by using AHP approach. Büyüközkan and Ruan (2007) employed fuzzy AHP and fuzzy TOPSIS methods for evaluating the quality of government websites. Dominic et al. (2013) considered to determine the best university website by using fuzzy AHP and linear weightage model.

We present the possibility degree based TOPSIS method with IT2F numbers as an extension of TOPSIS method. In contrast to precise numbers in TOPSIS method, the merit of fuzzy TOPSIS method is to handle the fuzzy numbers to evaluate the alternatives. Type-1 fuzzy numbers consider crisp membership degrees to express fuzzy numbers but IT2F numbers handle more uncertainties than type-1 fuzzy numbers. IT2F numbers ensure us with additional information to describe the fuzziness and the uncertainty of the real-life world. This study aims to extend the TOPSIS method by utilizing interval type-2 trapezoidal fuzzy (IT2TrF) numbers in order to model more uncertainties of the subjective judgments in complex problems. The aim of this study is to introduce a novel IT2F TOPSIS method based on possibility mean value and possibility degree. This study uses the approximate positive and negative ideal solutions with IT2TrF numbers to evaluate the alternatives. This study presents the possibility mean value and possibility degree measures instead of distance measures in current TOPSIS to define a comparative index. The closeness coefficient based on the possibility degree of each alternative is calculated according to the approximate positive and negative ideal solutions. This study also uses the IT2F number operations to aggregate the subjective judgments of the decision makers about the relative importance of criteria and criteria based alternative evaluations. The subjective judgments of the decision makers are aggregated by using the IT2F number operations to determine the weights of the criteria. These weights with IT2TrF numbers are used into IT2TrF numbers based TOPSIS phase to rank the alternatives. The proposed method is applied to evaluate the university websites.

PRELIMINARIES

If a IT2FS $\tilde{\tilde{A}} = (\tilde{A}^U, \tilde{A}^L)$, $\tilde{A}^U$ and $\tilde{A}^L$ show the upper membership function and the lower membership function, respectively. These upper and lower membership functions are type-1 membership functions.

$H_j(\tilde{A}^L)$ shows the membership value of the element a_{j+1}^L in the upper trapezoidal membership function:

$\tilde{A}^L$,

$1 \le j \le 2$. $H_1(\tilde{A}^U) \in [0,1], H_2(\tilde{A}^U) \in [0,1], H_1(\tilde{A}^L) \in [0,1], H_2(\tilde{A}^L) \in [0,1]$,

and

$1 \le i \le n$.

Chen and Lee (2010) introduced some arithmetic operations between trapezoidal IT2F sets. Let $\tilde{\tilde{A}}_1$ and $\tilde{\tilde{A}}_2$ be trapezoidal IT2F sets, where:

$$\tilde{\tilde{A}}_1 = (\tilde{A}_1^U, \tilde{A}_1^L) = ((a_{11}^U, a_{12}^U, a_{13}^U, a_{14}^U; H_1(\tilde{A}_1^U), H_2(\tilde{A}_1^U)), (a_{11}^L, a_{12}^L, a_{13}^L, a_{14}^L; H_1(\tilde{A}_1^L), H_2(\tilde{A}_1^L)))$$

and:

$$\tilde{\tilde{A}}_2 = (\tilde{A}_2^U, \tilde{A}_2^L) = ((a_{21}^U, a_{22}^U, a_{23}^U, a_{24}^U; H_1(\tilde{A}_2^U), H_2(\tilde{A}_2^U)), (a_{21}^L, a_{22}^L, a_{23}^L, a_{24}^L; H_1(\tilde{A}_2^L), H_2(\tilde{A}_2^L)))$$

The addition operation between the trapezoidal IT2F numbers $\tilde{\tilde{A}}_1$ and $\tilde{\tilde{A}}_2$ is defined as follows:

$$\tilde{\tilde{A}}_1 \oplus \tilde{\tilde{A}}_2 = (\tilde{A}_1^U, \tilde{A}_1^L) \oplus (\tilde{A}_2^U, \tilde{A}_2^L) = ((a_{11}^U + a_{21}^U, a_{12}^U + a_{22}^U, a_{13}^U + a_{23}^U, a_{14}^U + a_{24}^U;$$
$$\min\{H_1(\tilde{A}_1^U), H_2(\tilde{A}_1^U)\}), (a_{11}^L + a_{21}^L, a_{12}^L + a_{22}^L, a_{13}^L + a_{23}^L, a_{14}^L + a_{24}^L; \min\{H_1(\tilde{A}_1^L), H_2(\tilde{A}_1^L)\}))$$

The multiplication operation between the trapezoidal IT2F numbers $\tilde{\tilde{A}}_1$ and $\tilde{\tilde{A}}_2$ is defined as follows:

$$\tilde{\tilde{A}}_1 \otimes \tilde{\tilde{A}}_2 = (\tilde{A}_1^U, \tilde{A}_1^L) \otimes (\tilde{A}_2^U, \tilde{A}_2^L) = ((a_{11}^U \times a_{21}^U, a_{12}^U \times a_{22}^U, a_{13}^U \times a_{23}^U, a_{14}^U \times a_{24}^U;$$
$$\min\{H_1(\tilde{A}_1^U), H_2(\tilde{A}_1^U)\}), (a_{11}^L \times a_{21}^L, a_{12}^L \times a_{22}^L, a_{13}^L \times a_{23}^L, a_{14}^L \times a_{24}^L; \min\{H_1(\tilde{A}_1^L), H_2(\tilde{A}_1^L)\}))$$

If k is a crisp value, the multiplication operation between k and $\tilde{\tilde{A}}_1$ is defined as follows:

$$k \times \tilde{\tilde{A}}_1 = k \times (\tilde{A}_1^U, \tilde{A}_1^L) = ((k \times a_{11}^U, k \times a_{12}^U, k \times a_{13}^U, k \times a_{14}^U; H_1(\tilde{A}_1^U)), (k \times a_{11}^L, k \times a_{12}^L, k \times a_{13}^L, k \times a_{14}^L; H_1(\tilde{A}_1^L)))$$

where $k>0$.

The Interval-Valued Possibility Mean Value and Possibility Degree of IT2FS

This study used the possibility mean value and possibility degree of IT2F numbers proposed by Gong et al. (2015). Let $\tilde{\tilde{A}}$ be a trapezoidal IT2F set, where:

$$\tilde{\tilde{A}} = (\tilde{A}^U, \tilde{A}^L) = ((a_1^U, a_2^U, a_3^U, a_4^U; h_U), (a_1^L, a_2^L, a_3^L, a_4^L; h_L))$$

The lower possibility mean value is defined as follows:

$$M_*(\tilde{A}) = \frac{1}{6}(a_1^U + 2a_2^U)h_U^2 + \frac{1}{6}(a_1^L + 2a_2^L)h_L^2$$

The upper possibility mean value is defined as follows:

$$M^*(\tilde{A}) = \frac{1}{6}(a_4^U + 2a_3^U)h_U^2 + \frac{1}{6}(a_4^L + 2a_3^L)h_L^2$$

Let $M(\tilde{A}_1) = [M_*(\tilde{A}_1), M^*(\tilde{A}_1)]$ and $M(\tilde{A}_2) = [M_*(\tilde{A}_2), M^*(\tilde{A}_2)]$ be interval valued possibility mean values of IT2F numbers $\tilde{A}_1$ and $\tilde{A}_2$, respectively.

The possibility degree of IT2F numbers is defined as follows (Gong et al., 2015):

$$p(\tilde{A}_1 \succ \tilde{A}_2) = \min\left\{\max\left(\frac{M^*(\tilde{A}_1) - M_*(\tilde{A}_2)}{M^*(\tilde{A}_1) - M_*(\tilde{A}_1) + M^*(\tilde{A}_2) - M_*(\tilde{A}_2)}, 0\right), 1\right\}$$

METHODOLOGY

Interval Type-2 Fuzzy TOPSIS Method

TOPSIS, which is developed by Hwang and Yoon (1981), ranks suitable solutions presenting the farthest distance from negative ideal solution (NIS) and the shortest distance from positive ideal solution (PIS) simultaneously (Hwang and Yoon, 1981). In this study, we propose the possibility degree based TOPSIS method with IT2F numbers as an extension of TOPSIS method. Let X be a set of alternatives $X=\{x_1, x_2, ..., x_n\}$, F be a set of attributes $F=\{f_1, f_2, ..., f_m\}$, and D be a set of decision makers $D=\{D_1, D_2, ..., D_l\}$. The set F of attributes can be separated into two sets: benefit and cost attributes. The proposed method is now introduced as follows:

Step 1: Define the weighting matrix W_1 of the attributes:

$$W_l = \left(\tilde{\tilde{w}}_i^l\right)_{1 \times m} = \begin{array}{c} f_1 \quad f_2 \quad \cdots \quad f_m \\ \left[\tilde{\tilde{w}}_1^l \quad \tilde{\tilde{w}}_2^l \quad \cdots \quad \tilde{\tilde{w}}_m^l\right] \end{array}$$

$$\tilde{\tilde{w}}_i = \sum_{l=1}^{k} w_l \tilde{\tilde{w}}_i^l$$

$\tilde{\tilde{w}}_i$ is a trapezoidal IT2F number, $1 \le i \le m$, $1 \le l \le k$. k is the number of decision makers. w_l is the importance degree of the decision maker D_l. $\tilde{\tilde{w}}_i^l$ is the importance degree of attribute f_i according to the decision maker D_l.

Step 2: Define the decision matrix Y_1 of the decision maker D_1 and construct the average decision matrix $\bar{Y}$, respectively:

$$Y_l = \left(\tilde{\tilde{f}}_{ij}^l\right)_{m \times n} = \begin{array}{c} \quad\quad x_1 \quad\; x_2 \quad \cdots \quad x_n \\ \begin{array}{c} f_1 \\ f_2 \\ \vdots \\ f_m \end{array} \left[\begin{array}{cccc} \tilde{\tilde{f}}_{11}^l & \tilde{\tilde{f}}_{12}^l & \cdots & \tilde{\tilde{f}}_{1n}^l \\ \tilde{\tilde{f}}_{21}^l & \tilde{\tilde{f}}_{22}^l & \cdots & \tilde{\tilde{f}}_{2n}^l \\ \vdots & \vdots & \vdots & \vdots \\ \tilde{\tilde{f}}_{m1}^l & \tilde{\tilde{f}}_{m2}^l & \cdots & \tilde{\tilde{f}}_{mn}^l \end{array}\right] \end{array}$$

$$\bar{Y} = \left(\tilde{\tilde{f}}_{ij}\right)_{m \times n}$$

$$\tilde{\tilde{f}}_{ij} = \sum_{l=1}^{k} w_l \cdot \tilde{\tilde{f}}_{ij}^l$$

$\tilde{\tilde{f}}_{ij}$ is a trapezoidal IT2F number, $1 \le i \le m, 1 \le j \le n, 1 \le l \le k$. k is the number of decision makers.

w_l is the importance degree of the decision maker D_l. $\tilde{\tilde{f}}_{ij}^l$ is the judgment of the decision maker D_l for $\tilde{\tilde{f}}_{ij}$.

Step 3: Define the average weighting matrix $\bar{W}$:

$$\overline{W} = (\tilde{\tilde{v}}_{ij})_{m \times n} = \begin{array}{c} f_1 \\ f_2 \\ \vdots \\ f_m \end{array} \begin{array}{c} \quad x_1 \quad\quad x_2 \quad \cdots \quad x_n \\ \begin{bmatrix} \tilde{\tilde{v}}_{11} & \tilde{\tilde{v}}_{12} & \cdots & \tilde{\tilde{v}}_{1n} \\ \tilde{\tilde{v}}_{21} & \tilde{\tilde{v}}_{22} & \cdots & \tilde{\tilde{v}}_{2n} \\ \vdots & \vdots & \vdots & \vdots \\ \tilde{\tilde{v}}_{m1} & \tilde{\tilde{v}}_{m2} & \cdots & \tilde{\tilde{v}}_{mn} \end{bmatrix} \end{array}$$

where $\tilde{\tilde{v}}_{ij} = \tilde{\tilde{w}}_i \otimes \tilde{\tilde{f}}_{ij}, 1 \leq i \leq m$, and $1 \leq j \leq n$. $\tilde{\tilde{v}}_{ij}$ is a trapezoidal IT2F number.

Step 4: Define the approximate positive and negative ideal solution $x^+ = (v_1^+, v_2^+, ..., v_m^+)$ and $x^- = (v_1^-, v_2^-, ..., v_m^-)$ with respect to benefit and cost attributes. Let $\tilde{\tilde{A}}$ be a trapezoidal IT2F set, where:

$$\tilde{\tilde{v}} = (\tilde{v}^U, \tilde{v}^L) = ((v_1^U, v_2^U, v_3^U, v_4^U; h_U), (v_1^L, v_2^L, v_3^L, v_4^L; h_L))$$

It is shown as follows:

$$\tilde{\tilde{v}}_i^+ = \begin{cases} \bigvee_{j=1}^{n} \tilde{v}_{1ij}^L, \bigvee_{j=1}^{n} \tilde{v}_{2ij}^L, \bigvee_{j=1}^{n} \tilde{v}_{3ij}^L, \bigvee_{j=1}^{n} \tilde{v}_{4ij}^L, \bigwedge_{j=1}^{n} \left\{ H(\tilde{A}_{ij}^L) \right\}, \bigvee_{j=1}^{n} \tilde{v}_{1ij}^U, \bigvee_{j=1}^{n} \tilde{v}_{2ij}^U, \bigvee_{j=1}^{n} \tilde{v}_{3ij}^U, \bigvee_{j=1}^{n} \tilde{v}_{4ij}^U, \bigwedge_{j=1}^{n} \left\{ H(\tilde{A}_{ij}^U) \right\}, \ if \ f_i \in F_1 \\ \bigwedge_{j=1}^{n} \tilde{v}_{1ij}^L, \bigwedge_{j=1}^{n} \tilde{v}_{2ij}^L, \bigwedge_{j=1}^{n} \tilde{v}_{3ij}^L, \bigwedge_{j=1}^{n} \tilde{v}_{4ij}^L, \bigwedge_{j=1}^{n} \left\{ H(\tilde{A}_{ij}^L) \right\}, \bigwedge_{j=1}^{n} \tilde{v}_{1ij}^U, \bigwedge_{j=1}^{n} \tilde{v}_{2ij}^U, \bigwedge_{j=1}^{n} \tilde{v}_{3ij}^U, \bigwedge_{j=1}^{n} \tilde{v}_{4ij}^U, \bigwedge_{j=1}^{n} \left\{ H(\tilde{A}_{ij}^U) \right\}, \ if \ f_i \in F_2 \end{cases}$$

$$\tilde{\tilde{v}}_i^- = \begin{cases} \bigwedge_{j=1}^{n} \tilde{v}_{1ij}^L, \bigwedge_{j=1}^{n} \tilde{v}_{2ij}^L, \bigwedge_{j=1}^{n} \tilde{v}_{3ij}^L, \bigwedge_{j=1}^{n} \tilde{v}_{4ij}^L, \bigwedge_{j=1}^{n} \left\{ H(\tilde{A}_{ij}^L) \right\}, \bigwedge_{j=1}^{n} \tilde{v}_{1ij}^U, \bigwedge_{j=1}^{n} \tilde{v}_{2ij}^U, \bigwedge_{j=1}^{n} \tilde{v}_{3ij}^U, \bigwedge_{j=1}^{n} \tilde{v}_{4ij}^U, \bigwedge_{j=1}^{n} \left\{ H(\tilde{A}_{ij}^U) \right\}, \ if \ f_i \in F_1 \\ \bigvee_{j=1}^{n} \tilde{v}_{1ij}^L, \bigvee_{j=1}^{n} \tilde{v}_{2ij}^L, \bigvee_{j=1}^{n} \tilde{v}_{3ij}^L, \bigvee_{j=1}^{n} \tilde{v}_{4ij}^L, \bigwedge_{j=1}^{n} \left\{ H(\tilde{A}_{ij}^L) \right\}, \bigvee_{j=1}^{n} \tilde{v}_{1ij}^U, \bigvee_{j=1}^{n} \tilde{v}_{2ij}^U, \bigvee_{j=1}^{n} \tilde{v}_{3ij}^U, \bigvee_{j=1}^{n} \tilde{v}_{4ij}^U, \bigwedge_{j=1}^{n} \left\{ H(\tilde{A}_{ij}^U) \right\}, \ if \ f_i \in F_2 \end{cases}$$

where F_1 and F_2 show the set of benefit and cost attributes, respectively, $\vee$ and $\wedge$ show max and min, respectively, and $1 \leq i \leq m$.

Step 5: Define the possibility degree $p(\tilde{\tilde{v}}_i \succ \tilde{\tilde{v}}_i^+)$ between each alternative $\tilde{\tilde{v}}_i$ and the approximate positive ideal solution $\tilde{\tilde{v}}_i^+$, the possibility degree $p(\tilde{\tilde{v}}_i \succ \tilde{\tilde{v}}_i^-)$ between each alternative $\tilde{\tilde{v}}_i$ and the approximate negative ideal solution $\tilde{\tilde{v}}_i^-$, shown as follows:

$$p(\tilde{\tilde{v}}_i \succ \tilde{\tilde{v}}_i^+) = \min\left\{\max\left(\frac{M^*(\tilde{\tilde{v}}_i) - M_*(\tilde{\tilde{v}}_i^+)}{M^*(\tilde{\tilde{v}}_i) - M_*(\tilde{\tilde{v}}_i) + M^*(\tilde{\tilde{v}}_i^+) - M_*(\tilde{\tilde{v}}_i^+)}, 0\right), 1\right\}$$

$$p(\tilde{\tilde{v}}_i \succ \tilde{\tilde{v}}_i^-) = \min\left\{\max\left(\frac{M^*(\tilde{\tilde{v}}_i) - M_*(\tilde{\tilde{v}}_i^-)}{M^*(\tilde{\tilde{v}}_i) - M_*(\tilde{\tilde{v}}_i) + M^*(\tilde{\tilde{v}}_i^-) - M_*(\tilde{\tilde{v}}_i^-)}, 0\right), 1\right\}$$

where:

$$M_*(\tilde{\tilde{v}}_i) = \frac{1}{6}(v_{i1}^U + 2v_{i2}^U)H(\tilde{A}_i^U)^2 + \frac{1}{6}(v_{i1}^L + 2v_{i2}^L)H(\tilde{A}_i^L)^2$$

and:

$$M^*(\tilde{\tilde{v}}_i) = \frac{1}{6}(v_{i4}^U + 2v_{i3}^U)H(\tilde{A}_i^U)^2 + \frac{1}{6}(v_{i4}^L + 2v_{i3}^L)H(\tilde{A}_i^L)^2$$

Step 6: Define the possibility degree based closeness coefficient PC_i for each alternative, shown as follows:

$$PC_i = \frac{\sum_{j=1}^m p(\tilde{\tilde{v}}_i \succ \tilde{\tilde{v}}_i^-)}{\sum_{j=1}^m \left(p(\tilde{\tilde{v}}_i \succ \tilde{\tilde{v}}_i^-) + p(\tilde{\tilde{v}}_i \succ \tilde{\tilde{v}}_i^+)\right)}$$

where $1 \leq i \leq n$.

Step 7: Rank the values of PC_i in a decreasing order, where $1 \leq i \leq n$. The higher the possibility degree based closeness coefficient PC_i, the better alternative x_i.

APPLICATION OF THE MOST APPROPRIATE WEBSITE SELECTION

A website evaluation process includes defining of expert decision makers to make selection, determining suitable website alternatives, determining criteria that examined in evaluation phases, weighting the criteria and evaluation of alternatives phases. A real-life application is presented in order to provide the better understanding of the proposed approach.

A questionnaire study was presented to fill to five decision makers E1, E2, E3, E4 and E5 in order to determine the most appropriate university website for the students. E1, E2 and E3 are a software engineering, a computer engineering and an electronic engineering, respectively while E4 and E5 are academicians. They worked in website area for least 5 years so that they have enough knowledge and experience about website evaluation. Firstly, evaluation criteria for a university website are determined by five experts. These criteria are content (C1), authority (C2), search ability (C3), usability (C4), appearance (C5), security/privacy (C6) and interactivity (C7). Seven criteria based fifteen university websites are evaluated according to five experts' judgments.

Results

The subjective judgments of experts are established to obtain priorities of evaluation criteria by employing the linguistic scale, which is demonstrated in Table 1.

The five decision makers construct the importance degrees of evaluation criteria as showing in Table 2. The importance degree of decision makers are assigned in order to show their differences in the group decision making problem so that the importance degrees of E1, E2, E3, E4, and E5 decision makers can be defined as (0.15, 0.25, 0.15, 0.20, 0.25), respectively.

Table 1. Transformation between linguistic terms and IT2TrF numbers

Linguistic Term	IT2TrF Numbers
Very low (VL)	(0.08,0.11,0.15,0.18;0.8),(0.04,0.09,0.17,0.22;1)
Low (L)	(0.20,0.25,0.33,0.36;0.8),(0.17,0.22,0.38,0.43;1)
Medium (M)	(0.40,0.45,0.54,0.57;0.8),(0.30,0.40,0.60,0.66;1)
High (H)	(0.77,0.80,0.86,0.90;0.8),(0.72,0.75,0.90,0.95;1)
Very high (VH)	(0.95,0.97,0.98,0.99;0.8),(0.92,0.96,0.99,1.00;1)

Table 2. The importance degrees of criteria for five decision makers

Decision Makers	Criteria						
	C1	**C2**	**C3**	**C4**	**C5**	**C6**	**C7**
DM1	VL	M	H	L	M	VH	VL
DM2	M	H	H	VL	VH	M	L
DM3	M	M	VH	M	VH	H	L
DM4	L	L	M	VL	M	H	VL
DM5	M	VH	VL	M	H	H	L

The subjective judgments of experts based on importance degrees of experts are aggregated. After aggregation process, the importance degrees of the criteria for the combining result of five decision makers are defined and shown in Table 3.

TOPSIS approach is proposed to evaluate the university websites under IT2F set environment. Five decision makers utilize the linguistic rating variables indicated in Table 1 to determine the rating of university websites based on each criteria. The rating of fifteen university websites based on the seven criteria from the five decision makers are presented in Table 4.

The linguistic evaluations indicated in Table 4 are converted into the IT2TrF numbers by using Table 1. The group decision of the five decision makers based on their importance is obtained with using IT2F number operations and the aggregated IT2TrF evaluative rating of university websites under the seven criteria is shown in Table 5. The weighted aggregated IT2TrF evaluative rating of university websites is obtained and is indicated in Table 6.

Table 3. Importance degrees of criteria for the combining result of five decision makers

Criteria	IT2TrF Numbers
C1	((0.312,0.359,0.440,0.470;0.800),(0.235,0.318,0.492,0.548;1.000))
C2	((0.590,0.628,0.688,0.716;0.800),(0.534,0.592,0.729,0.772;1.000))
C3	((0.551,0.583,0.637,0.668;0.800),(0.496,0.547,0.671,0.717;1.000))
C4	((0.226,0.267,0.333,0.363;0.800),(0.164,0.234,0.374,0.428;1.000))
C5	((0.713,0.746,0.796,0.821;0.800),(0.653,0.712,0.831,0.869;1.000))
C6	((0.705,0.738,0.798,0.831;0.800),(0.645,0.694,0.839,0.885;1.000))
C7	((0.158,0.201,0.267,0.297;0.800),(0.125,0.175,0.307,0.357;1.000))

Table 4. Evaluation data of alternatives

		A1	A2	A3	A4	A5	A6	A7	A8	A9	A10	A11	A12	A13	A14	A15
DM1	C1	VH	H	L	L	H	VH	M	M	H	H	H	L	H	H	M
	C2	M	VL	M	M	VH	H	M	VL	L	H	H	M	M	VH	L
	C3	L	VH	M	M	VL	H	M	M	VH	H	H	M	L	H	H
	C4	M	L	M	L	VL	L	H	H	H	M	VH	M	H	H	M
	C5	VH	M	L	L	VL	L	L	M	H	M	H	H	L	H	L
	C6	M	VL	M	M	L	L	H	M	H	L	H	H	VH	VH	M
	C7	L	L	L	M	VL	L	M	M	VH	H	L	L	H	M	H
DM2	C1	VH	M	L	L	L	VH	VH	M	H	M	M	L	L	H	H
	C2	L	H	M	M	VH	H	M	H	H	H	H	M	L	H	M
	C3	L	VH	H	H	H	H	M	H	M	M	M	M	L	H	M
	C4	M	L	M	L	VL	L	H	H	L	VH	VH	M	H	H	L
	C5	VH	M	L	L	VL	H	L	L	L	M	L	H	H	H	M
	C6	M	VL	M	M	L	M	H	L	H	L	L	H	VH	H	H
	C7	L	L	L	M	VL	M	L	M	H	H	M	H	L	L	M
DM3	C1	M	M	M	L	M	M	M	L	M	H	M	M	H	H	M
	C2	L	L	M	M	VH	H	VH	H	M	H	H	L	M	VH	L
	C3	M	H	H	H	VH	H	H	H	H	VH	H	M	L	M	H
	C4	M	L	M	L	VL	L	L	M	M	VH	VH	H	H	M	L
	C5	VH	M	L	L	VL	H	H	L	M	M	L	M	L	H	H
	C6	M	VL	M	M	L	M	H	L	M	L	L	M	H	VH	M
	C7	L	L	L	M	VL	H	L	M	M	M	M	H	H	M	H
DM4	C1	H	L	M	VL	M	M	M	H	VH	H	H	H	H	H	L
	C2	H	L	M	VL	L	M	L	L	M	M	H	M	L	H	M
	C3	H	M	M	VL	VH	H	VH	H	VH	VH	VH	L	L	L	H
	C4	M	L	M	L	VL	L	L	H	L	VH	VH	H	H	M	L
	C5	VH	M	L	L	VL	H	H	L	H	L	H	H	L	H	VH
	C6	M	VL	M	M	L	L	H	L	H	L	H	L	VH	VH	H
	C7	L	L	L	M	VL	H	L	H	L	H	L	H	H	M	VH
DM5	C1	VL	M	VL	VL	M	L	VL	VL	H	H	M	L	L	L	M
	C2	H	H	M	M	H	M	H	M	M	H	H	M	M	VH	M
	C3	VH	L	VH	VH	VH	VH	VH	VH	VH	VH	VH	L	L	L	L
	C4	M	H	L	L	M	M	L	M	M	L	M	M	M	H	M
	C5	H	L	M	H	M	L	L	H	L	M	L	L	L	M	L
	C6	M	H	L	M	L	M	M	L	M	M	L	M	H	H	M
	C7	H	L	M	M	M	H	H	M	H	L	M	M	M	L	L

Table 5. The aggregated IT2TrF evaluative rating of university websites

A1	C1	(((0.614,0.643,0.683,0.707;0.800),(0.567,0.617,0.709,0.744;1.000))
	C2	(((0.487,0.528,0.600,0.635;0.800),(0.437,0.486,0.647,0.699;1.000))
	C3	(((0.532,0.570,0.630,0.657;0.800),(0.487,0.538,0.670,0.711;1.000))
	C4	(((0.400,0.450,0.540,0.570;0.800),(0.300,0.400,0.600,0.660;1.000))
	C5	(((0.905,0.928,0.950,0.968;0.800),(0.870,0.908,0.968,0.988;1.000))
	C6	(((0.400,0.450,0.540,0.570;0.800),(0.300,0.400,0.600,0.660;1.000))
	C7	(((0.343,0.388,0.463,0.495;0.800),(0.308,0.353,0.510,0.560;1.000))
A2	C1	(((0.416,0.463,0.546,0.578;0.800),(0.337,0.417,0.601,0.658;1.000))
	C2	(((0.467,0.504,0.568,0.603;0.800),(0.426,0.466,0.609,0.659;1.000))
	C3	(((0.626,0.661,0.712,0.735;0.800),(0.579,0.632,0.746,0.782;1.000))
	C4	(((0.343,0.388,0.463,0.495;0.800),(0.308,0.353,0.510,0.560;1.000))
	C5	(((0.350,0.400,0.488,0.518;0.800),(0.268,0.355,0.545,0.603;1.000))
	C6	(((0.253,0.283,0.328,0.360;0.800),(0.210,0.255,0.353,0.403;1.000))
	C7	(((0.200,0.250,0.330,0.360;0.800),(0.170,0.220,0.380,0.430;1.000))
⋮	⋮	⋮ ⋮ ⋮ ⋮ ⋮ ⋮ ⋮ ⋮ ⋮
A14	C1	(((0.628,0.663,0.728,0.765;0.800),(0.583,0.618,0.770,0.820;1.000))
	C2	(((0.869,0.894,0.926,0.950;0.800),(0.830,0.866,0.950,0.978;1.000))
	C3	(((0.458,0.500,0.574,0.608;0.800),(0.410,0.459,0.621,0.673;1.000))
	C4	(((0.641,0.678,0.748,0.785;0.800),(0.573,0.628,0.795,0.849;1.000))
	C5	(((0.678,0.713,0.780,0.818;0.800),(0.615,0.663,0.825,0.878;1.000))
	C6	(((0.860,0.885,0.920,0.945;0.800),(0.820,0.855,0.945,0.975;1.000))
	C7	(((0.300,0.350,0.435,0.465;0.800),(0.235,0.310,0.490,0.545;1.000))
A15	C1	(((0.453,0.498,0.578,0.611;0.800),(0.379,0.452,0.631,0.687;1.000))
	C2	(((0.340,0.390,0.477,0.507;0.800),(0.261,0.346,0.534,0.591;1.000))
	C3	(((0.535,0.575,0.648,0.683;0.800),(0.478,0.530,0.695,0.748;1.000))
	C4	(((0.280,0.330,0.414,0.444;0.800),(0.222,0.292,0.468,0.522;1.000))
	C5	(((0.486,0.527,0.592,0.620;0.800),(0.435,0.493,0.635,0.680;1.000))
	C6	(((0.567,0.608,0.684,0.719;0.800),(0.489,0.558,0.735,0.791;1.000))
	C7	(((0.571,0.609,0.672,0.701;0.800),(0.518,0.572,0.713,0.758;1.000))

Table 6. The weighted aggregated IT2TrF evaluative rating of university websites

		A1									
A1	C1	((0.192,0.231,0.300,0.332;0.800),(0.133,0.196,0.348,0.408;1,000)									
	C2	((0.287,0.331,0.413,0.454;0.800),(0.233,0.287,0.471,0.539;1,000)									
	C3	((0.293,0.332,0.401,0.439;0.800),(0.242,0.294,0.449,0.510;1,000)									
	C4	((0.090,0.120,0.180,0.207;0.800),(0.049,0.093,0.224,0.282;1,000)									
	C5	((0.645,0.691,0.756,0.794;0.800),(0.568,0.646,0.804,0.858;1,000)									
	C6	((0.282,0.332,0.431,0.474;0.800),(0.194,0.278,0.503,0.584;1,000)									
	C7	((0.054,0.078,0.123,0.147;0.800),(0.038,0.062,0.156,0.200;1,000)									
A2	C1	((0.130,0.166,0.240,0.271;0.800),(0.079,0.132,0.295,0.360;1,000)									
	C2	((0.276,0.316,0.391,0.431;0.800),(0.227,0.275,0.443,0.508;1,000)									
	C3	((0.344,0.385,0.453,0.491;0.800),(0.287,0.345,0.501,0.561;1,000)									
	C4	((0.077,0.103,0.154,0.180;0.800),(0.050,0.082,0.190,0.239;1,000)									
	C5	((0.249,0.298,0.388,0.425;0.800),(0.175,0.253,0.453,0.523;1,000)									
	C6	((0.178,0.208,0.261,0.299;0.800),(0.135,0.177,0.296,0.356;1,000)									
	C7	((0.032,0.050,0.088,0.107;0.800),(0.021,0.038,0.116,0.153;1,000)									
⋮	⋮	⋮	⋮	⋮	⋮	⋮	⋮	⋮	⋮	⋮	⋮
A14	C1	((0.196,0.238,0.320,0.359;0.800),(0.137,0.196,0.378,0.449;1,000)									
	C2	((0.513,0.561,0.637,0.679;0.800),(0.443,0.512,0.692,0.754;1,000)									
	C3	((0.252,0.292,0.365,0.406;0.800),(0.203,0.251,0.417,0.482;1,000)									
	C4	((0.145,0.181,0.249,0.285;0.800),(0.094,0.147,0.297,0.363;1,000)									
	C5	((0.483,0.531,0.621,0.671;0.800),(0.402,0.471,0.686,0.762;1,000)									
	C6	((0.606,0.653,0.734,0.785;0.800),(0.529,0.593,0.792,0.863;1,000)									
	C7	((0.047,0.070,0.116,0.138;0.800),(0.029,0.054,0.150,0.194;1,000)									
A15	C1	((0.141,0.179,0.254,0.287;0.800),(0.089,0.143,0.310,0.376;1,000)									
	C2	((0.201,0.245,0.328,0.363;0.800),(0.139,0.205,0.389,0.456;1,000)									
	C3	((0.295,0.335,0.412,0.456;0.800),(0.237,0.290,0.466,0.536;1,000)									
	C4	((0.063,0.088,0.138,0.161;0.800),(0.036,0.068,0.175,0.223;1,000)									
	C5	((0.346,0.393,0.471,0.508;0.800),(0.284,0.350,0.528,0.590;1,000)									
	C6	((0.399,0.448,0.546,0.597;0.800),(0.315,0.387,0.616,0.700;1,000)									
	C7	((0.090,0.122,0.179,0.208;0.800),(0.064,0.100,0.219,0.270;1,000)									

The approximate positive and negative ideal solutions of each criterion are denoted in Table 7. The lower and upper possibility mean values of each criterion are calculated by using Eqs. - and shown in Table 8.

The possibility degrees $p(\tilde{\tilde{v}}_i \succ \tilde{\tilde{v}}_i^+)$ between each alternative $\tilde{\tilde{v}}_i$ and the approximate positive ideal solution $\tilde{\tilde{v}}_i^+$ are calculated by using Eq. and shown in Table 9. The possibility degrees between $p(\tilde{\tilde{v}}_i \succ \tilde{\tilde{v}}_i^-)$ each alternative $\tilde{\tilde{v}}_i$ and the approximate negative ideal solution $\tilde{\tilde{v}}_i^-$ are also calculated by using Eq. and shown in Table 9.

The possibility degree based closeness coefficient PC_i for each alternative is calculated by using Eq. and shown in Table 10.

CONCLUSION

This study aims to present a method, which is the possibility degree based TOPSIS method with IT2F numbers, to evaluate the university websites. In contrast to precise numbers in TOPSIS method, the merit of fuzzy TOPSIS method is to handle the fuzzy numbers to evaluate the alternatives. The IT2F numbers ensure us more additional information than type-1 fuzzy numbers to describe the fuzziness and the uncertainty of the real-life world so that it is preferred the IT2F numbers in this study.

Table 7. The approximate positive and negative ideal solutions

Approximate positive ideal solution	C1	((0.234,0.281,0.367,0.408;0.800),(0.164,0.235,0.429,0.502;1.000)
	C2	((0.513,0.561,0.637,0.679;0.800),(0.443,0.512,0.692,0.754;1.000)
	C3	((0.449,0.491,0.566,0.616;0.800),(0.382,0.439,0.619,0.690;1.000)
	C4	((0.184,0.224,0.290,0.321;0.800),(0.125,0.191,0.333,0.391;1.000)
	C5	((0.645,0.691,0.756,0.794;0.800),(0.568,0.646,0.804,0.858;1.000)
	C6	((0.619,0.666,0.744,0.793;0.800),(0.542,0.608,0.800,0.867;1.000)
	C7	((0.099,0.133,0.193,0.225;0.800),(0.072,0.109,0.234,0.289;1.000)
Approximate negative ideal solution	C1	((0.046,0.067,0.109,0.131;0.800),(0.026,0.051,0.140,0.184;1.000)
	C2	((0.183,0.226,0.307,0.340;0.800),(0.129,0.189,0.365,0.429;1.000)
	C3	((0.110,0.146,0.210,0.240;0.800),(0.084,0.120,0.255,0.308;1.000)
	C4	((0.036,0.052,0.082,0.101;0.800),(0.017,0.039,0.104,0.141;1.000)
	C5	((0.114,0.145,0.197,0.228;0.800),(0.069,0.119,0.231,0.287;1.000)
	C6	((0.141,0.185,0.261,0.299;0.800),(0.110,0.153,0.296,0.356;1.000)
	C7	((0.025,0.039,0.066,0.082;0.800),(0.013,0.029,0.085,0.118;1.000)

Table 8. The lower and upper possibility mean values

	C1	C2	C3	C4	C5	C6	C7
$M_*(A_{1i})$	0,157	0,236	0,240	0,075	0,526	0,226	0,049
$M^*(A_{1i})$	0,283	0,383	0,367	0,182	0,657	0,408	0,127
$M_*(A_{2i})$	0,107	0,227	0,282	0,066	0,204	0,145	0,030
$M^*(A_{2i})$	0,239	0,362	0,409	0,155	0,366	0,246	0,095
$M_*(A_{3i})$	0,063	0,191	0,305	0,066	0,152	0,200	0,037
$M^*(A_{3i})$	0,161	0,353	0,449	0,165	0,292	0,370	0,108
$M_*(A_{4i})$	0,041	0,161	0,277	0,041	0,205	0,226	0,056
$M^*(A_{4i})$	0,115	0,304	0,403	0,115	0,344	0,408	0,149
$M_*(A_{5i})$	0,104	0,366	0,347	0,031	0,094	0,124	0,023
$M^*(A_{5i})$	0,234	0,502	0,465	0,086	0,191	0,258	0,071
$M_*(A_{6i})$	0,147	0,288	0,362	0,049	0,315	0,190	0,082
$M^*(A_{6i})$	0,279	0,454	0,508	0,132	0,469	0,355	0,187
$M_*(A_{7i})$	0,117	0,258	0,314	0,081	0,236	0,382	0,053
$M^*(A_{7i})$	0,235	0,408	0,450	0,179	0,380	0,565	0,136
$M_*(A_{8i})$	0,094	0,222	0,338	0,115	0,220	0,139	0,066
$M^*(A_{8i})$	0,207	0,363	0,483	0,238	0,366	0,280	0,165
$M_*(A_{9i})$	0,190	0,222	0,352	0,070	0,252	0,351	0,087
$M^*(A_{9i})$	0,349	0,379	0,483	0,166	0,402	0,534	0,191

continued on following page

Table 8. Continued

	C1	C2	C3	C4	C5	C6	C7
$M_*(A_{10i})$	0,171	0,332	0,352	0,128	0,209	0,149	0,079
$M^*(A_{10i})$	0,329	0,499	0,483	0,238	0,374	0,295	0,182
$M_*(A_{11i})$	0,134	0,368	0,339	0,152	0,236	0,232	0,047
$M^*(A_{11i})$	0,281	0,536	0,475	0,272	0,380	0,384	0,130
$M_*(A_{12i})$	0,090	0,178	0,141	0,098	0,331	0,289	0,082
$M^*(A_{12i})$	0,205	0,334	0,273	0,215	0,491	0,462	0,187
$M_*(A_{13i})$	0,125	0,152	0,097	0,125	0,205	0,501	0,074
$M^*(A_{13i})$	0,255	0,295	0,207	0,252	0,344	0,654	0,174
$M_*(A_{14i})$	0,160	0,419	0,207	0,118	0,389	0,490	0,043
$M^*(A_{14i})$	0,308	0,565	0,340	0,243	0,560	0,648	0,122
$M_*(A_{15i})$	0,116	0,165	0,239	0,054	0,285	0,320	0,080
$M^*(A_{15i})$	0,251	0,314	0,381	0,142	0,429	0,502	0,178

All judgments of decision makers are characterized based on linguistic terms by the IT2F numbers, which deals with uncertainty. IT2F number operations are used to aggregate the individual judgments of decision makers into a group opinion about the relative importance degrees of criteria and criteria based alternative evaluations. These relative importance degrees of criteria are taken into account of IT2TrF numbers based TOPSIS phase, which ranks the university websites. This study considers the approximate positive and negative ideal solutions with IT2TrF numbers to evaluate the alternatives due to its effectiveness and simplicity.

Table 9. The possibility degrees

	C1	C2	C3	C4	C5	C6	C7
$p(\tilde{\tilde{v}}_{1i} \succ \tilde{\tilde{v}}_i^+)$	0,327	0,000	0,017	0,132	0,500	0,000	0,220
$p(\tilde{\tilde{v}}_{1i} \succ \tilde{\tilde{v}}_i^-)$	1,000	0,797	1,000	0,928	1,000	0,935	0,829
$p(\tilde{\tilde{v}}_{2i} \succ \tilde{\tilde{v}}_i^+)$	0,166	0,000	0,171	0,016	0,000	0,000	0,044
$p(\tilde{\tilde{v}}_{2i} \succ \tilde{\tilde{v}}_i^-)$	0,960	0,754	1,000	0,860	1,000	0,548	0,639
$p(\tilde{\tilde{v}}_{3i} \succ \tilde{\tilde{v}}_i^+)$	0,000	0,000	0,299	0,061	0,000	0,000	0,120
$p(\tilde{\tilde{v}}_{3i} \succ \tilde{\tilde{v}}_i^-)$	0,702	0,659	1,000	0,869	0,834	0,844	0,714
$p(\tilde{\tilde{v}}_{4i} \succ \tilde{\tilde{v}}_i^+)$	0,000	0,000	0,149	0,000	0,000	0,000	0,314
$p(\tilde{\tilde{v}}_{4i} \succ \tilde{\tilde{v}}_i^-)$	0,500	0,531	1,000	0,650	1,000	0,935	0,892
$p(\tilde{\tilde{v}}_{5i} \succ \tilde{\tilde{v}}_i^+)$	0,152	0,296	0,390	0,000	0,000	0,000	0,000
$p(\tilde{\tilde{v}}_{5i} \succ \tilde{\tilde{v}}_i^-)$	0,949	1,000	1,000	0,500	0,500	0,524	0,500
$p(\tilde{\tilde{v}}_{6i} \succ \tilde{\tilde{v}}_i^+)$	0,305	0,112	0,500	0,000	0,000	0,000	0,477
$p(\tilde{\tilde{v}}_{6i} \succ \tilde{\tilde{v}}_i^-)$	1,000	0,978	1,000	0,732	1,000	0,806	1,000
$p(\tilde{\tilde{v}}_{7i} \succ \tilde{\tilde{v}}_i^+)$	0,163	0,000	0,312	0,125	0,000	0,191	0,259
$p(\tilde{\tilde{v}}_{7i} \succ \tilde{\tilde{v}}_i^-)$	1,000	0,875	1,000	0,967	1,000	1,000	0,863
$p(\tilde{\tilde{v}}_{8i} \succ \tilde{\tilde{v}}_i^+)$	0,063	0,000	0,414	0,354	0,000	0,000	0,381
$p(\tilde{\tilde{v}}_{8i} \succ \tilde{\tilde{v}}_i^-)$	0,887	0,743	1,000	1,000	1,000	0,595	0,964
$p(\tilde{\tilde{v}}_{9i} \succ \tilde{\tilde{v}}_i^+)$	0,500	0,000	0,435	0,065	0,000	0,098	0,500
$p(\tilde{\tilde{v}}_{9i} \succ \tilde{\tilde{v}}_i^-)$	1,000	0,758	1,000	0,889	1,000	1,000	1,000

continued on following page

Table 9. Continued

	C1	C2	C3	C4	C5	C6	C7
$p(\tilde{\tilde{v}}_{10i} \succ \tilde{\tilde{v}}_i^+)$	0,439	0,257	0,435	0,372	0,000	0,000	0,457
$p(\tilde{\tilde{v}}_{10i} \succ \tilde{\tilde{v}}_i^-)$	1,000	1,000	1,000	1,000	1,000	0,640	1,000
$p(\tilde{\tilde{v}}_{11i} \succ \tilde{\tilde{v}}_i^+)$	0,296	0,372	0,401	0,500	0,000	0,000	0,229
$p(\tilde{\tilde{v}}_{11i} \succ \tilde{\tilde{v}}_i^-)$	1,000	1,000	1,000	1,000	1,000	0,952	0,816
$p(\tilde{\tilde{v}}_{12i} \succ \tilde{\tilde{v}}_i^+)$	0,055	0,000	0,000	0,265	0,000	0,000	0,477
$p(\tilde{\tilde{v}}_{12i} \succ \tilde{\tilde{v}}_i^-)$	0,871	0,609	0,728	1,000	1,000	1,000	1,000
$p(\tilde{\tilde{v}}_{13i} \succ \tilde{\tilde{v}}_i^+)$	0,225	0,000	0,000	0,405	0,000	0,500	0,426
$p(\tilde{\tilde{v}}_{13i} \succ \tilde{\tilde{v}}_i^-)$	1,000	0,500	0,500	1,000	1,000	1,000	1,000
$p(\tilde{\tilde{v}}_{14i} \succ \tilde{\tilde{v}}_i^+)$	0,383	0,500	0,000	0,371	0,111	0,473	0,190
$p(\tilde{\tilde{v}}_{14i} \succ \tilde{\tilde{v}}_i^-)$	1,000	1,000	0,999	1,000	1,000	1,000	0,780
$p(\tilde{\tilde{v}}_{15i} \succ \tilde{\tilde{v}}_i^+)$	0,206	0,000	0,065	0,000	0,000	0,004	0,449
$p(\tilde{\tilde{v}}_{15i} \succ \tilde{\tilde{v}}_i^-)$	1,000	0,556	1,000	0,776	1,000	1,000	1,000

Table 10. The possibility degree based closeness coefficient

	A1	A2	A3	A4	A5	A6	A7	A8	A9	A10	A11	A12	A13	A14	A15
PC_i	0,844	0,936	0,921	0,922	0,856	0,824	0,865	0,836	0,806	0,772	0,790	0,886	0,794	0,770	0,897
Rank	8	1	3	2	7	10	6	9	11	14	13	5	12	15	4

This study presents the possibility mean value and possibility degree measures instead of distance measures in current TOPSIS to define a comparative index. The closeness coefficient based on the possibility degree of each alternative is calculated according to the approximate positive and negative ideal solutions. In future papers, the proposed method can be utilized for dealing with vagueness under IT2TrF set environment in different applications such as personnel selection, software selection, and supplier selection.

REFERENCES

Akincilar, A., & Dagdeviren, M. (2014). A hybrid multi-criteria decision making model to evaluate hotel websites. *International Journal of Hospitality Management, 36*, 263–271. doi:10.1016/j.ijhm.2013.10.002

Bilsel, R. U., Büyüközkan, G., & Ruan, D. (2006). A fuzzy preference-ranking model for a quality evaluation of hospital web sites. *International Journal of Intelligent Systems, 21*(11), 1181–1197. doi:10.1002/int.20177

Buyukozkan, G., & Ruan, D. (2007). Evaluating government websites based on a fuzzy multiple criteria decision-making approach. *Int. J. Uncertainty. Fuzziness Knowledge-Based Syst., 15*(3), 321–343. doi:10.1142/S0218488507004704

Dominic, P. D. D., Jati, H., & Hanim, S. (2013). University website quality comparison by using non-parametric statistical test: A case study from Malaysia. *Int. J. Oper. Res., 16*(3), 349–374.

Hsu, C. Y., & Shih, S. C. (2016). An e-service quality assessment of house rental websites based on the Kano model and Multiple Criteria Decision Making method (MCDM) in Taiwan. *African Journal of Business Management, 10*(14), 340–351. doi:10.5897/AJBM2016.8034

Lee, Y., & Kozar, K. A. (2006). Investigating the effect of website quality on e-business success: An analytic hierarchy process (AHP) approach. *Decision Support Systems, 42*(3), 1383–1401. doi:10.1016/j.dss.2005.11.005

Pamučar, D., Stević, Ž., & Zavadskas, E. K. (2018). Integration of interval rough AHP and interval rough MABAC methods for evaluating university web pages. *Applied Soft Computing, 67*, 141–163. doi:10.1016/j.asoc.2018.02.057

Roy, S., Pattnaik, P. K., & Mall, R. (2017). Quality assurance of academic websites using usability testing: An experimental study with AHP. *International Journal of System Assurance Engineering and Management*, 8(1), 1–11. doi:10.100713198-016-0436-0

Stanujkic, D., Zavadskas, K. E., & Tamosaitiene, J. (2015). An approach to measuring website quality in the rural tourism industry based on Atanassov intuitionistic fuzzy sets. *Information & Management*, *18*, 184–199.

Tzeng, G. H., Yang, Y. P. O., Lin, C. T., & Chen, C. B. (2005). Hierarchical MADM with fuzzy integral for evaluating enterprise intranet web sites. *Information Sciences*, *169*(3-4), 409–426. doi:10.1016/j.ins.2004.07.001

Yu, X., Guo, S., Guo, J., & Huang, X. (2011). Rank B2C e-commerce websites in e-alliance based on AHP and fuzzy TOPSIS. *Expert Systems with Applications*, *38*(4), 3550–3557. doi:10.1016/j.eswa.2010.08.143

Glossary

BIST: İstanbul Stock Exchange.

C4.5: A well-known decision tree algorithm to select the best attribute for classification.

Data Mining: A process to extract information from big data.

Decision Tree Model: A convenient method for classification and estimation problem.

DEMATEL: It refers to the "decision making trial and evaluation laboratory."

Entropy: A measurement of uncertainty or randomness in a data set.

MCDM: Multi-criteria decision making model.

OpenCourseWare: (OCW): Course lessons created at universities and published for free via the internet.

TAM: Technology acceptance model.

TOPSIS: It is an acronym for "technique for order preference by similarity to ideal solution."

UPS: Universal power supply.

VIKOR: It is an acronym for "Vise Kriterijumska Optimizacija I Kompromisno Resenje".

Weka: A software program which includes most of the widely used data mining algorithms and methods.

Wikipedia: Is one of the world's most visited and used online encyclopedias.

Compilation of References

Abdel-Basset, M., Zhou, Y., Mohamed, M., & Chang, V. (2018). A group decision making framework based on neutrosophic VIKOR approach for e-government website evaluation. *Journal of Intelligent & Fuzzy Systems*, *34*(6), 4213–4224. doi:10.3233/JIFS-171952

Adalı, E. A., & Işık, A. T. (2017). The Multi-Objective Decision Making Methods Based on MULTIMOORA and MOOSRA for the Laptop Selection Problem. *Journal of Industrial Engineering International*, *13*(2), 229–237. doi:10.100740092-016-0175-5

Adhatrao, K., Gaykar, A., Dhawan, A., Jha, R., & Honrao, V. (2013). Predicting students' performance using ID3 and C4.5 classification algorithms. *International Journal of Data Mining & Knowledge Management Process*, *3*(5), 39–52. doi:10.5121/ijdkp.2013.3504

Agarwal, R., & Venkatesh, V. (2002). Assessing a firm's web presence: A heuristic evaluation procedure for the measurement of usability. *Information Systems Research*, *13*(2), 168–186. doi:10.1287/isre.13.2.168.84

Aggarwal, A. G., & Aakash. (2017). *An Innovative B2C E-commerce Websites Selection using the ME-OWA and Fuzzy AHP*. New Delhi, India: Academic Press.

Aggarwal, A. G., Sharma, H., & Tandon, A. (2017). *An Intuitionistic Approach for Ranking OTA Websites under Multi Criteria Group Decision Making Framework*. Paper presented at the Proceedings of the First International Conference on Information Technology and Knowledge Management, New Delhi, India.

Aggarwal, A. G., & Aakash. (2018). A Multi-attribute Online Advertising Budget Allocation Under Uncertain Preferences. *Journal of Engineering and Education*, *14*(25), 10. doi:10.16925/.v14i0.2225

Aggarwal, A., & Aakash, N. A. (2018). Multi-criteria based Prioritization of B2C E-Commerce Website. *International Journal of Society Systems Science, 10*(3), 201. doi:10.1504/IJSSS.2018.093940

Aghdaie, M. H., Zolfani, S. H., & Zavadskas, E. K. (2013). Market segment evaluation and selection based on application of fuzzy AHP and COPRAS-G methods. *Journal of Business Economics and Management, 14*(1), 213–233. doi:10.3846/16111699.2012.721392

Agrawal, G. L., & Gupta, H. (2013). Optimization of C4.5 decision tree algorithm for data mining application. *International Journal of Emerging Technology and Advanced Engineering, 3*(3), 341–345.

Ahmad, S. Z., Abu Bakar, A. R., Faziharudean, T. M., & Mohamad Zaki, K. A. (2015). An empirical study of factors affecting e-commerce adoption among small- and medium-sized enterprises in a developing country: Evidence from Malaysia. *Information Technology for Development, 21*(4), 555–572. doi:10.1080/02681102.2014.899961

Aibar, E., Lerga, M., Lladós-Masllorens, J., Meseguer-Artola, A., & Minguillón, J. (2013). Wikipedia in higher education: an empirical study on faculty perceptions and practices. In L. Gómez Chova, A. López Martínez, & I. Candel Torres (Eds.), *EDULEARN13 Proceedings, International Association for Technology, Education and Development, IATED* (pp. 4269-4275). Academic Press.

Akincilar, A., & Dagdeviren, M. (2014). A hybrid multi-criteria decision making model to evaluate hotel websites. *International Journal of Hospitality Management, 36*, 263–271. doi:10.1016/j.ijhm.2013.10.002

Al-Manasraa, E. A., Khair, M., Zaid, S.A., & TaherQutaishatc, F. (2013). Investigating the Impact of Website Quality on Consumers' Satisfaction in Jordanian Telecommunication Sector. *Arab Economic and Business Journal, 8*, 31–37.

An Introduction to Data Mining. (1998). Pilot Software Whitepaper, Pilot Software. Retrieved from http://iproject.online.fr/intro1.htm

Anand, A. (2007). E-satisfaction—A comprehensive framework. *Second international conference on internet and web applications and service (ICIW'07)*, 13–19, 55–60.

Andam, Z. R. (2003). *E-commerce and e-business, e-primer for the information economy*. Society and Polity Series, UNDP-APDIP and e-ASEAN Task Force.

Andreou, A. S., Leonidou, C., Chrysostomou, C., Pitsillides, A., Samaras, G., Schizas, C., & Mavromous, S. M. (2005). Key issues for the design and development of mobile commerce services and applications. *International Journal of Mobile Communications*, *3*(3), 303–323. doi:10.1504/IJMC.2005.006586

Angelie, L. (2014). *Types of Ad Layout on Behance*. Retrieved from https://www.behance.net/gallery/14774035/Types-of-Ad-Layout

Apostolou, G., & Economides, A. A. (2008). *Airlines websites evaluation around the world*. Paper presented at the World Summit on Knowledge Society. 10.1007/978-3-540-87783-7_78

Asl, M. B., Khalilzadeh, A., Youshanlouei, H. R., & Mood, M. M. (2012). Identifying and ranking the effective factors on selecting Enterprise Resource Planning (ERP) system using the combined Delphi and Shannon Entropy approach. *Procedia: Social and Behavioral Sciences*, *41*, 513–520. doi:10.1016/j.sbspro.2012.04.063

Ataburo, H., Muntaka, A. S., & Quansah, E. K. (2017). Linkages among E-Service Quality, Satisfaction, and Usage of E-Services within Higher Educational Environments. *International Journal of Business and Social Research*, *7*(3), 10–26. doi:10.18533/ijbsr.v7i3.1040

Atanassov, K. T. (1986). Intuitionistic fuzzy sets. *Fuzzy Sets and Systems*, *20*(1), 87–96. doi:10.1016/S0165-0114(86)80034-3

Ayağ, Z., & Özdemİr, R. G. (2007). An intelligent approach to ERP software selection through fuzzy ANP. *International Journal of Production Research*, *45*(10), 2169–2194. doi:10.1080/00207540600724849

Aydin, S., & Kahraman, C. (2012). Evaluation of e-commerce website quality using fuzzy multi-criteria decision making approach. *IAENG International Journal of Computer Science, 39*(1).

Ayeh, J. K. (2015). Travellers' acceptance of consumer-generated media: An integrated model of technology acceptance and source credibility theories. *Computers in Human Behavior*, *48*, 173–180. doi:10.1016/j.chb.2014.12.049

Baek, H., Oh, S., Yang, H.-D., & Ahn, J. (2017). Electronic word-of-mouth, box office revenue and social media. *Electronic Commerce Research and Applications*, *22*, 13–23. doi:10.1016/j.elerap.2017.02.001

Bai, B., Law, R., & Wen, L. (2008). The impact of website quality on customer satisfaction and purchase intentions: Evidence from Chinese online visitors. *International Journal of Hospitality Management, 27*(3), 391–402. doi:10.1016/j.ijhm.2007.10.008

Barnes, S. J., & Vidgen, R. (2001). An evaluation of cyber-bookshops: The WebQual method. *International Journal of Electronic Commerce, 6*(1), 11–30. doi:10.1080/10864415.2001.11044225

Barnes, S. J., & Vidgen, R. T. (2006). Data triangulation and web quality metrics: A case study in e-government. *Information & Management, 43*(6), 767–777. doi:10.1016/j.im.2006.06.001

Basfirinci, C., & Mitra, A. (2015). A cross cultural investigation of airlines service quality through integration of Servqual and the Kano model. *Journal of Air Transport Management, 42*, 239–248. doi:10.1016/j.jairtraman.2014.11.005

Bauer, H. H., Hammerschmidt, M., & Falk, T. (2005). Measuring the quality of e-banking portals. *International Journal of Bank Marketing, 23*(2), 153–175. doi:10.1108/02652320510584395

Behboudi, Hanzaee, K. H., Koshksaray, A. A., Tabar, M. J. S., & Taheri, Z. (2012). A Review of the Activities of Advertising Agencies in Online World. *International Journal of Marketing Studies, 4*(1), 138–150. doi:10.5539/ijms.v4n1p138

Belanger, F., Hiller, J. S., & Smith, W. J. (2002). Trustworthiness in electronic commerce: The role of privacy, security, and site attributes. *The Journal of Strategic Information Systems, 11*(3-4), 245–270. doi:10.1016/S0963-8687(02)00018-5

Bell, H., & Tang, N. K. (1998). The effectiveness of commercial Internet Web sites: A user's perspective. *Internet Research, 8*(3), 219–228. doi:10.1108/10662249810217768

Berger, B., & Matt, C. (2016). *Media Meets Retail-Re-Evaluating Content Quality in the Context of B2C E-Commerce.* Paper presented at the ECIS.

Bhati, A., Thu, Y. T., Woon, S. K. H., Phuong, L. L., & Lynn, M. M. (2017). E-Commerce Usage and User Perspectives in Myanmar: An Exploratory Study. *Advanced Science Letters, 23*(1), 519–523. doi:10.1166/asl.2017.7241

Bigus, P. J. (1996). *Data mining with neural networks: solving business problems from application development to decision support.* McGraw-Hill.

Bilsel, R. U., Büyüközkan, G., & Ruan, D. (2006). A fuzzy preference-ranking model for a quality evaluation of hospital web sites. *International Journal of Intelligent Systems*, *21*(11), 1181–1197. doi:10.1002/int.20177

Bolumole, Y. A., Grawe, S. J., & Daugherty, P. J. (2016). Customer service responsiveness in logistics outsourcing contracts: The influence of job autonomy and role clarity among on-site representatives. *Transportation Journal*, *55*(2), 124–148. doi:10.5325/transportationj.55.2.0124

Bombiak, E., & Marciniuk-Kluska, A. (2018). Green Human Resource Management as a Tool for the Sustainable Development of Enterprises: Polish Young Company Experience. *Sustainability*, *10*(6), 1739. doi:10.3390u10061739

Borissova, D., Mustakerov, I., Korsemov, D., & Dimitrova, V. (2016). Evaluation and selection of ERP software by SMART and combinatorial optimization. *Int. Journal Advanced Modeling and Optimization*, *18*(1), 145–152.

Brandon-Jones, A., & Kauppi, K. (2018). Examining the antecedents of the technology acceptance model within e-procurement. *International Journal of Operations & Production Management*, *38*(1), 22–42. doi:10.1108/IJOPM-06-2015-0346

Brucks, M., Zeithaml, V. A., & Naylor, G. (2000). Price and Brand name as indicators of quality dimensions for consumer durables. *Journal of the Academy of Marketing Science*, *25*, 139–374.

Bueyuekoezkan, G., & Ruan, D. (2007). Evaluating government websites based on a fuzzy multiple criteria decision-making approach. *International Journal of Uncertainty, Fuzziness and Knowledge-based Systems*, *15*(03), 321–343. doi:10.1142/S0218488507004704

Burmaoglu, S., & Kazancoglu, Y. (2012). E-government website evaluation with hybrid MCDM method in fuzzy environment. *International Journal of Applied Decision Sciences*, *5*(2), 163–181. doi:10.1504/IJADS.2012.046504

Büyüközkan, G., Feyzioğlu, O., & Gocer, F. (2016, December). Evaluation of hospital web services using intuitionistic fuzzy AHP and intuitionistic fuzzy VIKOR. In *Industrial Engineering and Engineering Management (IEEM), 2016 IEEE International Conference on* (pp. 607-611). IEEE. 10.1109/IEEM.2016.7797947

Büyüközkan, G., Arsenyan, J., & Ertek, G. (2010). Evaluation of e-learning web sites using fuzzy axiomatic design based approach. *International Journal of Computational Intelligence Systems*, *3*(1), 28–42. doi:10.1080/18756891.2010.9727675

Çakır, S. (2016). Selecting appropriate ERP software using integrated fuzzy linguistic preference relations–fuzzy TOPSIS method. *International Journal of Computational Intelligence Systems*, *9*(3), 433–449. doi:10.1080/18756891.2016.1175810

Calitz M.G. (2009). *Pilot Study*. University of South Africa. doi:10.1097/IGC.0b013e3182842efa.End-of-Life

Carlos Martins Rodrigues Pinho, J., & Soares, A. M. (2011). Examining the technology acceptance model in the adoption of social networks. *Journal of Research in Interactive Marketing*, *5*(2/3), 116–129. doi:10.1108/17505931111187767

Čáslavová, E., & Čmakalová, H. (2015). Competition and customer loyalty of fitness centres in the Prague region compared to the Prague-West area. *Studia sportiva*, *9*(1), 144-150.

Chang, B., Chang, C. W., & Wu, C. H. (2011). Fuzzy DEMATEL method for developing supplier selection criteria. *Expert Systems with Applications*, *38*(3), 1850–1858. doi:10.1016/j.eswa.2010.07.114

Chang, D. Y. (1996). Applications of the extent analysis method on fuzzy AHP. *European Journal of Operational Research*, *95*(3), 649–655. doi:10.1016/0377-2217(95)00300-2

Chankong, V., & Haimes, Y. Y. (2008). *Multiobjective Decision Making: Theory And Methodology*. Courier Dover Publications.

Chatterjee, K., Kar, M. B., & Kar, S. (2013). Strategic Decisions Using Intuitionistic Fuzzy Vikor Method for Information System (IS) Outsourcing. *2013 International Symposium on Computational and Business Intelligence*, 123-126. 10.1109/ISCBI.2013.33

Chatterjee, P. (2008). Are Unclicked Ads Wasted? Enduring Effects of Banner and Pop-Up Ad Exposures on Brand Memory and Attitudes. *Journal of Electronic Commerce Research*, *9*(1), 51–61.

Chen, J. V., Rungruengsamrit, D., Rajkumar, T., & Yen, D. C. (2013). Success of electronic commerce Web sites: A comparative study in two countries. *Information & Management*, *50*(6), 344–355. doi:10.1016/j.im.2013.02.007

Cherfi, A., Nouira, K., & Ferchichi, A. (2018). Very fast C4.5 decision tree algorithm. *Applied Artificial Intelligence*, *32*(2), 119–137. doi:10.1080/08839514.2018.1447479

Cheung, R., & Vogel, D. (2013). Predicting user acceptance of collaborative technologies: An extension of the technology acceptance model for e-learning. *Computers & Education, 63*, 160–175. doi:10.1016/j.compedu.2012.12.003

Chiou, W. C., Lin, C. C., & Perng, C. (2010). A strategic framework for website evaluation based on a review of the literature from 1995–2006. *Information & Management, 47*(5-6), 282–290. doi:10.1016/j.im.2010.06.002

Chong, S., & Law, R. (2018). Review of studies on airline website evaluation. *Journal of Travel & Tourism Marketing*, 1–16. doi:10.1080/10548408.2018.1494084

Choshin, M., & Ghaffari, A. (2017). An investigation of the impact of effective factors on the success of e-commerce in small-and medium-sized companies. *Computers in Human Behavior, 66*, 67–74. doi:10.1016/j.chb.2016.09.026

Chu, T. C. (2002a). Facility location selection using fuzzy TOPSIS under group decisions. *International Journal of Uncertainty, Fuzziness and Knowledge-based Systems, 10*(6), 687–701. doi:10.1142/S0218488502001739

Chu, T. C., & Lin, Y. C. (2003). A fuzzy TOPSIS method for robot selection. *International Journal of Advanced Manufacturing Technology, 21*(4), 284–290. doi:10.1007001700300033

Cronin, J. J. Jr, & Taylor, S. A. (1994). SERVPERF versus SERVQUAL: Reconciling performance-based and perceptions-minus-expectations measurement of service quality. *Journal of Marketing, 58*(1), 125–131. doi:10.1177/002224299405800110

Dachyar, M., & Rusydina, A. (2015). Measuring customer satisfaction and its relationship towards taxi's service quality around capital City Jakarta. *IACSIT International Journal of Engineering and Technology, 15*(1), 24–27.

Dagdeviren, M. (2008). Decision making in equipment selection: An integrated approach with AHP and PROMETHEE. *Journal of Intelligent Manufacturing, 19*(4), 397–406. doi:10.100710845-008-0091-7

Davis, F. D. (1985). *A technology acceptance model for empirically testing new end-user information systems: Theory and results* (Doctoral dissertation). Massachusetts Institute of Technology.

Davis, F. D. (1985). *A technology acceptance model for empirically testing new end-user information systems: Theory and results* (Unpublished Doctoral dissertation). Massachusetts Institute of Technology, Cambridge, MA.

Davis, F. D. (1989). Perceived Usefulness, Perceived Ease of Use, and User Acceptance of Information Technology. *Management Information Systems Quarterly*, *13*(3), 319–340. doi:10.2307/249008

DeLone, W. H., & McLean, E. R. (1992). Information systems success: The quest for the dependent variable. *Information Systems Research*, *3*(1), 60–95. doi:10.1287/isre.3.1.60

Delone, W. H., & McLean, E. R. (2003). The DeLone and McLean model of information systems success: A ten-year update. *Journal of Management Information Systems*, *19*(4), 9–30. doi:10.1080/07421222.2003.11045748

Delone, W. H., & Mclean, E. R. (2004). Measuring e-commerce success: Applying the DeLone & McLean information systems success model. *International Journal of Electronic Commerce*, *9*(1), 31–47. doi:10.1080/10864415.2004.11044317

Demircioğlu, M., & Coşkun, İ. T. (2018). CRITIC-MOOSRA Yöntemi ve UPS Seçimi Üzerine Bir Uygulama. *Çukurova Üniversitesi Sosyal Bilimler Enstitüsü Dergisi*, *27*(1), 183-195.

Díaz, E., & Martín-Consuegra, D. (2016). A latent class segmentation analysis of airlines based on website evaluation. *Journal of Air Transport Management*, *55*, 20–40. doi:10.1016/j.jairtraman.2016.04.007

Dincer, H., Hacioglu, U., & Yuksel, S. (2016). Balanced scorecard-based performance assessment of Turkish banking sector with analytic network process. *International Journal of Decision Sciences & Applications-IJDSA*, *1*(1), 1–21.

Dinçer, H., Yuksel, S., & Bozaykut-Buk, T. (2018). Evaluation of Financial and Economic Effects on Green Supply Chain Management With Multi-Criteria Decision-Making Approach: Evidence From Companies Listed in BIST. In *Handbook of Research on Supply Chain Management for Sustainable Development* (pp. 144–175). IGI Global. doi:10.4018/978-1-5225-5757-9.ch009

Dominic, P. D. D., Jati, H., & Hanim, S. (2013). University website quality comparison by using non-parametric statistical test: A case study from Malaysia. *Int. J. Oper. Res.*, *16*(3), 349–374.

Dorfeshan, Y., Mousavi, S. M., Mohagheghi, V., & Vahdani, B. (2018). Selecting Project-Critical Path by a New Interval Type-2 Fuzzy Decision Methodology Based on MULTIMOORA, MOOSRA and TPOP methods. *Computers & Industrial Engineering*, *120*, 160–178. doi:10.1016/j.cie.2018.04.015

Dündar, S., Ecer, F., & Özdemir, Ş. (2007). Fuzzy Topsis Yöntemi İle Sanal Mağazalarin Web Sitelerinin Değerlendirilmesi. *Atatürk Üniversitesi İktisadi ve İdari Bilimler Dergisi, 21*(1).

Dunham, M. H. (2002). *Data mining, introductory and advanced topics.* Prentice Hall.

Ecer, F. (2014). A hybrid banking websites quality evaluation model using AHP and COPRAS-G: A Turkey case. *Technological and Economic Development of Economy, 20*(4), 758–782. doi:10.3846/20294913.2014.915596

Efe, B. (2016). An integrated fuzzy multi criteria group decision making approach for ERP system selection. *Applied Soft Computing, 38*, 106–117. doi:10.1016/j.asoc.2015.09.037

Efe, B., Boran, F. E., & Kurt, M. (2015). Sezgisel Bulanik Topsis Yöntemi Kullanilarak Ergonomik Ürün Konsept Seçimi. *Mühendislik Bilimleri ve Tasarım Dergisi, 3*(3), 433–440.

Elibol, H., & Kesici, B. (2004). Çağdaş İşletmecilik Açisindan Elektronik Ticaret. *Selçuk Üniversitesi Sosyal Bilimler Enstitüsü Dergisi*, (11), 303-329.

Eroğlu, Ö. (2014). *Assessment of Maintenance/Repair Alternatives With The Fuzzy Dematel And Smaa-2 Methods* (Unpublished Master dissertation). Turkish Military Academy Defense Science Institute, Department of Supply and Logistics Management, Ankara, Turkey.

Ersoy, İ. (2011). The impact of financial openness on financial development, growth and volatility in Turkey: Evidence from the ARDL bounds tests. Economic research-. *Ekonomska Istrazivanja, 24*(3), 33–44.

Evangelos, T. (2000). Multi-Criteria Decision Making Methods: a Comparative Study. Kluwer Academic Publication.

Evans, K. (2015). *The number of global online shoppers will grow 50% by 2018.* Academic Press.

Fakhimi, E. (2015). Data mining techniques for web mining: A review. *Applied Mathematics in Engineering. Management and Technology, 3*(5), 81–90.

Fayyad, U., Piatetsky-Shapiro, G., & Smyth, P. (1996). From data mining to knowledge discovery in databases. *The Alumni Magazine, 17*(3), 37–54.

Filardi, F., Berti, D., & Moreno, V. (2015). Implementation analysis of Lean Sigma in IT applications. A multinational oil company experience in Brazil. *Procedia Computer Science, 55*, 1221–1230. doi:10.1016/j.procs.2015.07.128

Gabus, A., & Fontela, E. (1972). *World Problems, An Invitation to Further Thought within The Framework of DEMATEL.* Geneva, Switzerland: Battelle Geneva Research Centre.

Gani, A. N., & Assarudeen, S. M. (2012). A new operation on triangular fuzzy number for solving fuzzy linear programming problem. *Applied Mathematical Sciences, 6*(11), 525–532.

Gao, L., & Bai, X. (2014). A unified perspective on the factors influencing consumer acceptance of internet of things technology. *Asia Pacific Journal of Marketing and Logistics, 26*(2), 211–231. doi:10.1108/APJML-06-2013-0061

Garca Laencina, P. J., Abreu, P. H., Abreu, M. H., & Afonoso, N. (2015). Missing data imputation on the 5-year survival prediction of breast cancer patients with unknown discrete values. *Computers in Biology and Medicine, 59*, 125–133. doi:10.1016/j.compbiomed.2015.02.006 PMID:25725446

Garg, R., Kumar, R., & Garg, S. (2018). MADM-Based Parametric Selection and Ranking of E-Learning Websites Using Fuzzy COPRAS. *IEEE Transactions on Education*, (99): 1–8. doi:10.1109/TE.2018.2814611

Genç, H. (2010). İnternetteki etkileşim merkezi sosyal ağlar ve e-iş 2.0 uygulamaları. *Akademik Bilişim*, 481-487.

Glass, A. D. (1998). A countdown to the age of secure electronic commerce. *Credit World, 86*, 29–31.

Guo, M., & Zhao, Y. (2009). AHP-Based Evaluation of Information Service Quality of Information Center Web Portals in High-Tech Industry. In *Management and Service Science, 2009. MASS'09. International Conference on* (pp. 1-4). IEEE. 10.1109/ICMSS.2009.5301245

Guo, S., & Shao, B. (2005). Quantitative evaluation of e-commercial Web sites of foreign trade enterprises in Chongqing. *Proceedings of ICSSSM, 05*, 2005.

Gupta, A. (2016). Redefining service quality scale with customer experience quality scale: A critical review. *International Journal of Services and Operations Management, 25*(1), 48–64. doi:10.1504/IJSOM.2016.078070

Gupta, R., & Naqvi, S. K. (2017). A Framework for Applying CSFs to ERP Software Selection: An Extension of Fuzzy TOPSIS Approach. *International Journal of Intelligent Information Technologies, 13*(2), 41–62. doi:10.4018/IJIIT.2017040103

Gürbüz, F., & Çavdarcı, S. (2018). Evaluation of problem areas related to the recycling sector via DEMATEL and Grey DEMATEL Method. *Sakarya University Journal of the Institute of Science and Technology, 22*(2), 285–301.

Gürbüz, T., Alptekin, S. E., & Alptekin, G. I. (2012). A hybrid MCDM methodology for ERP selection problem with interacting criteria. *Decision Support Systems, 54*(1), 206–214. doi:10.1016/j.dss.2012.05.006

Hamzah, N., Ishak, N. M., & Nor, N. I. M. (2015). Customer satisfactions on Islamic banking system. *Journal of Economics. Business and Management, 3*(1), 140–144.

Han, B., Liu, H., & Wang, R. (2015). Urban Ecological Security Assessment for Cities in the Beijing–Tianjin–Hebei Metropolitan Region Based on Fuzzy And Entropy Methods. *Ecological Modelling, 318*, 217–225. doi:10.1016/j.ecolmodel.2014.12.015

Hand, D. J. (1981). *Discrimination and Classification*. Chichester, UK: Wiley.

Han, J., Kamber, M., & Pei, J. (2012). *Data mining: concepts and techniques* (3rd ed.). Morgan Kaufmann.

Ha, S., & Stoel, L. (2009). Consumer e-shopping acceptance: Antecedents in a technology acceptance model. *Journal of Business Research, 62*(5), 565–571. doi:10.1016/j.jbusres.2008.06.016

Hasanov, J., & Khalid, H. (2015). The Impact of Website Quality on Online Purchase Intention of Organic Food in Malaysia: A WebQual Model Approach. *Procedia Computer Science, 72*, 382–389. doi:10.1016/j.procs.2015.12.153

Hidayanto, A. N., Herbowo, A., Budi, N. F. A., & Sucahyo, Y. G. (2014). Determinant of customer trust on e-commerce and its impact to purchase and word of mouth intention: A case of Indonesia. *Journal of Computational Science, 10*(12), 2395–2407. doi:10.3844/jcssp.2014.2395.2407

Hssina, B., Merbouha, A., Ezzikouri, H. & Erritali, M. (2014). A comparative study of decision tree ID3 and C4.5. *International Journal of Advanced Computer Science and Applications,* 13-19.

Hsu, C. Y., & Shih, S. C. (2016). An e-service quality assessment of house rental websites based on the Kano model and Multiple Criteria Decision Making method (MCDM) in Taiwan. *African Journal of Business Management, 10*(14), 340–351. doi:10.5897/AJBM2016.8034

Huang, C. Y., Shyu, J. Z., & Tzeng, G. H. (2007). Reconfiguring The Innovation Policy Portfolios For Taiwan's SIP Mall Industry. *Technovation, 27*(12), 744–765. doi:10.1016/j.technovation.2007.04.002

Hunt, E., Martin, J., & Stone, P. (1966). *Experiments in induction.* Academic Press.

Hwang, C. L., & Yoon, K. (1981). Methods for multiple attribute decision making. In *Multiple attribute decision making* (pp. 58–191). Berlin: Springer. doi:10.1007/978-3-642-48318-9_3

İbrahim, S. H., Duraisamy, S., & Sridevi, U. K. (2018). Flexible and reliable ERP project customization framework to improve user satisfaction level. *Cluster Computing*, 1–7.

Ip, C., Law, R., & Lee, H. A. (2012). The evaluation of hotel website functionality by fuzzy analytic hierarchy process. *Journal of Travel & Tourism Marketing, 29*(3), 263–278. doi:10.1080/10548408.2012.666173

Izogo, E. E. (2017). Customer loyalty in telecom service sector: The role of service quality and customer commitment. *The TQM Journal, 29*(1), 19–36. doi:10.1108/TQM-10-2014-0089

Jayawardhena, C. (2004). Measurement of service quality in internet banking: The development of an instrument. *Journal of Marketing Management, 20*(1-2), 185–207. doi:10.1362/0267257704773041177

Jeong, J. S., & Ramírez-Gómez, Á. (2018). Optimizing the location of a biomass plant with a fuzzy-DEcision-MAking Trial and Evaluation Laboratory (F-DEMATEL) and multi-criteria spatial decision assessment for renewable energy management and long-term sustainability. *Journal of Cleaner Production, 182*, 509–520. doi:10.1016/j.jclepro.2017.12.072

Jones, M., & Kayworth, T. (1999). Corporate web performance evaluation: An exploratory assessment. *AMCIS 1999 Proceedings*, 88.

Jordan, T. (2018). Quality Assurance: Applying Methodologies for Launching New Products, Services and Customer Satisfaction. *Quality Progress, 51*(2), 60–60.

Kabak, M., & Burmaoğlu, S. (2013). A holistic evaluation of the e-procurement website by using a hybrid MCDM methodology. *Electronic Government, an International Journal, 10*(2), 125-150.

Kahraman, C., Keshavarz Ghorabaee, M., Zavadskas, E. K., Cevik Onar, S., Yazdani, M., & Oztaysi, B. (2017). Intuitionistic fuzzy EDAS method: An application to solid waste disposal site selection. *Journal of Environmental Engineering and Landscape Management, 25*(1), 1–12. doi:10.3846/16486897.2017.1281139

Kalia, G. (2018). *Effect of Online Advertising on Consumers: A Study.* Ph.D Thesis.

Kang, D., Jang, W., & Park, Y. (2016). Evaluation of e-commerce websites using fuzzy hierarchical TOPSIS based on ES-QUAL. *Applied Soft Computing, 42*, 53–65. doi:10.1016/j.asoc.2016.01.017

Kannan, D., Lopes de Sousa Jabbour, A. B., & Chiappetta Jabbour, C. J. (2014). Selecting green suppliers based on GSCM practices: Using fuzzy TOPSIS applied to a Brazilian electronics company. *European Journal of Operational Research, 233*(2), 432–447. doi:10.1016/j.ejor.2013.07.023

Karami, A., & Johansson, R. (2014). Utilization of Multi Attribute Decision Making Techniques to Integrate Automatic and Manual Ranking of Options. *Journal of Information Science and Engineering, 30*, 519–534.

Karar ağacı (decison tree) nedir? (n.d.). Retrieved from http://mail.baskent. edu. tr/~20410964/DM_8.pdf

Kardaras, D., & Karakostas, V. (1999). Measuring the Electronic Commerce Impact on Customer Satisfaction: Experiences, Problems and expectations of the banking sector in the UK. *Proceeding of the International conference of the Measurement of Electronic Commerce.*

Karsak, E. E., & Ozogul, C. O. (2009). An integrated decision making approach for ERP system selection. *Expert Systems with Applications, 36*(1), 660–667. doi:10.1016/j.eswa.2007.09.016

Kaya, R. (2017). *Integration Of Bayesian Networks With Dematel For Causal Risk Analysis: A Supplier Selection Case Study In Automotive Industry* (Unpublished doctoral dissertation). University of Hacettepe, Ankara, Turkey.

Kaya, T., & Kahraman, C. (2011). A fuzzy approach to e-banking website quality assessment based on an integrated AHP-ELECTRE method. *Technological and Economic Development of Economy*, *17*(2), 313–334. doi:10.3846/20294913.2011.583727

Keršuliene, V., Zavadskas, E. K., & Turskis, Z. (2010). Selection of rational dispute resolution method by applying new step-wise weight assessment ratio analysis (SWARA). *Journal of business economics and management*, *11*(2), 243–258. doi:10.3846/jbem.2010.12

Khan, H., & Faisal, M. N. (2015). A Grey-based approach for ERP vendor selection in small and medium enterprises in Qatar. *International Journal of Business Information Systems*, *19*(4), 465–487. doi:10.1504/IJBIS.2015.070205

Kim, E. (1999). A model of an effective web. *AMCIS 1999 Proceedings*, 181.

Kim, C., Galliers, R. D., Shin, N., Ryoo, J.-H., & Kim, J. (2012). Factors influencing Internet shopping value and customer repurchase intention. *Electronic Commerce Research and Applications*, *11*(4), 374–387. doi:10.1016/j.elerap.2012.04.002

Kim, S., & Lee, Y. (2006). Global online marketplace: A cross-cultural comparison of website quality. *International Journal of Consumer Studies*, *30*(6), 533–543. doi:10.1111/j.1470-6431.2006.00522.x

Kim, S., & Stoel, L. (2004). Apparel retailers: Website quality dimensions and satisfaction. *Journal of Retailing and Consumer Services*, *11*(2), 109–117. doi:10.1016/S0969-6989(03)00010-9

Kim, T. G., Lee, J. H., & Law, R. (2008). An empirical examination of the acceptance behaviour of hotel front office systems: An extended technology acceptance model. *Tourism Management*, *29*(3), 500–513. doi:10.1016/j.tourman.2007.05.016

King, W. R., & He, J. (2006). A meta-analysis of the technology acceptance model. *Information & Management*, *43*(6), 740–755. doi:10.1016/j.im.2006.05.003

Kocabulut, Ö., & Albayrak, T. (2017). The E*ffect of Website Service Quality on Customer Satisfaction. Anatolia: Journal of Tourism Research*, *28*(2), 293–303.

Koufaris, M. (2002). Applying the technology acceptance model and flow theory to online consumer behavior. *Information Systems Research*, *13*(2), 205–223. doi:10.1287/isre.13.2.205.83

Kumar, R., & Ray, A. (2015). Optimal Selection of Material: an Eclectic Decision. *Journal of The Institution of Engineers (India): Series C, 96*(1), 29-33.

Kumar, R. D., & Zayaraz, G. (2011). A QoS aware quantitative web service selection model. *International Journal on Computer Science and Engineering, 3*(4), 1534–1538.

Law, R. (2007). A fuzzy multiple criteria decision-making model for evaluating travel websites. *Asia Pacific Journal of Tourism Research, 12*(2), 147–159. doi:10.1080/10941660701243372

Lee, H. S., Shen, P. D., & Chih, W. L. (2004). A Fuzzy Multiple Criteria Decision Making Model for Software Selection. *Fuzz- IEEE, 3*, 1709-1713.

Lee, N. Y., & Choi, E. H. (2001). *Appling the AHP techniques to electronic commerce in a special attention to Fashion website selection.* Paper presented at the International Conference Human Society@ Internet.

Lee, Y., & Kozar, K. A. (2006). Investigating the effect of website quality on e-business success: An analytic hierarchy process (AHP) approach. *Decision Support Systems, 42*(3), 1383–1401. doi:10.1016/j.dss.2005.11.005

Legris, P., Ingham, J., & Collerette, P. (2003). Why do people use information technology? A critical review of the technology acceptance model. *Information & Management, 40*(3), 191–204. doi:10.1016/S0378-7206(01)00143-4

Liang, R., Wang, J., & Zhang, H. (2017). Evaluation of e-commerce websites: An integrated approach under a single-valued trapezoidal neutrosophic environment. *Knowledge-Based Systems, 135*, 44–59. doi:10.1016/j.knosys.2017.08.002

Liao, X., Li, Y., & Lu, B. (2007). A model for selecting an ERP system based on linguistic information processing. *Information Systems, 32*(7), 1005–1017. doi:10.1016/j.is.2006.10.005

Li, L., Peng, M., Jiang, N., & Law, R. (2017). An empirical study on the influence of economy hotel website quality on online booking intentions. *International Journal of Hospitality Management, 63*, 1–10. doi:10.1016/j.ijhm.2017.01.001

Lim, T. S., Loh, W. Y., & Shih, Y. S. (2000). A comparison of prediction accuracy, complexity,and training time of thirty-three old and new classification algorithms. *Machine Learning, 40*(3), 203–228. doi:10.1023/A:1007608224229

Lin, H. F. (2010). An application of fuzzy AHP for evaluating course website quality. *Computers & Education*, *54*(4), 877–888. doi:10.1016/j.compedu.2009.09.017

Liou, J. J. H., Yen, L., & Tzeng, G. H. (2008). Building An Effective Safety Management system for Airlines. *Journal of Air Transport Management*, *14*, 20–26. doi:10.1016/j.jairtraman.2007.10.002

Liou, J. J., Tsai, C. Y., Lin, R. H., & Tzeng, G. H. (2011). A modified VIKOR multiple-criteria decision method for improving domestic airlines service quality. *Journal of Air Transport Management*, *17*(2), 57–61. doi:10.1016/j.jairtraman.2010.03.004

Liu, C., & Arnett, K. P. (2000). Exploring the factors associated with Web site success in the context of electronic commerce. *Information & Management*, *38*(1), 23–33. doi:10.1016/S0378-7206(00)00049-5

Liu, C., & Arnett, K. P. (2000). Exploring The Factors Associated With Web Site Success In the Context of Electronic Commerce. *Information & Management*, *38*(1), 23–33. doi:10.1016/S0378-7206(00)00049-5

Li, X., & Claramount, C. (2006). A spatial entropy-based decision tree for classification of geographical information. *Transactions in GIS*, *10*(3), 451–467. doi:10.1111/j.1467-9671.2006.01006.x

Loiacono, E., Chen, D., & Goodhue, D. (2002). WebQual TM revisited: Predicting the intent to reuse a web site. *AMCIS 2002 Proceedings*, 46.

López, C., & Ishizaka, A. (2017). GAHPSort: A new group multi-criteria decision method for sorting a large number of the cloud-based ERP solutions. *Computers in Industry*, *92*, 12–24. doi:10.1016/j.compind.2017.06.007

Macnamara, J. (2003). Media Content Analysis: Its Uses; Benefits and Best Practice Methodology. *Asia Pacific Public Relations Journal*, *6*(1), 1–23.

Maditinos, D., Chatzoudes, D., & Sarigiannidis, L. (2013). An examination of the critical factors affecting consumer acceptance of online banking: A focus on the dimensions of risk. *Journal of Systems and Information Technology*, *15*(1), 97–116. doi:10.1108/13287261311322602

Mavi, R. K., Goh, M., & Zarbakhshnia, N. (2017). Sustainable third-party reverse logistic provider selection with fuzzy SWARA and fuzzy MOORA in plastic industry. *International Journal of Advanced Manufacturing Technology, 91*(5-8), 2401–2418. doi:10.100700170-016-9880-x

Mayew, W. J. (2012). Disclosure Outlets and Corporate Financial Communication: A Discussion of "Managers' Use of Language Across Alternative Disclosure Outlets: Earnings Press Releases versus MD&A". *Contemporary Accounting Research, 29*(3), 838–844. doi:10.1111/j.1911-3846.2011.01126.x

Meseguer-Artola, A., Aibar, E., Liadós, J., Minguillón, J., & Lerga, M. (2016). Factors That Influence the Teaching Use of Wikipedia in Higher Education. *Journal of the Association for Information Science and Technology, 67*(5), 1224–1232. doi:10.1002/asi.23488

Méxas, M. P., Quelhas, O. L. G., & Costa, H. G. (2012). Prioritization of enterprise resource planning systems criteria: Focusing on construction industry. *International Journal of Production Economics, 139*(1), 340–350. doi:10.1016/j.ijpe.2012.05.025

Mitchel, K. (2012). *Uncluttered Web Pages Make Ads Work Better.* SAY Media and IPG Media Lab _ Business Wire. Retrieved from http://www.businesswire.com/news/home/20120607005281/en/Uncluttered-Web-Pages-Ads-Work-Research-Media

Molla, A., & Licker, P. S. (2001). E-commerce systems success: An attempt to extend and respecify the Delone and MacLean model of IS success. *Journal of Electronic Commerce Research, 2*(4), 131–141.

Moritz, S., Berna, F., Jaeger, S., Westermann, S., & Nagel, M. (2017). The customer is always right? Subjective target symptoms and treatment preferences in patients with psychosis. *European Archives of Psychiatry and Clinical Neuroscience, 267*(4), 335–339. doi:10.100700406-016-0694-5 PMID:27194554

Moustakis, V., Litos, C., Dalivigas, A., & Tsironis, L. (2004). *Website Quality Assessment Criteria. IQ, 5,* 59–73.

Moustakis, V., Tsironis, L., & Litos, C. (2006). A model of web site quality assessment. *The Quality Management Journal, 13*(2), 22–37. doi:10.1080/10686967.2006.11918547

Mulfari, D., Celesti, A., & Villari, M. (2015). A computer system architecture providing a user-friendly man machine interface for accessing assistive technology in cloud computing. *Journal of Systems and Software, 100,* 129–138. doi:10.1016/j.jss.2014.10.035

Nagpal, R., Mehrotra, D., Bhatia, P. K., & Sharma, A. (2015). Rank university websites using fuzzy AHP and fuzzy TOPSIS approach on usability. *International Journal of Information Engineering and Electronic Business, 7*(1), 29.

Nagpal, R., Mehrotra, D., & Bhatia, P. K. (2016). Usability evaluation of website using combined weighted method: Fuzzy AHP and entropy approach. *International Journal of System Assurance Engineering and Management, 7*(4), 408–417. doi:10.100713198-016-0462-y

Naor, M., & Coman, A. (2017). Offshore responsiveness: Theory of Constraints innovates customer services. *Service Industries Journal, 37*(3-4), 155–166. doi:10.1080/02642069.2017.1303047

Ngai, E. (2003). Selection of web sites for online advertising using the AHP. *Information & Management, 40*(4), 233–242. doi:10.1016/S0378-7206(02)00004-6

Nielsen, J. (1999). *Designing web usability: The practice of simplicity.* New Riders Publishing.

Nosratabadi, H. E., Pourdarab, S., & Nadali, A. (2011). Credit Risk Assessment of Bank Customers using DEMATEL and Fuzzy Expert System. *Economics and Finance Research, 4*, 255–259.

Oenuet, S., & Soner, S. (2008). Transshipment site selection using the AHP and TOPSIS approaches under fuzzy environment. *Waste Management (New York, N.Y.), 28*(9), 1552–1559. doi:10.1016/j.wasman.2007.05.019 PMID:17768038

Ömürbek, N., Eren, H & Dağ, O. (2017). Entropi-ARAS ve Entropi-MOOSRA Yöntemleri İle Yaşam Kalitesi Açısından AB Ülkelerinin Değerlendirilmesi. *Ömer Halisdemir Üniversitesi, İktisadi Ve İdari Bilimler Fakültesi Dergisi, 10*(2), 29-48.

Ömürbek, N., Karaatlı, M., & Balcı, H. F. (2016). Entropi Temelli MAUT ve SAW Yöntemleri ile Otomotiv Firmalarının Performans Değerlemesi. *Dokuz Eylül Üniversitesi İktisadi ve İdari Bilimler Fakültesi Dergisi, 31*(1).

Ömürbek, V., Aksoy, E., & Akçakanat, Ö. (2017). Bankaların Sürdürülebilirlik Performanslarının ARAS, MOOSRA ve COPRAS Yöntemleri İle Değerlendirilmesi. *Visionary E-Journal/Vizyoner Dergisi, 8*(19).

Opricovic, S. (1998). *Multi-criteria optimization of civil engineering systems.* Belgrade: Faculty of Civil Engineering.

Opricovic, S., & Tzeng, G. H. (2004). Compromise solution by MCDM methods: A comparative analysis of VIKOR and TOPSIS. *European Journal of Operational Research, 156*(2), 445–455. doi:10.1016/S0377-2217(03)00020-1

Opricovic, S., & Tzeng, G. H. (2007). Extended VIKOR method in comparison with outranking methods. *European Journal of Operational Research, 178*(2), 514–529. doi:10.1016/j.ejor.2006.01.020

Osgood, A., & Angela, D. (2010). *Intro to Google Adwords*. Retrieved from https://www.slideshare.net/BostonLogic/logic-classroom-google-adwordsv2

Ou Yang, Y. P., Shieh, H. M., Leu, J. D., & Tzeng, G. H. (2009). A VIKOR-based multiple criteria decision method for improving information security risk. *International Journal of Information Technology & Decision Making, 8*(02), 267–287. doi:10.1142/S0219622009003375

Özsarı, S. H., & Hoşgör, H. (2016). ve Gündüz Hoşgör, D., (2016). Hastane Web Site Performanslarının Halkla İlişkiler ve Tanıtım Açısından İncelenmesi: Türkiye, Hindistan ve Irlanda Örnekleri. *ACU Sağlık Bil. Dergisi, 4,* 209–217.

Oztaysi, B. (2015). A Group Decision Making Approach Using Interval Type-2 Fuzzy AHP for Enterprise Information Systems Project Selection. *Journal of Multiple-Valued Logic & Soft Computing, 24*(5).

Pai, F. Y., & Huang, K. I. (2011). Applying the technology acceptance model to the introduction of healthcare information systems. *Technological Forecasting and Social Change, 78*(4), 650–660. doi:10.1016/j.techfore.2010.11.007

Pallud, J., & Straub, D. W. (2014). Effective website design for experience-influenced environments: The case of high culture museums. *Information & Management, 51*(3), 359–373. doi:10.1016/j.im.2014.02.010

Palmer, J. W. (2002). Web site usability, design, and performance metrics. *Information Systems Research, 13*(2), 151–167. doi:10.1287/isre.13.2.151.88

Pamučar, D., Stević, Ž., & Zavadskas, E. K. (2018). Integration of interval rough AHP and interval rough MABAC methods for evaluating university web pages. *Applied Soft Computing, 67,* 141–163. doi:10.1016/j.asoc.2018.02.057

Panigrahi, R., & Srivastava, P. R. (2015). *Evaluation of travel websites: A fuzzy analytical hierarchy process approach.* Paper presented at the Electrical Computer and Electronics (UPCON), 2015 IEEE UP Section Conference on. 10.1109/UPCON.2015.7456743

Parasuraman, A., Zeithaml, V. A., & Berry, L. L. (1988). Servqual: A multiple-item scale for measuring consumer perc. *Journal of Retailing, 64*(1), 12.

Park, E. J., Kim, E. Y., Funches, V. M., & Foxx, W. (2012). Apparel product attributes, web browsing, and e-impulse buying on shopping websites. *Journal of Business Research, 65*(11), 1583–1589. doi:10.1016/j.jbusres.2011.02.043

Park, E., & Kim, K. J. (2014). An integrated adoption model of mobile cloud services: Exploration of key determinants and extension of technology acceptance model. *Telematics and Informatics, 31*(3), 376–385. doi:10.1016/j.tele.2013.11.008

Park, Y. A., & Gretzel, U. (2007). Success factors for destination marketing web sites: A qualitative meta-analysis. *Journal of Travel Research, 46*(1), 46–63. doi:10.1177/0047287507302381

Patel, N., & Singh, D. (2015). An algorithm to construct decision tree for machine learning based on similarity factor. *International Journal of Computers and Applications, 111*(10), 22–26. doi:10.5120/19575-1376

Pavlou, P. A. (2003). Consumer acceptance of electronic commerce: Integrating trust and risk with the technology acceptance model. *International Journal of Electronic Commerce, 7*(3), 101–134. doi:10.1080/10864415.2003.11044275

Peng, H. G., & Wang, J. Q. (2017). Hesitant uncertain linguistic Z-numbers and their application in multi-criteria group decision-making problems. *International Journal of Fuzzy Systems, 19*(5), 1300–1316. doi:10.100740815-016-0257-y

Peng, X., Yuan, H., & Yang, Y. (2017). Pythagorean fuzzy information measures and their applications. *International Journal of Intelligent Systems, 32*(10), 991–1029. doi:10.1002/int.21880

Perçin, S., & Sönmez, Ö. (2018). Bütünleşik Entropi Ağırlık ve TOPSIS Yöntemleri Kullanılarak Türk Sigorta Şirketlerinin Performansının Ölçülmesi. *Uluslararası İktisadi ve İdari İncelemeler Dergisi*, 565-582.

Pérez, I. J., Alonso, S., Cabrerizo, F. J., Lu, J., & Herrera-Viedma, E. (2011). *Modelling heterogeneity among experts in multi-criteria group decision making problems.* Paper presented at the International Conference on Modeling Decisions for Artificial Intelligence. 10.1007/978-3-642-22589-5_7

Pérez-Domínguez, L., Rodríguez-Picón, L. A., Alvarado-Iniesta, A., Luviano Cruz, D., & Xu, Z. (2018). MOORA under Pythagorean Fuzzy Set for Multiple Criteria Decision Making. *Complexity*.

Priyanka, S. (2012). A Study on Impact of Online Advertising on Consumer Behavior (With Special Reference to E-mails). *International Journal of Engineering and Management Sciences*, *3*(4), 461–465.

Qi, S., Law, R., & Buhalis, D. (2008). Usability of Chinese destination management organization websites. *Journal of Travel & Tourism Marketing*, *25*(2), 182–198. doi:10.1080/10548400802402933

Qi, S., Law, R., & Buhalis, D. (2013). A modified fuzzy hierarchical TOPSIS model for hotel website evaluation. *International Journal of Fuzzy System Applications*, *3*(3), 82–101. doi:10.4018/ijfsa.2013070105

Qi, S., Law, R., & Buhalis, D. (2017). Comparative evaluation study of the websites of China-based and international luxury hotels. *Journal of China Tourism Research*, *13*(1), 1–25. doi:10.1080/19388160.2017.1289135

Quinlan, J. R. (1986). Induction of decision trees. *Machine Learning*, *1*(1), 81–106. doi:10.1007/BF00116251

Quinlan, J. R. (1993). *C4.5: Programs for machine learning*. Morgan Kaufmann.

Ramanathan, R. (2010). E-commerce success criteria: Determining which criteria count most. *Electronic Commerce Research*, *10*(2), 191–208. doi:10.100710660-010-9051-3

Rana, N. P., Dwivedi, Y. K., Williams, M. D., & Weerakkody, V. (2015). Investigating success of an e-government initiative: Validation of an integrated IS success model. *Information Systems Frontiers*, *17*(1), 127–142. doi:10.100710796-014-9504-7

Ranganathan, C., & Ganapathy, S. (2002). Key dimensions of business to consumer web sites. *Information & Management*, *39*(6), 457–465. doi:10.1016/S0378-7206(01)00112-4

Raut, R. D., Bhasin, H. V., & Kamble, S. S. (2011). Evaluation of supplier selection criteria by combination of AHP and fuzzy DEMATEL method. *International Journal of Business Innovation and Research*, *5*(4), 359–392. doi:10.1504/IJBIR.2011.041056

Ray, A. (2014). Green Cutting Fluid Selection Using MOOSRA Method. *International Journal of Research in Engineering and Technology, 3*(3), 559–563.

Rensburg, R., & Botha, E. (2014). Is integrated reporting the silver bullet of financial communication? A stakeholder perspective from South Africa. *Public Relations Review, 40*(2), 144–152. doi:10.1016/j.pubrev.2013.11.016

Rostamzadeh, R., Govindan, K., Esmaeili, A., & Sabaghi, M. (2015). Application of fuzzy VIKOR for evaluation of green supply chain management practices. *Ecological Indicators, 49*, 188–203. doi:10.1016/j.ecolind.2014.09.045

Rouyendegh, B. D., Topuz, K., Dag, A., & Oztekin, A. (2018). An AHP-IFT Integrated Model for Performance Evaluation of E-Commerce Web Sites. *Information Systems Frontiers*, 1–11.

Roy, S., Pattnaik, P. K., & Mall, R. (2017). Quality assurance of academic websites using usability testing: An experimental study with AHP. *International Journal of System Assurance Engineering and Management, 8*(1), 1–11. doi:10.100713198-016-0436-0

Saaty, A. (1980). *The analytic hierarchy process*. Mc Graw Hill, Inc.

San Lim, Y., Heng, P. C., Ng, T. H., & Cheah, C. S. (2016). Customers' online website satisfaction in online apparel purchase: A study of Generation Y in Malaysia. *Asia Pacific Management Review, 21*(2), 74–78. doi:10.1016/j.apmrv.2015.10.002

Sarkar, A., Panja, S. C., Das, D., & Sarkar, B. (2015). Developing An Efficient Decision Support System for Non-Traditional Machine Selection: An Application of MOORA and MOOSRA. *Production & Manufacturing Research, 3*(1), 324–342. doi:10.1080/21693277.2014.895688

Schaupp, L. C., & Belanger, F. (2005). A conjoint analysis of online consumer satisfaction. *Journal of Electronic Commerce Research, 6*(2), 95–111.

Schmitz, S. W., & Latzer, M. (2002). Competition in B2C e-Commerce: Analytical issues and empirical evidence. *Electronic Markets, 12*(3), 163–174. doi:10.1080/101967802320245938

Schubert, P., & Selz, D. (2001). Measuring the effectiveness of e-commerce Web sites. In E-commerce and V-Business. Oxford, UK: Butterworth Heinemann.

Sen, C. G., & Baraçlı, H. (2010). Fuzzy quality function deployment based methodology for acquiring enterprise software selection requirements. *Expert Systems with Applications, 37*(4), 3415–3426. doi:10.1016/j.eswa.2009.10.006

Şengül, Ü., Eren, M., Shiraz, S. E., Gezder, V., & Şengül, A. B. (2015). Fuzzy TOPSIS method for ranking renewable energy supply systems in Turkey. *Renewable Energy, 75*, 617–625. doi:10.1016/j.renene.2014.10.045

Shamdasani, P. N., Stanaland, A. J. S., & Tan, J. (2001). Location, Location, Location: Insights for Advertising Placement on the Web. *Journal of Advertising Research, 41*(4), 7 LP-21. Retrieved from http://www.journalofadvertisingresearch.com/content/41/4/7.abstract

Shannon, C. E. (1948). A mathematical theory of communication. *The Bell System Technical Journal, 27*(3), 379–423, 623–656. doi:10.1002/j.1538-7305.1948.tb01338.x

Singh, S. N., & Dalal, N. P. (1999). Web Home Pages as Home Page as Advertisments. *Magazine Communications of the ACM, 42*(8), 91–98. doi:10.1145/310930.310978

Si, S. L., You, X. Y., Liu, H. C., & Zhang, P. (2018). DEMATEL Technique: A Systematic Review of the State-of-the-Art Literature on Methodologies and Applications. *Mathematical Problems in Engineering*, 1–33.

Smith, A. G. (2001). Applying evaluation criteria to New Zealand government websites. *International Journal of Information Management, 21*(2), 137–149. doi:10.1016/S0268-4012(01)00006-8

Sreedhar, G., Chari, A. A., & Ramana, V. (2010). A qualitative and quantitative frame work for effective website design. *International Journal of Computers and Applications, 2*(1), 71–79. doi:10.5120/610-860

Stamatis, D. H. (2015). *Quality Assurance: Applying Methodologies for Launching New Products, Services, and Customer Satisfaction.* CRC Press. doi:10.1201/b18887

Stanujkic, D., & Jovanovic, R. (2012). Measuring a quality of faculty website using ARAS method. In *Proceeding of the International Scientific Conference Contemporary Issues in Business, Management and Education* (pp. 545-554). Academic Press.

Stanujkic, D., Zavadskas, E. K., Karabasevic, D., Urosevic, S., & Maksimovic, M. (2017). An approach for evaluating website quality in hotel industry based on triangular intuitionistic fuzzy numbers. *Informatica*, *28*(4), 725–748. doi:10.15388/Informatica.2017.153

Stanujkic, D., Zavadskas, K. E., & Tamosaitiene, J. (2015). An approach to measuring website quality in the rural tourism industry based on Atanassov intuitionistic fuzzy sets. *Information & Management*, *18*, 184–199.

Steinhoff, L., Witte, C., & Eggert, A. (2018). Mixed Effects of Company-Initiated Customer Engagement on Customer Loyalty: The Contingency Role of Service Category Involvement. *SMR-Journal of Service Management Research*, *2*(2), 22–35. doi:10.15358/2511-8676-2018-2-22

Studio, D. (2017). *Banner Design final.pdf*. Retrieved from http://studiodejavu.photo/banner-design

Sumrit, D., & Anuntavoranich, P. (2013). Using DEMATEL method to analyze the causal relations on technological innovation capability evaluation factors in Thai technology-based firms. *International Transaction Journal of Engineering, Management, & Applied Sciences & Technologies*, *4*(2), 81–103.

Sun, C.-C., & Lin, G. T. (2009). Using fuzzy TOPSIS method for evaluating the competitive advantages of shopping websites. *Expert Systems with Applications*, *36*(9), 11764–11771. doi:10.1016/j.eswa.2009.04.017

Sun, P., Cárdenas, D. A., & Harrill, R. (2016). Chinese customers' evaluation of travel website quality: A decision-tree analysis. *Journal of Hospitality Marketing & Management*, *25*(4), 476–497. doi:10.1080/19368623.2015.1037977

Tadić, S., Zečević, S., & Krstić, M. (2014). A novel hybrid MCDM model based on fuzzy DEMATEL, fuzzy ANP and fuzzy VIKOR for city logistics concept selection. *Expert Systems with Applications*, *41*(18), 8112–8128. doi:10.1016/j.eswa.2014.07.021

Tan, G. W., & Wei, K. K. (2006). An empirical study of Web browsing behaviour: Towards an effective Website design. *Electronic Commerce Research and Applications*, *5*(4), 261–271. doi:10.1016/j.elerap.2006.04.007

Tarasewich, P., & Warkentin, M. (2000). Issues in wireless E-commerce. *ACM SIGEcom Exchanges*, *1*(1), 21–25. doi:10.1145/844302.844307

Taylan, O., Bafail, A. O., Abdulaal, R. M. S., & Kabli, M. R. (2014). Construction projects selection and risk assessment by fuzzy AHP and fuzzy TOPSIS methodologies. *Applied Soft Computing*, *17*, 105–116. doi:10.1016/j.asoc.2014.01.003

Temur, G. T., & Bolat, B. (2018). A robust MCDM approach for ERP system selection under uncertain environment based on worst case scenario. *Journal of Enterprise Information Management*, *31*(3), 405–425. doi:10.1108/JEIM-12-2017-0175

Tonidandel, S., & LeBreton, J. M. (2015). RWA web: A free, comprehensive, web-based, and user-friendly tool for relative weight analyses. *Journal of Business and Psychology*, *30*(2), 207–216. doi:10.100710869-014-9351-z

Torkzadeh, G., & Dhillon, G. (2002). Measuring factors that influence the success of Internet commerce. *Information Systems Research*, *13*(2), 187–204. doi:10.1287/isre.13.2.187.87

Tung, V. W. S., Chen, P. J., & Schuckert, M. (2017). Managing customer citizenship behaviour: The moderating roles of employee responsiveness and organizational reassurance. *Tourism Management*, *59*, 23–35. doi:10.1016/j.tourman.2016.07.010

Turskis, Z., Zavadskas, E. K., Antucheviciene, J., & Kosareva, N. (2015). A hybrid model based on fuzzy AHP and fuzzy WASPAS for construction site selection. *International Journal of Computers, Communications & Control*, *10*(6), 113–128. doi:10.15837/ijccc.2015.6.2078

Tzeng, G. H., Yang, Y. P. O., Lin, C. T., & Chen, C. B. (2005). Hierarchical MADM with fuzzy integral for evaluating enterprise intranet web sites. *Information Sciences*, *169*(3-4), 409–426. doi:10.1016/j.ins.2004.07.001

Ulutaş, A., Karaköy, Ç., Arıç, K.H., & Cengiz, E. (2018). Çok Kriterli Karar Verme Yöntemleri ile Lojistik Merkezi Yeri Seçimi. *İktisadi Yenilik Dergisi, 5*(2), 45-53.

Ureña, R., Chiclana, F., Fujita, H., & Herrera-Viedma, E. (2015). Confidence-consistency driven group decision making approach with incomplete reciprocal intuitionistic preference relations. *Knowledge-Based Systems*, *89*, 86–96. doi:10.1016/j.knosys.2015.06.020

Vafadarnikjoo, A., Mobin, M., Allahi, S., & Rastegari, A. (2015, January). A hybrid approach of intuitionistic fuzzy set theory and DEMATEL method to prioritize selection criteria of bank branches locations. In *Proceedings of the International Annual Conference of the American Society for Engineering Management* (p. 1). American Society for Engineering Management (ASEM).

Van Iwaarden, J., Van Der Wiele, T., Ball, L., & Millen, R. (2004). Perceptions about the quality of web sites: A survey amongst students at Northeastern University and Erasmus University. *Information & Management, 41*(8), 947–959. doi:10.1016/j.im.2003.10.002

Vatansever, K., & Akgül, Y. (2017). Evaluation of Information Management Infrastructure and factors affecting process competencies with Dematerial method. *International Symposium on Social Sciences.*

Vatansever, K., & Akgul, Y. (2014). Applying fuzzy analytic hierarchy process for evaluating service quality of private shopping website quality: A case study in Turkey. *Journal of Business Economics and Finance, 3*(3), 283–301.

Vatansever, K., & Akgül, Y. (2018). Performance evaluation of websites using entropy and grey relational analysis methods: The case of airline companies. *Decision Science Letters, 7*(2), 119–130. doi:10.5267/j.dsl.2017.6.005

Venkatesh, V., Morris, M. G., Davis, G. B., & Davis, F. D. (2003). User acceptance of information technology: Toward a unified view. *Management Information Systems Quarterly, 27*(3), 425–478. doi:10.2307/30036540

Vihonen, J. (2013). *The Effects of Internet Pages and Online Advertising in Consumer behaviour Case IKEA Tampere. Department of Applied sciences.* Tampere University.

Wang, J.-W., Cheng, C.-H., & Kun-Cheng, H. (2009). Fuzzy hierarchical TOPSIS for supplier selection. *Applied Soft Computing, 9*(1), 377–386. doi:10.1016/j.asoc.2008.04.014

Wang, Y. S. (2008). Assessing e-commerce systems success: A respecification and validation of the DeLone and McLean model of IS success. *Information Systems Journal, 18*(5), 529–557. doi:10.1111/j.1365-2575.2007.00268.x

Wei, C. C., Chien, C. F., & Wang, M. J. J. (2005). An AHP-based approach to ERP system selection. *International Journal of Production Economics, 96*(1), 47–62. doi:10.1016/j.ijpe.2004.03.004

Weiss, S. I., & Kulikowski, C. (1991). *Computer systems that learn: classification and prediction methods from statistics, neural networks, machine learning, and expert systems.* San Francisco, CA: Morgan Kaufmann.

Weka. (n.d.). Retrieved from https://tr.wikipedia.org/wiki/Weka

Wu, F., Mahajan, V., & Balasubramanian, S. (2003). An analysis of e-business adoption and its impact on business performance. *Journal of the Academy of Marketing Science, 31*(4), 425–447. doi:10.1177/0092070303255379

Wu, J., Sun, J., Liang, L., & Zha, Y. (2011). Determination of Weights for Ultimate Cross Efficiency Using Shannon Entropy. *Expert Systems with Applications, 38*(5), 5162–5165. doi:10.1016/j.eswa.2010.10.046

Wu, W. W., & Lee, Y. T. (2007). Developing Global Managers' Competencies Using The Fuzzy DEMATEL Method. *Expert Systems with Applications, 32*(2), 499–507. doi:10.1016/j.eswa.2005.12.005

Wuyts, S., Rindfleisch, A., & Citrin, A. (2015). Outsourcing customer support: The role of provider customer focus. *Journal of Operations Management, 35*(1), 40–55. doi:10.1016/j.jom.2014.10.004

Xiaoliang, Z., Jian, W., Hongcan, Y., & Shangzhuo, W. (2009). Research and application of the improved algorithm C4.5 on decision tree. In *International Conference on Test and Measurement (ICTM)* (*vol. 2*, pp184-187). Academic Press. 10.1109/ICTM.2009.5413078

Xu, J. D., Benbasat, I., & Cenfetelli, R. T. (2013). Integrating service quality with system and information quality: An empirical test in the e-service context. *Management Information Systems Quarterly, 37*(3), 777–794. doi:10.25300/MISQ/2013/37.3.05

Xu, Z. S. (2007). Intuitionistic fuzzy aggregation operators. *IEEE Transactions on Fuzzy Systems, 15*(6), 1179–1187. doi:10.1109/TFUZZ.2006.890678

Yager, R. R. (2013). *Pythagorean fuzzy subsets*. Paper presented at the IFSA World Congress and NAFIPS Annual Meeting (IFSA/NAFIPS), 2013 Joint. 10.1109/IFSA-NAFIPS.2013.6608375

Yager, R. R. (2014). Pythagorean membership grades in multicriteria decision making. *IEEE Transactions on Fuzzy Systems*, 22(4), 958–965. doi:10.1109/TFUZZ.2013.2278989

Yalçın, F. & Mehmet, B. A. Ş. (2012). Elektronik Ticarette Müşteri Memnuniyeti: Fırsat Siteleri Üzerine Bir Araştırma. *İktisadi ve İdari Bilimler Fakültesi Dergisi, 14*(3), 1-16.

Yang, Z., Cai, S., Zhou, Z., & Zhou, N. (2005). Development and validation of an instrument to measure user perceived service quality of information presenting web portals. *Information & Management, 42*(4), 575–589. doi:10.1016/S0378-7206(04)00073-4

Yang, Z., Jun, M., & Peterson, R. (2004). Measuring Customer Perceived Online Service Quality, Scale Development and Managerial Implications. *International Journal of Operations & Production Management, 24*(11), 1149–1174. doi:10.1108/01443570410563278

Yavuz, V. A. (2016). Coğrafi Pazar Seçiminde PROMETHEE ve Entropi Yöntemlerine Dayalı Çok Kriterli Bir Analiz: Mobilya Sektöründe Bir Uygulama. *Ömer Halisdemir Üniversitesi İktisadi ve İdari Bilimler Fakültesi Dergisi, 9*(2), 163-177.

Yeh, T. M., & Huang, Y. L. (2014). Factors in determining wind farm location: Integrating GQM, fuzzy DEMATEL, and ANP. *Renewable Energy, 66*, 159–169. doi:10.1016/j.renene.2013.12.003

Yen, B., Hu, P. J. H., & Wang, M. (2007). Toward an analytical approach for effective Web site design: A framework for modeling, evaluation and enhancement. *Electronic Commerce Research and Applications, 6*(2), 159–170. doi:10.1016/j.elerap.2006.11.004

Ye, Q., Law, R., & Gu, B. (2009). The impact of online user reviews on hotel room sales. *International Journal of Hospitality Management, 28*(1), 180–182. doi:10.1016/j.ijhm.2008.06.011

Yılmaz, V., Arı, E., & Doğan, R. (2016). Online alışverişte müşteri şikayet niyetleri ve davranışlarının yapısal eşitlik modeli ile incelenmesi. *Journal of Yaşar University*, *11*(42), 102–112.

Yong, D. (2006). Plant location selection based on fuzzy TOPSIS. *International Journal of Advanced Manufacturing Technology*, *28*(7–8), 839–844. doi:10.100700170-004-2436-5

Young, D., & Benamati, J. (2000). Differences in public web sites: The current state of large US firms. *Journal of Electronic Commerce Research*, *1*(3), 94–105.

Yücenur, G. N., & Demirel, N. Ç. (2012). Group decision making process for insurance company selection problem with extended VIKOR method under fuzzy environment. *Expert Systems with Applications*, *39*(3), 3702–3707. doi:10.1016/j.eswa.2011.09.065

Yüksel, H. (2007). Evaluation Of Quality Dimensions Of Web Sites. *Anadolu University Journal of Social Sciences*, *7*(1), 519–536.

Yüksel, S., Dinçer, H., & Emir, Ş. (2017). Comparing the performance of Turkish deposit banks by using DEMATEL, Grey Relational Analysis (GRA) and MOORA approaches. *World Journal of Applied Economics*, *3*(2), 26–47. doi:10.22440/wjae.3.2.2

Yüksel, S., Mukhtarov, S., Mammadov, E., & Özsarı, M. (2018). Determinants of Profitability in the Banking Sector: An Analysis of Post-Soviet Countries. *Economies*, *6*(3), 1–15. doi:10.3390/economies6030041

Yusuf, Y., Gunasekaran, A., & Abthorpe, M. S. (2004). Enterprise information Systems Project implementation: A case study of ERP in Rolls-Royce. *International Journal of Production Economics*, *87*(3), 251–266. doi:10.1016/j.ijpe.2003.10.004

Yu, X., Guo, S., Guo, J., & Huang, X. (2011). Rank B2C e-commerce websites in e-alliance based on AHP and fuzzy TOPSIS. *Expert Systems with Applications*, *38*(4), 3550–3557. doi:10.1016/j.eswa.2010.08.143

Zadeh, L. A. (1965). Fuzzy sets. *Information and Control*, *8*(3), 338–353. doi:10.1016/S0019-9958(65)90241-X

Zameer, H., Tara, A., Kausar, U., & Mohsin, A. (2015). Impact of service quality, corporate image and customer satisfaction towards customers' perceived value in the banking sector in Pakistan. *International Journal of Bank Marketing, 33*(4), 442–456. doi:10.1108/IJBM-01-2014-0015

Zarbakhshnia, N., Soleimani, H., & Ghaderi, H. (2018). Sustainable third-party reverse logistics provider evaluation and selection using fuzzy SWARA and developed fuzzy COPRAS in the presence of risk criteria. *Applied Soft Computing, 65*, 307–319. doi:10.1016/j.asoc.2018.01.023

Zavadskas, E. K., Kaklauskas, A., Turskis, Z., & Tamošaitiene, J. (2008). Selection of the effective dwelling house walls by applying attributes values determined at intervals. *Journal of Civil Engineering and Management, 14*(2), 85–93. doi:10.3846/1392-3730.2008.14.3

Zavadskas, E. K., Turskis, Z., Antucheviciene, J., & Zakarevicius, A. (2012). Optimization of weighted aggregated sum product assessment. *Elektronika ir Elektrotechnika, 122*(6), 3–6. doi:10.5755/j01.eee.122.6.1810

Zhang, H.-y., Peng, H., Wang, J., & Wang, J. (2017). An extended outranking approach for multi-criteria decision-making problems with linguistic intuitionistic fuzzy numbers. *Applied Soft Computing, 59*, 462–474. doi:10.1016/j.asoc.2017.06.013

Zhang, T., Cheung, C., & Law, R. (2018). Functionality Evaluation for Destination Marketing Websites in Smart Tourism Cities. *Journal of China Tourism Research*, 1–16.

Zhang, X., Keeling, K. B., & Pavur, R. J. (2000). Information quality of commericial web site home pages: an explorative analysis. *Proceedings of the twenty first international conference on Information systems.*

Zhu, Y., & Buchmann, A. (2002). Evaluating and selecting web sources as external information resources of a data warehouse. *Web Information Systems Engineering, 2002. WISE 2002. Proceedings of the Third International Conference on.*

Zhu, X., Zhang, Q., Zhang, L., & Yang, J. (2013). Online Promotion of the E-Commerce Websites in Retail Market in China: An Empirical Study. *Journal of Electronic Commerce in Organizations, 11*(2), 23–40. doi:10.4018/jeco.2013040103

Zolfani, S. H., Chen, I.-S., Rezaeiniya, N., & Tamošaitienė, J. (2012). A hybrid MCDM model encompassing AHP and COPRAS-G methods for selecting company supplier in Iran. *Technological and Economic Development of Economy, 18*(3), 529–543. doi:10.3846/20294913.2012.709472

Related References

To continue our tradition of advancing information science and technology research, we have compiled a list of recommended IGI Global readings. These references will provide additional information and guidance to further enrich your knowledge and assist you with your own research and future publications.

Aasi, P., Rusu, L., & Vieru, D. (2017). The Role of Culture in IT Governance Five Focus Areas: A Literature Review. *International Journal of IT/Business Alignment and Governance, 8*(2), 42-61. doi:10.4018/IJITBAG.2017070103

Abdrabo, A. A. (2018). Egypt's Knowledge-Based Development: Opportunities, Challenges, and Future Possibilities. In A. Alraouf (Ed.), *Knowledge-Based Urban Development in the Middle East* (pp. 80–101). Hershey, PA: IGI Global. doi:10.4018/978-1-5225-3734-2.ch005

Abu Doush, I., & Alhami, I. (2018). Evaluating the Accessibility of Computer Laboratories, Libraries, and Websites in Jordanian Universities and Colleges. *International Journal of Information Systems and Social Change, 9*(2), 44–60. doi:10.4018/IJISSC.2018040104

Adeboye, A. (2016). Perceived Use and Acceptance of Cloud Enterprise Resource Planning (ERP) Implementation in the Manufacturing Industries. *International Journal of Strategic Information Technology and Applications, 7*(3), 24–40. doi:10.4018/IJSITA.2016070102

Adegbore, A. M., Quadri, M. O., & Oyewo, O. R. (2018). A Theoretical Approach to the Adoption of Electronic Resource Management Systems (ERMS) in Nigerian University Libraries. In A. Tella & T. Kwanya (Eds.), *Handbook of Research on Managing Intellectual Property in Digital Libraries* (pp. 292–311). Hershey, PA: IGI Global. doi:10.4018/978-1-5225-3093-0.ch015

Adhikari, M., & Roy, D. (2016). Green Computing. In G. Deka, G. Siddesh, K. Srinivasa, & L. Patnaik (Eds.), *Emerging Research Surrounding Power Consumption and Performance Issues in Utility Computing* (pp. 84–108). Hershey, PA: IGI Global. doi:10.4018/978-1-4666-8853-7.ch005

Afolabi, O. A. (2018). Myths and Challenges of Building an Effective Digital Library in Developing Nations: An African Perspective. In A. Tella & T. Kwanya (Eds.), *Handbook of Research on Managing Intellectual Property in Digital Libraries* (pp. 51–79). Hershey, PA: IGI Global. doi:10.4018/978-1-5225-3093-0.ch004

Agarwal, R., Singh, A., & Sen, S. (2016). Role of Molecular Docking in Computer-Aided Drug Design and Development. In S. Dastmalchi, M. Hamzeh-Mivehroud, & B. Sokouti (Eds.), *Applied Case Studies and Solutions in Molecular Docking-Based Drug Design* (pp. 1–28). Hershey, PA: IGI Global. doi:10.4018/978-1-5225-0362-0.ch001

Ali, O., & Soar, J. (2016). Technology Innovation Adoption Theories. In L. Al-Hakim, X. Wu, A. Koronios, & Y. Shou (Eds.), *Handbook of Research on Driving Competitive Advantage through Sustainable, Lean, and Disruptive Innovation* (pp. 1–38). Hershey, PA: IGI Global. doi:10.4018/978-1-5225-0135-0.ch001

Alsharo, M. (2017). Attitudes Towards Cloud Computing Adoption in Emerging Economies. *International Journal of Cloud Applications and Computing*, 7(3), 44–58. doi:10.4018/IJCAC.2017070102

Amer, T. S., & Johnson, T. L. (2016). Information Technology Progress Indicators: Temporal Expectancy, User Preference, and the Perception of Process Duration. *International Journal of Technology and Human Interaction*, 12(4), 1–14. doi:10.4018/IJTHI.2016100101

Amer, T. S., & Johnson, T. L. (2017). Information Technology Progress Indicators: Research Employing Psychological Frameworks. In A. Mesquita (Ed.), *Research Paradigms and Contemporary Perspectives on Human-Technology Interaction* (pp. 168–186). Hershey, PA: IGI Global. doi:10.4018/978-1-5225-1868-6.ch008

Anchugam, C. V., & Thangadurai, K. (2016). Introduction to Network Security. In D. G., M. Singh, & M. Jayanthi (Eds.), Network Security Attacks and Countermeasures (pp. 1-48). Hershey, PA: IGI Global. doi:10.4018/978-1-4666-8761-5.ch001

Anchugam, C. V., & Thangadurai, K. (2016). Classification of Network Attacks and Countermeasures of Different Attacks. In D. G., M. Singh, & M. Jayanthi (Eds.), Network Security Attacks and Countermeasures (pp. 115-156). Hershey, PA: IGI Global. doi:10.4018/978-1-4666-8761-5.ch004

Anohah, E. (2016). Pedagogy and Design of Online Learning Environment in Computer Science Education for High Schools. *International Journal of Online Pedagogy and Course Design*, *6*(3), 39–51. doi:10.4018/IJOPCD.2016070104

Anohah, E. (2017). Paradigm and Architecture of Computing Augmented Learning Management System for Computer Science Education. *International Journal of Online Pedagogy and Course Design*, *7*(2), 60–70. doi:10.4018/IJOPCD.2017040105

Anohah, E., & Suhonen, J. (2017). Trends of Mobile Learning in Computing Education from 2006 to 2014: A Systematic Review of Research Publications. *International Journal of Mobile and Blended Learning*, *9*(1), 16–33. doi:10.4018/IJMBL.2017010102

Assis-Hassid, S., Heart, T., Reychav, I., & Pliskin, J. S. (2016). Modelling Factors Affecting Patient-Doctor-Computer Communication in Primary Care. *International Journal of Reliable and Quality E-Healthcare*, *5*(1), 1–17. doi:10.4018/IJRQEH.2016010101

Bailey, E. K. (2017). Applying Learning Theories to Computer Technology Supported Instruction. In M. Grassetti & S. Brookby (Eds.), *Advancing Next-Generation Teacher Education through Digital Tools and Applications* (pp. 61–81). Hershey, PA: IGI Global. doi:10.4018/978-1-5225-0965-3.ch004

Balasubramanian, K. (2016). Attacks on Online Banking and Commerce. In K. Balasubramanian, K. Mala, & M. Rajakani (Eds.), *Cryptographic Solutions for Secure Online Banking and Commerce* (pp. 1–19). Hershey, PA: IGI Global. doi:10.4018/978-1-5225-0273-9.ch001

Baldwin, S., Opoku-Agyemang, K., & Roy, D. (2016). Games People Play: A Trilateral Collaboration Researching Computer Gaming across Cultures. In K. Valentine & L. Jensen (Eds.), *Examining the Evolution of Gaming and Its Impact on Social, Cultural, and Political Perspectives* (pp. 364–376). Hershey, PA: IGI Global. doi:10.4018/978-1-5225-0261-6.ch017

Banerjee, S., Sing, T. Y., Chowdhury, A. R., & Anwar, H. (2018). Let's Go Green: Towards a Taxonomy of Green Computing Enablers for Business Sustainability. In M. Khosrow-Pour (Ed.), *Green Computing Strategies for Competitive Advantage and Business Sustainability* (pp. 89–109). Hershey, PA: IGI Global. doi:10.4018/978-1-5225-5017-4.ch005

Basham, R. (2018). Information Science and Technology in Crisis Response and Management. In M. Khosrow-Pour, D.B.A. (Ed.), Encyclopedia of Information Science and Technology, Fourth Edition (pp. 1407-1418). Hershey, PA: IGI Global. doi:10.4018/978-1-5225-2255-3.ch121

Batyashe, T., & Iyamu, T. (2018). Architectural Framework for the Implementation of Information Technology Governance in Organisations. In M. Khosrow-Pour, D.B.A. (Ed.), Encyclopedia of Information Science and Technology, Fourth Edition (pp. 810-819). Hershey, PA: IGI Global. doi:10.4018/978-1-5225-2255-3.ch070

Bekleyen, N., & Çelik, S. (2017). Attitudes of Adult EFL Learners towards Preparing for a Language Test via CALL. In D. Tafazoli & M. Romero (Eds.), *Multiculturalism and Technology-Enhanced Language Learning* (pp. 214–229). Hershey, PA: IGI Global. doi:10.4018/978-1-5225-1882-2.ch013

Bennett, A., Eglash, R., Lachney, M., & Babbitt, W. (2016). Design Agency: Diversifying Computer Science at the Intersections of Creativity and Culture. In M. Raisinghani (Ed.), *Revolutionizing Education through Web-Based Instruction* (pp. 35–56). Hershey, PA: IGI Global. doi:10.4018/978-1-4666-9932-8.ch003

Bergeron, F., Croteau, A., Uwizeyemungu, S., & Raymond, L. (2017). A Framework for Research on Information Technology Governance in SMEs. In S. De Haes & W. Van Grembergen (Eds.), *Strategic IT Governance and Alignment in Business Settings* (pp. 53–81). Hershey, PA: IGI Global. doi:10.4018/978-1-5225-0861-8.ch003

Bhatt, G. D., Wang, Z., & Rodger, J. A. (2017). Information Systems Capabilities and Their Effects on Competitive Advantages: A Study of Chinese Companies. *Information Resources Management Journal*, *30*(3), 41–57. doi:10.4018/IRMJ.2017070103

Bogdanoski, M., Stoilkovski, M., & Risteski, A. (2016). Novel First Responder Digital Forensics Tool as a Support to Law Enforcement. In M. Hadji-Janev & M. Bogdanoski (Eds.), *Handbook of Research on Civil Society and National Security in the Era of Cyber Warfare* (pp. 352–376). Hershey, PA: IGI Global. doi:10.4018/978-1-4666-8793-6.ch016

Boontarig, W., Papasratorn, B., & Chutimaskul, W. (2016). The Unified Model for Acceptance and Use of Health Information on Online Social Networks: Evidence from Thailand. *International Journal of E-Health and Medical Communications*, *7*(1), 31–47. doi:10.4018/IJEHMC.2016010102

Brown, S., & Yuan, X. (2016). Techniques for Retaining Computer Science Students at Historical Black Colleges and Universities. In C. Prince & R. Ford (Eds.), *Setting a New Agenda for Student Engagement and Retention in Historically Black Colleges and Universities* (pp. 251–268). Hershey, PA: IGI Global. doi:10.4018/978-1-5225-0308-8.ch014

Burcoff, A., & Shamir, L. (2017). Computer Analysis of Pablo Picasso's Artistic Style. *International Journal of Art, Culture and Design Technologies*, *6*(1), 1–18. doi:10.4018/IJACDT.2017010101

Byker, E. J. (2017). I Play I Learn: Introducing Technological Play Theory. In C. Martin & D. Polly (Eds.), *Handbook of Research on Teacher Education and Professional Development* (pp. 297–306). Hershey, PA: IGI Global. doi:10.4018/978-1-5225-1067-3.ch016

Calongne, C. M., Stricker, A. G., Truman, B., & Arenas, F. J. (2017). Cognitive Apprenticeship and Computer Science Education in Cyberspace: Reimagining the Past. In A. Stricker, C. Calongne, B. Truman, & F. Arenas (Eds.), *Integrating an Awareness of Selfhood and Society into Virtual Learning* (pp. 180–197). Hershey, PA: IGI Global. doi:10.4018/978-1-5225-2182-2.ch013

Carlton, E. L., Holsinger, J. W. Jr, & Anunobi, N. (2016). Physician Engagement with Health Information Technology: Implications for Practice and Professionalism. *International Journal of Computers in Clinical Practice*, *1*(2), 51–73. doi:10.4018/IJCCP.2016070103

Carneiro, A. D. (2017). Defending Information Networks in Cyberspace: Some Notes on Security Needs. In M. Dawson, D. Kisku, P. Gupta, J. Sing, & W. Li (Eds.), Developing Next-Generation Countermeasures for Homeland Security Threat Prevention (pp. 354-375). Hershey, PA: IGI Global. doi:10.4018/978-1-5225-0703-1.ch016

Cavalcanti, J. C. (2016). The New "ABC" of ICTs (Analytics + Big Data + Cloud Computing): A Complex Trade-Off between IT and CT Costs. In J. Martins & A. Molnar (Eds.), *Handbook of Research on Innovations in Information Retrieval, Analysis, and Management* (pp. 152–186). Hershey, PA: IGI Global. doi:10.4018/978-1-4666-8833-9.ch006

Chase, J. P., & Yan, Z. (2017). Affect in Statistics Cognition. In *Assessing and Measuring Statistics Cognition in Higher Education Online Environments: Emerging Research and Opportunities* (pp. 144–187). Hershey, PA: IGI Global. doi:10.4018/978-1-5225-2420-5.ch005

Chen, C. (2016). Effective Learning Strategies for the 21st Century: Implications for the E-Learning. In M. Anderson & C. Gavan (Eds.), *Developing Effective Educational Experiences through Learning Analytics* (pp. 143–169). Hershey, PA: IGI Global. doi:10.4018/978-1-4666-9983-0.ch006

Chen, E. T. (2016). Examining the Influence of Information Technology on Modern Health Care. In P. Manolitzas, E. Grigoroudis, N. Matsatsinis, & D. Yannacopoulos (Eds.), *Effective Methods for Modern Healthcare Service Quality and Evaluation* (pp. 110–136). Hershey, PA: IGI Global. doi:10.4018/978-1-4666-9961-8.ch006

Cimermanova, I. (2017). Computer-Assisted Learning in Slovakia. In D. Tafazoli & M. Romero (Eds.), *Multiculturalism and Technology-Enhanced Language Learning* (pp. 252–270). Hershey, PA: IGI Global. doi:10.4018/978-1-5225-1882-2.ch015

Cipolla-Ficarra, F. V., & Cipolla-Ficarra, M. (2018). Computer Animation for Ingenious Revival. In F. Cipolla-Ficarra, M. Ficarra, M. Cipolla-Ficarra, A. Quiroga, J. Alma, & J. Carré (Eds.), *Technology-Enhanced Human Interaction in Modern Society* (pp. 159–181). Hershey, PA: IGI Global. doi:10.4018/978-1-5225-3437-2.ch008

Cockrell, S., Damron, T. S., Melton, A. M., & Smith, A. D. (2018). Offshoring IT. In M. Khosrow-Pour, D.B.A. (Ed.), Encyclopedia of Information Science and Technology, Fourth Edition (pp. 5476-5489). Hershey, PA: IGI Global. doi:10.4018/978-1-5225-2255-3.ch476

Coffey, J. W. (2018). Logic and Proof in Computer Science: Categories and Limits of Proof Techniques. In J. Horne (Ed.), *Philosophical Perceptions on Logic and Order* (pp. 218–240). Hershey, PA: IGI Global. doi:10.4018/978-1-5225-2443-4.ch007

Dale, M. (2017). Re-Thinking the Challenges of Enterprise Architecture Implementation. In M. Tavana (Ed.), *Enterprise Information Systems and the Digitalization of Business Functions* (pp. 205–221). Hershey, PA: IGI Global. doi:10.4018/978-1-5225-2382-6.ch009

Das, A., Dasgupta, R., & Bagchi, A. (2016). Overview of Cellular Computing-Basic Principles and Applications. In J. Mandal, S. Mukhopadhyay, & T. Pal (Eds.), *Handbook of Research on Natural Computing for Optimization Problems* (pp. 637–662). Hershey, PA: IGI Global. doi:10.4018/978-1-5225-0058-2.ch026

De Maere, K., De Haes, S., & von Kutzschenbach, M. (2017). CIO Perspectives on Organizational Learning within the Context of IT Governance. *International Journal of IT/Business Alignment and Governance, 8*(1), 32-47. doi:10.4018/IJITBAG.2017010103

Demir, K., Çaka, C., Yaman, N. D., İslamoğlu, H., & Kuzu, A. (2018). Examining the Current Definitions of Computational Thinking. In H. Ozcinar, G. Wong, & H. Ozturk (Eds.), *Teaching Computational Thinking in Primary Education* (pp. 36–64). Hershey, PA: IGI Global. doi:10.4018/978-1-5225-3200-2.ch003

Deng, X., Hung, Y., & Lin, C. D. (2017). Design and Analysis of Computer Experiments. In S. Saha, A. Mandal, A. Narasimhamurthy, S. V, & S. Sangam (Eds.), Handbook of Research on Applied Cybernetics and Systems Science (pp. 264-279). Hershey, PA: IGI Global. doi:10.4018/978-1-5225-2498-4.ch013

Denner, J., Martinez, J., & Thiry, H. (2017). Strategies for Engaging Hispanic/Latino Youth in the US in Computer Science. In Y. Rankin & J. Thomas (Eds.), *Moving Students of Color from Consumers to Producers of Technology* (pp. 24–48). Hershey, PA: IGI Global. doi:10.4018/978-1-5225-2005-4.ch002

Devi, A. (2017). Cyber Crime and Cyber Security: A Quick Glance. In R. Kumar, P. Pattnaik, & P. Pandey (Eds.), *Detecting and Mitigating Robotic Cyber Security Risks* (pp. 160–171). Hershey, PA: IGI Global. doi:10.4018/978-1-5225-2154-9.ch011

Dores, A. R., Barbosa, F., Guerreiro, S., Almeida, I., & Carvalho, I. P. (2016). Computer-Based Neuropsychological Rehabilitation: Virtual Reality and Serious Games. In M. Cruz-Cunha, I. Miranda, R. Martinho, & R. Rijo (Eds.), *Encyclopedia of E-Health and Telemedicine* (pp. 473–485). Hershey, PA: IGI Global. doi:10.4018/978-1-4666-9978-6.ch037

Doshi, N., & Schaefer, G. (2016). Computer-Aided Analysis of Nailfold Capillaroscopy Images. In D. Fotiadis (Ed.), *Handbook of Research on Trends in the Diagnosis and Treatment of Chronic Conditions* (pp. 146–158). Hershey, PA: IGI Global. doi:10.4018/978-1-4666-8828-5.ch007

Doyle, D. J., & Fahy, P. J. (2018). Interactivity in Distance Education and Computer-Aided Learning, With Medical Education Examples. In M. Khosrow-Pour, D.B.A. (Ed.), Encyclopedia of Information Science and Technology, Fourth Edition (pp. 5829-5840). Hershey, PA: IGI Global. doi:10.4018/978-1-5225-2255-3.ch507

Elias, N. I., & Walker, T. W. (2017). Factors that Contribute to Continued Use of E-Training among Healthcare Professionals. In F. Topor (Ed.), *Handbook of Research on Individualism and Identity in the Globalized Digital Age* (pp. 403–429). Hershey, PA: IGI Global. doi:10.4018/978-1-5225-0522-8.ch018

Eloy, S., Dias, M. S., Lopes, P. F., & Vilar, E. (2016). Digital Technologies in Architecture and Engineering: Exploring an Engaged Interaction within Curricula. In D. Fonseca & E. Redondo (Eds.), *Handbook of Research on Applied E-Learning in Engineering and Architecture Education* (pp. 368–402). Hershey, PA: IGI Global. doi:10.4018/978-1-4666-8803-2.ch017

Estrela, V. V., Magalhães, H. A., & Saotome, O. (2016). Total Variation Applications in Computer Vision. In N. Kamila (Ed.), *Handbook of Research on Emerging Perspectives in Intelligent Pattern Recognition, Analysis, and Image Processing* (pp. 41–64). Hershey, PA: IGI Global. doi:10.4018/978-1-4666-8654-0.ch002

Filipovic, N., Radovic, M., Nikolic, D. D., Saveljic, I., Milosevic, Z., Exarchos, T. P., ... Parodi, O. (2016). Computer Predictive Model for Plaque Formation and Progression in the Artery. In D. Fotiadis (Ed.), *Handbook of Research on Trends in the Diagnosis and Treatment of Chronic Conditions* (pp. 279–300). Hershey, PA: IGI Global. doi:10.4018/978-1-4666-8828-5.ch013

Fisher, R. L. (2018). Computer-Assisted Indian Matrimonial Services. In M. Khosrow-Pour, D.B.A. (Ed.), Encyclopedia of Information Science and Technology, Fourth Edition (pp. 4136-4145). Hershey, PA: IGI Global. doi:10.4018/978-1-5225-2255-3.ch358

Fleenor, H. G., & Hodhod, R. (2016). Assessment of Learning and Technology: Computer Science Education. In V. Wang (Ed.), *Handbook of Research on Learning Outcomes and Opportunities in the Digital Age* (pp. 51–78). Hershey, PA: IGI Global. doi:10.4018/978-1-4666-9577-1.ch003

García-Valcárcel, A., & Mena, J. (2016). Information Technology as a Way To Support Collaborative Learning: What In-Service Teachers Think, Know and Do. *Journal of Information Technology Research*, 9(1), 1–17. doi:10.4018/JITR.2016010101

Gardner-McCune, C., & Jimenez, Y. (2017). Historical App Developers: Integrating CS into K-12 through Cross-Disciplinary Projects. In Y. Rankin & J. Thomas (Eds.), *Moving Students of Color from Consumers to Producers of Technology* (pp. 85–112). Hershey, PA: IGI Global. doi:10.4018/978-1-5225-2005-4.ch005

Garvey, G. P. (2016). Exploring Perception, Cognition, and Neural Pathways of Stereo Vision and the Split–Brain Human Computer Interface. In A. Ursyn (Ed.), *Knowledge Visualization and Visual Literacy in Science Education* (pp. 28–76). Hershey, PA: IGI Global. doi:10.4018/978-1-5225-0480-1.ch002

Ghafele, R., & Gibert, B. (2018). Open Growth: The Economic Impact of Open Source Software in the USA. In M. Khosrow-Pour (Ed.), *Optimizing Contemporary Application and Processes in Open Source Software* (pp. 164–197). Hershey, PA: IGI Global. doi:10.4018/978-1-5225-5314-4.ch007

Ghobakhloo, M., & Azar, A. (2018). Information Technology Resources, the Organizational Capability of Lean-Agile Manufacturing, and Business Performance. *Information Resources Management Journal*, 31(2), 47–74. doi:10.4018/IRMJ.2018040103

Gianni, M., & Gotzamani, K. (2016). Integrated Management Systems and Information Management Systems: Common Threads. In P. Papajorgji, F. Pinet, A. Guimarães, & J. Papathanasiou (Eds.), *Automated Enterprise Systems for Maximizing Business Performance* (pp. 195–214). Hershey, PA: IGI Global. doi:10.4018/978-1-4666-8841-4.ch011

Gikandi, J. W. (2017). Computer-Supported Collaborative Learning and Assessment: A Strategy for Developing Online Learning Communities in Continuing Education. In J. Keengwe & G. Onchwari (Eds.), *Handbook of Research on Learner-Centered Pedagogy in Teacher Education and Professional Development* (pp. 309–333). Hershey, PA: IGI Global. doi:10.4018/978-1-5225-0892-2.ch017

Gokhale, A. A., & Machina, K. F. (2017). Development of a Scale to Measure Attitudes toward Information Technology. In L. Tomei (Ed.), *Exploring the New Era of Technology-Infused Education* (pp. 49–64). Hershey, PA: IGI Global. doi:10.4018/978-1-5225-1709-2.ch004

Grace, A., O'Donoghue, J., Mahony, C., Heffernan, T., Molony, D., & Carroll, T. (2016). Computerized Decision Support Systems for Multimorbidity Care: An Urgent Call for Research and Development. In M. Cruz-Cunha, I. Miranda, R. Martinho, & R. Rijo (Eds.), *Encyclopedia of E-Health and Telemedicine* (pp. 486–494). Hershey, PA: IGI Global. doi:10.4018/978-1-4666-9978-6.ch038

Gupta, A., & Singh, O. (2016). Computer Aided Modeling and Finite Element Analysis of Human Elbow. *International Journal of Biomedical and Clinical Engineering*, 5(1), 31–38. doi:10.4018/IJBCE.2016010104

H., S. K. (2016). Classification of Cybercrimes and Punishments under the Information Technology Act, 2000. In S. Geetha, & A. Phamila (Eds.), *Combating Security Breaches and Criminal Activity in the Digital Sphere* (pp. 57-66). Hershey, PA: IGI Global. doi:10.4018/978-1-5225-0193-0.ch004

Hafeez-Baig, A., Gururajan, R., & Wickramasinghe, N. (2017). Readiness as a Novel Construct of Readiness Acceptance Model (RAM) for the Wireless Handheld Technology. In N. Wickramasinghe (Ed.), *Handbook of Research on Healthcare Administration and Management* (pp. 578–595). Hershey, PA: IGI Global. doi:10.4018/978-1-5225-0920-2.ch035

Hanafizadeh, P., Ghandchi, S., & Asgarimehr, M. (2017). Impact of Information Technology on Lifestyle: A Literature Review and Classification. *International Journal of Virtual Communities and Social Networking*, 9(2), 1–23. doi:10.4018/IJVCSN.2017040101

Harlow, D. B., Dwyer, H., Hansen, A. K., Hill, C., Iveland, A., Leak, A. E., & Franklin, D. M. (2016). Computer Programming in Elementary and Middle School: Connections across Content. In M. Urban & D. Falvo (Eds.), *Improving K-12 STEM Education Outcomes through Technological Integration* (pp. 337–361). Hershey, PA: IGI Global. doi:10.4018/978-1-4666-9616-7.ch015

Haseski, H. İ., Ilic, U., & Tuğtekin, U. (2018). Computational Thinking in Educational Digital Games: An Assessment Tool Proposal. In H. Ozcinar, G. Wong, & H. Ozturk (Eds.), *Teaching Computational Thinking in Primary Education* (pp. 256–287). Hershey, PA: IGI Global. doi:10.4018/978-1-5225-3200-2.ch013

Hee, W. J., Jalleh, G., Lai, H., & Lin, C. (2017). E-Commerce and IT Projects: Evaluation and Management Issues in Australian and Taiwanese Hospitals. *International Journal of Public Health Management and Ethics*, 2(1), 69–90. doi:10.4018/IJPHME.2017010104

Hernandez, A. A. (2017). Green Information Technology Usage: Awareness and Practices of Philippine IT Professionals. *International Journal of Enterprise Information Systems*, *13*(4), 90–103. doi:10.4018/IJEIS.2017100106

Hernandez, A. A., & Ona, S. E. (2016). Green IT Adoption: Lessons from the Philippines Business Process Outsourcing Industry. *International Journal of Social Ecology and Sustainable Development*, *7*(1), 1–34. doi:10.4018/IJSESD.2016010101

Hernandez, M. A., Marin, E. C., Garcia-Rodriguez, J., Azorin-Lopez, J., & Cazorla, M. (2017). Automatic Learning Improves Human-Robot Interaction in Productive Environments: A Review. *International Journal of Computer Vision and Image Processing*, *7*(3), 65–75. doi:10.4018/IJCVIP.2017070106

Horne-Popp, L. M., Tessone, E. B., & Welker, J. (2018). If You Build It, They Will Come: Creating a Library Statistics Dashboard for Decision-Making. In L. Costello & M. Powers (Eds.), *Developing In-House Digital Tools in Library Spaces* (pp. 177–203). Hershey, PA: IGI Global. doi:10.4018/978-1-5225-2676-6.ch009

Hossan, C. G., & Ryan, J. C. (2016). Factors Affecting e-Government Technology Adoption Behaviour in a Voluntary Environment. *International Journal of Electronic Government Research*, *12*(1), 24–49. doi:10.4018/IJEGR.2016010102

Hu, H., Hu, P. J., & Al-Gahtani, S. S. (2017). User Acceptance of Computer Technology at Work in Arabian Culture: A Model Comparison Approach. In M. Khosrow-Pour (Ed.), *Handbook of Research on Technology Adoption, Social Policy, and Global Integration* (pp. 205–228). Hershey, PA: IGI Global. doi:10.4018/978-1-5225-2668-1.ch011

Huie, C. P. (2016). Perceptions of Business Intelligence Professionals about Factors Related to Business Intelligence input in Decision Making. *International Journal of Business Analytics*, *3*(3), 1–24. doi:10.4018/IJBAN.2016070101

Hung, S., Huang, W., Yen, D. C., Chang, S., & Lu, C. (2016). Effect of Information Service Competence and Contextual Factors on the Effectiveness of Strategic Information Systems Planning in Hospitals. *Journal of Global Information Management*, *24*(1), 14–36. doi:10.4018/JGIM.2016010102

Ifinedo, P. (2017). Using an Extended Theory of Planned Behavior to Study Nurses' Adoption of Healthcare Information Systems in Nova Scotia. *International Journal of Technology Diffusion*, *8*(1), 1–17. doi:10.4018/IJTD.2017010101

Ilie, V., & Sneha, S. (2018). A Three Country Study for Understanding Physicians' Engagement With Electronic Information Resources Pre and Post System Implementation. *Journal of Global Information Management*, 26(2), 48–73. doi:10.4018/JGIM.2018040103

Inoue-Smith, Y. (2017). Perceived Ease in Using Technology Predicts Teacher Candidates' Preferences for Online Resources. *International Journal of Online Pedagogy and Course Design*, 7(3), 17–28. doi:10.4018/IJOPCD.2017070102

Islam, A. A. (2016). Development and Validation of the Technology Adoption and Gratification (TAG) Model in Higher Education: A Cross-Cultural Study Between Malaysia and China. *International Journal of Technology and Human Interaction*, 12(3), 78–105. doi:10.4018/IJTHI.2016070106

Islam, A. Y. (2017). Technology Satisfaction in an Academic Context: Moderating Effect of Gender. In A. Mesquita (Ed.), *Research Paradigms and Contemporary Perspectives on Human-Technology Interaction* (pp. 187–211). Hershey, PA: IGI Global. doi:10.4018/978-1-5225-1868-6.ch009

Jamil, G. L., & Jamil, C. C. (2017). Information and Knowledge Management Perspective Contributions for Fashion Studies: Observing Logistics and Supply Chain Management Processes. In G. Jamil, A. Soares, & C. Pessoa (Eds.), *Handbook of Research on Information Management for Effective Logistics and Supply Chains* (pp. 199–221). Hershey, PA: IGI Global. doi:10.4018/978-1-5225-0973-8.ch011

Jamil, G. L., Jamil, L. C., Vieira, A. A., & Xavier, A. J. (2016). Challenges in Modelling Healthcare Services: A Study Case of Information Architecture Perspectives. In G. Jamil, J. Poças Rascão, F. Ribeiro, & A. Malheiro da Silva (Eds.), *Handbook of Research on Information Architecture and Management in Modern Organizations* (pp. 1–23). Hershey, PA: IGI Global. doi:10.4018/978-1-4666-8637-3.ch001

Janakova, M. (2018). Big Data and Simulations for the Solution of Controversies in Small Businesses. In M. Khosrow-Pour, D.B.A. (Ed.), Encyclopedia of Information Science and Technology, Fourth Edition (pp. 6907-6915). Hershey, PA: IGI Global. doi:10.4018/978-1-5225-2255-3.ch598

Jha, D. G. (2016). Preparing for Information Technology Driven Changes. In S. Tiwari & L. Nafees (Eds.), *Innovative Management Education Pedagogies for Preparing Next-Generation Leaders* (pp. 258–274). Hershey, PA: IGI Global. doi:10.4018/978-1-4666-9691-4.ch015

Jhawar, A., & Garg, S. K. (2018). Logistics Improvement by Investment in Information Technology Using System Dynamics. In A. Azar & S. Vaidyanathan (Eds.), *Advances in System Dynamics and Control* (pp. 528–567). Hershey, PA: IGI Global. doi:10.4018/978-1-5225-4077-9.ch017

Kalelioğlu, F., Gülbahar, Y., & Doğan, D. (2018). Teaching How to Think Like a Programmer: Emerging Insights. In H. Ozcinar, G. Wong, & H. Ozturk (Eds.), *Teaching Computational Thinking in Primary Education* (pp. 18–35). Hershey, PA: IGI Global. doi:10.4018/978-1-5225-3200-2.ch002

Kamberi, S. (2017). A Girls-Only Online Virtual World Environment and its Implications for Game-Based Learning. In A. Stricker, C. Calongne, B. Truman, & F. Arenas (Eds.), *Integrating an Awareness of Selfhood and Society into Virtual Learning* (pp. 74–95). Hershey, PA: IGI Global. doi:10.4018/978-1-5225-2182-2.ch006

Kamel, S., & Rizk, N. (2017). ICT Strategy Development: From Design to Implementation – Case of Egypt. In C. Howard & K. Hargiss (Eds.), *Strategic Information Systems and Technologies in Modern Organizations* (pp. 239–257). Hershey, PA: IGI Global. doi:10.4018/978-1-5225-1680-4.ch010

Kamel, S. H. (2018). The Potential Role of the Software Industry in Supporting Economic Development. In M. Khosrow-Pour, D.B.A. (Ed.), Encyclopedia of Information Science and Technology, Fourth Edition (pp. 7259-7269). Hershey, PA: IGI Global. doi:10.4018/978-1-5225-2255-3.ch631

Karon, R. (2016). Utilisation of Health Information Systems for Service Delivery in the Namibian Environment. In T. Iyamu & A. Tatnall (Eds.), *Maximizing Healthcare Delivery and Management through Technology Integration* (pp. 169–183). Hershey, PA: IGI Global. doi:10.4018/978-1-4666-9446-0.ch011

Kawata, S. (2018). Computer-Assisted Parallel Program Generation. In M. Khosrow-Pour, D.B.A. (Ed.), Encyclopedia of Information Science and Technology, Fourth Edition (pp. 4583-4593). Hershey, PA: IGI Global. doi:10.4018/978-1-5225-2255-3.ch398

Khanam, S., Siddiqui, J., & Talib, F. (2016). A DEMATEL Approach for Prioritizing the TQM Enablers and IT Resources in the Indian ICT Industry. *International Journal of Applied Management Sciences and Engineering, 3*(1), 11–29. doi:10.4018/IJAMSE.2016010102

Khari, M., Shrivastava, G., Gupta, S., & Gupta, R. (2017). Role of Cyber Security in Today's Scenario. In R. Kumar, P. Pattnaik, & P. Pandey (Eds.), *Detecting and Mitigating Robotic Cyber Security Risks* (pp. 177–191). Hershey, PA: IGI Global. doi:10.4018/978-1-5225-2154-9.ch013

Khouja, M., Rodriguez, I. B., Ben Halima, Y., & Moalla, S. (2018). IT Governance in Higher Education Institutions: A Systematic Literature Review. *International Journal of Human Capital and Information Technology Professionals*, 9(2), 52–67. doi:10.4018/IJHCITP.2018040104

Kim, S., Chang, M., Choi, N., Park, J., & Kim, H. (2016). The Direct and Indirect Effects of Computer Uses on Student Success in Math. *International Journal of Cyber Behavior, Psychology and Learning*, 6(3), 48–64. doi:10.4018/IJCBPL.2016070104

Kiourt, C., Pavlidis, G., Koutsoudis, A., & Kalles, D. (2017). Realistic Simulation of Cultural Heritage. *International Journal of Computational Methods in Heritage Science*, 1(1), 10–40. doi:10.4018/IJCMHS.2017010102

Korikov, A., & Krivtsov, O. (2016). System of People-Computer: On the Way of Creation of Human-Oriented Interface. In V. Mkrttchian, A. Bershadsky, A. Bozhday, M. Kataev, & S. Kataev (Eds.), *Handbook of Research on Estimation and Control Techniques in E-Learning Systems* (pp. 458–470). Hershey, PA: IGI Global. doi:10.4018/978-1-4666-9489-7.ch032

Köse, U. (2017). An Augmented-Reality-Based Intelligent Mobile Application for Open Computer Education. In G. Kurubacak & H. Altinpulluk (Eds.), *Mobile Technologies and Augmented Reality in Open Education* (pp. 154–174). Hershey, PA: IGI Global. doi:10.4018/978-1-5225-2110-5.ch008

Lahmiri, S. (2018). Information Technology Outsourcing Risk Factors and Provider Selection. In M. Gupta, R. Sharman, J. Walp, & P. Mulgund (Eds.), *Information Technology Risk Management and Compliance in Modern Organizations* (pp. 214–228). Hershey, PA: IGI Global. doi:10.4018/978-1-5225-2604-9.ch008

Landriscina, F. (2017). Computer-Supported Imagination: The Interplay Between Computer and Mental Simulation in Understanding Scientific Concepts. In I. Levin & D. Tsybulsky (Eds.), *Digital Tools and Solutions for Inquiry-Based STEM Learning* (pp. 33–60). Hershey, PA: IGI Global. doi:10.4018/978-1-5225-2525-7.ch002

Lau, S. K., Winley, G. K., Leung, N. K., Tsang, N., & Lau, S. Y. (2016). An Exploratory Study of Expectation in IT Skills in a Developing Nation: Vietnam. *Journal of Global Information Management*, 24(1), 1–13. doi:10.4018/JGIM.2016010101

Lavranos, C., Kostagiolas, P., & Papadatos, J. (2016). Information Retrieval Technologies and the "Realities" of Music Information Seeking. In I. Deliyannis, P. Kostagiolas, & C. Banou (Eds.), *Experimental Multimedia Systems for Interactivity and Strategic Innovation* (pp. 102–121). Hershey, PA: IGI Global. doi:10.4018/978-1-4666-8659-5.ch005

Lee, W. W. (2018). Ethical Computing Continues From Problem to Solution. In M. Khosrow-Pour, D.B.A. (Ed.), Encyclopedia of Information Science and Technology, Fourth Edition (pp. 4884-4897). Hershey, PA: IGI Global. doi:10.4018/978-1-5225-2255-3.ch423

Lehto, M. (2016). Cyber Security Education and Research in the Finland's Universities and Universities of Applied Sciences. *International Journal of Cyber Warfare & Terrorism*, 6(2), 15–31. doi:10.4018/IJCWT.2016040102

Lin, C., Jalleh, G., & Huang, Y. (2016). Evaluating and Managing Electronic Commerce and Outsourcing Projects in Hospitals. In A. Dwivedi (Ed.), *Reshaping Medical Practice and Care with Health Information Systems* (pp. 132–172). Hershey, PA: IGI Global. doi:10.4018/978-1-4666-9870-3.ch005

Lin, S., Chen, S., & Chuang, S. (2017). Perceived Innovation and Quick Response Codes in an Online-to-Offline E-Commerce Service Model. *International Journal of E-Adoption*, 9(2), 1–16. doi:10.4018/IJEA.2017070101

Liu, M., Wang, Y., Xu, W., & Liu, L. (2017). Automated Scoring of Chinese Engineering Students' English Essays. *International Journal of Distance Education Technologies*, 15(1), 52–68. doi:10.4018/IJDET.2017010104

Luciano, E. M., Wiedenhöft, G. C., Macadar, M. A., & Pinheiro dos Santos, F. (2016). Information Technology Governance Adoption: Understanding its Expectations Through the Lens of Organizational Citizenship. *International Journal of IT/Business Alignment and Governance,* 7(2), 22-32. doi:10.4018/IJITBAG.2016070102

Mabe, L. K., & Oladele, O. I. (2017). Application of Information Communication Technologies for Agricultural Development through Extension Services: A Review. In T. Tossy (Ed.), *Information Technology Integration for Socio-Economic Development* (pp. 52–101). Hershey, PA: IGI Global. doi:10.4018/978-1-5225-0539-6.ch003

Manogaran, G., Thota, C., & Lopez, D. (2018). Human-Computer Interaction With Big Data Analytics. In D. Lopez & M. Durai (Eds.), *HCI Challenges and Privacy Preservation in Big Data Security* (pp. 1–22). Hershey, PA: IGI Global. doi:10.4018/978-1-5225-2863-0.ch001

Margolis, J., Goode, J., & Flapan, J. (2017). A Critical Crossroads for Computer Science for All: "Identifying Talent" or "Building Talent," and What Difference Does It Make? In Y. Rankin & J. Thomas (Eds.), *Moving Students of Color from Consumers to Producers of Technology* (pp. 1–23). Hershey, PA: IGI Global. doi:10.4018/978-1-5225-2005-4.ch001

Mbale, J. (2018). Computer Centres Resource Cloud Elasticity-Scalability (CRECES): Copperbelt University Case Study. In S. Aljawarneh & M. Malhotra (Eds.), *Critical Research on Scalability and Security Issues in Virtual Cloud Environments* (pp. 48–70). Hershey, PA: IGI Global. doi:10.4018/978-1-5225-3029-9.ch003

McKee, J. (2018). The Right Information: The Key to Effective Business Planning. In *Business Architectures for Risk Assessment and Strategic Planning: Emerging Research and Opportunities* (pp. 38–52). Hershey, PA: IGI Global. doi:10.4018/978-1-5225-3392-4.ch003

Mensah, I. K., & Mi, J. (2018). Determinants of Intention to Use Local E-Government Services in Ghana: The Perspective of Local Government Workers. *International Journal of Technology Diffusion*, *9*(2), 41–60. doi:10.4018/IJTD.2018040103

Mohamed, J. H. (2018). Scientograph-Based Visualization of Computer Forensics Research Literature. In J. Jeyasekar & P. Saravanan (Eds.), *Innovations in Measuring and Evaluating Scientific Information* (pp. 148–162). Hershey, PA: IGI Global. doi:10.4018/978-1-5225-3457-0.ch010

Moore, R. L., & Johnson, N. (2017). Earning a Seat at the Table: How IT Departments Can Partner in Organizational Change and Innovation. *International Journal of Knowledge-Based Organizations*, *7*(2), 1–12. doi:10.4018/IJKBO.2017040101

Mtebe, J. S., & Kissaka, M. M. (2016). Enhancing the Quality of Computer Science Education with MOOCs in Sub-Saharan Africa. In J. Keengwe & G. Onchwari (Eds.), *Handbook of Research on Active Learning and the Flipped Classroom Model in the Digital Age* (pp. 366–377). Hershey, PA: IGI Global. doi:10.4018/978-1-4666-9680-8.ch019

Mukul, M. K., & Bhattaharyya, S. (2017). Brain-Machine Interface: Human-Computer Interaction. In E. Noughabi, B. Raahemi, A. Albadvi, & B. Far (Eds.), *Handbook of Research on Data Science for Effective Healthcare Practice and Administration* (pp. 417–443). Hershey, PA: IGI Global. doi:10.4018/978-1-5225-2515-8.ch018

Na, L. (2017). Library and Information Science Education and Graduate Programs in Academic Libraries. In L. Ruan, Q. Zhu, & Y. Ye (Eds.), *Academic Library Development and Administration in China* (pp. 218–229). Hershey, PA: IGI Global. doi:10.4018/978-1-5225-0550-1.ch013

Nabavi, A., Taghavi-Fard, M. T., Hanafizadeh, P., & Taghva, M. R. (2016). Information Technology Continuance Intention: A Systematic Literature Review. *International Journal of E-Business Research, 12*(1), 58–95. doi:10.4018/IJEBR.2016010104

Nath, R., & Murthy, V. N. (2018). What Accounts for the Differences in Internet Diffusion Rates Around the World? In M. Khosrow-Pour, D.B.A. (Ed.), Encyclopedia of Information Science and Technology, Fourth Edition (pp. 8095-8104). Hershey, PA: IGI Global. doi:10.4018/978-1-5225-2255-3.ch705

Nedelko, Z., & Potocan, V. (2018). The Role of Emerging Information Technologies for Supporting Supply Chain Management. In M. Khosrow-Pour, D.B.A. (Ed.), Encyclopedia of Information Science and Technology, Fourth Edition (pp. 5559-5569). Hershey, PA: IGI Global. doi:10.4018/978-1-5225-2255-3.ch483

Ngafeeson, M. N. (2018). User Resistance to Health Information Technology. In M. Khosrow-Pour, D.B.A. (Ed.), Encyclopedia of Information Science and Technology, Fourth Edition (pp. 3816-3825). Hershey, PA: IGI Global. doi:10.4018/978-1-5225-2255-3.ch331

Nozari, H., Najafi, S. E., Jafari-Eskandari, M., & Aliahmadi, A. (2016). Providing a Model for Virtual Project Management with an Emphasis on IT Projects. In C. Graham (Ed.), *Strategic Management and Leadership for Systems Development in Virtual Spaces* (pp. 43–63). Hershey, PA: IGI Global. doi:10.4018/978-1-4666-9688-4.ch003

Nurdin, N., Stockdale, R., & Scheepers, H. (2016). Influence of Organizational Factors in the Sustainability of E-Government: A Case Study of Local E-Government in Indonesia. In I. Sodhi (Ed.), *Trends, Prospects, and Challenges in Asian E-Governance* (pp. 281–323). Hershey, PA: IGI Global. doi:10.4018/978-1-4666-9536-8.ch014

Odagiri, K. (2017). Introduction of Individual Technology to Constitute the Current Internet. In *Strategic Policy-Based Network Management in Contemporary Organizations* (pp. 20–96). Hershey, PA: IGI Global. doi:10.4018/978-1-68318-003-6.ch003

Okike, E. U. (2018). Computer Science and Prison Education. In I. Biao (Ed.), *Strategic Learning Ideologies in Prison Education Programs* (pp. 246–264). Hershey, PA: IGI Global. doi:10.4018/978-1-5225-2909-5.ch012

Olelewe, C. J., & Nwafor, I. P. (2017). Level of Computer Appreciation Skills Acquired for Sustainable Development by Secondary School Students in Nsukka LGA of Enugu State, Nigeria. In C. Ayo & V. Mbarika (Eds.), *Sustainable ICT Adoption and Integration for Socio-Economic Development* (pp. 214–233). Hershey, PA: IGI Global. doi:10.4018/978-1-5225-2565-3.ch010

Oliveira, M., Maçada, A. C., Curado, C., & Nodari, F. (2017). Infrastructure Profiles and Knowledge Sharing. *International Journal of Technology and Human Interaction*, *13*(3), 1–12. doi:10.4018/IJTHI.2017070101

Otarkhani, A., Shokouhyar, S., & Pour, S. S. (2017). Analyzing the Impact of Governance of Enterprise IT on Hospital Performance: Tehran's (Iran) Hospitals – A Case Study. *International Journal of Healthcare Information Systems and Informatics*, *12*(3), 1–20. doi:10.4018/IJHISI.2017070101

Otunla, A. O., & Amuda, C. O. (2018). Nigerian Undergraduate Students' Computer Competencies and Use of Information Technology Tools and Resources for Study Skills and Habits' Enhancement. In M. Khosrow-Pour, D.B.A. (Ed.), Encyclopedia of Information Science and Technology, Fourth Edition (pp. 2303-2313). Hershey, PA: IGI Global. doi:10.4018/978-1-5225-2255-3.ch200

Özçınar, H. (2018). A Brief Discussion on Incentives and Barriers to Computational Thinking Education. In H. Ozcinar, G. Wong, & H. Ozturk (Eds.), *Teaching Computational Thinking in Primary Education* (pp. 1–17). Hershey, PA: IGI Global. doi:10.4018/978-1-5225-3200-2.ch001

Pandey, J. M., Garg, S., Mishra, P., & Mishra, B. P. (2017). Computer Based Psychological Interventions: Subject to the Efficacy of Psychological Services. *International Journal of Computers in Clinical Practice*, *2*(1), 25–33. doi:10.4018/IJCCP.2017010102

Parry, V. K., & Lind, M. L. (2016). Alignment of Business Strategy and Information Technology Considering Information Technology Governance, Project Portfolio Control, and Risk Management. *International Journal of Information Technology Project Management*, *7*(4), 21–37. doi:10.4018/IJITPM.2016100102

Patro, C. (2017). Impulsion of Information Technology on Human Resource Practices. In P. Ordóñez de Pablos (Ed.), *Managerial Strategies and Solutions for Business Success in Asia* (pp. 231–254). Hershey, PA: IGI Global. doi:10.4018/978-1-5225-1886-0.ch013

Patro, C. S., & Raghunath, K. M. (2017). Information Technology Paraphernalia for Supply Chain Management Decisions. In M. Tavana (Ed.), *Enterprise Information Systems and the Digitalization of Business Functions* (pp. 294–320). Hershey, PA: IGI Global. doi:10.4018/978-1-5225-2382-6.ch014

Paul, P. K. (2016). Cloud Computing: An Agent of Promoting Interdisciplinary Sciences, Especially Information Science and I-Schools – Emerging Techno-Educational Scenario. In L. Chao (Ed.), *Handbook of Research on Cloud-Based STEM Education for Improved Learning Outcomes* (pp. 247–258). Hershey, PA: IGI Global. doi:10.4018/978-1-4666-9924-3.ch016

Paul, P. K. (2018). The Context of IST for Solid Information Retrieval and Infrastructure Building: Study of Developing Country. *International Journal of Information Retrieval Research*, 8(1), 86–100. doi:10.4018/IJIRR.2018010106

Paul, P. K., & Chatterjee, D. (2018). iSchools Promoting "Information Science and Technology" (IST) Domain Towards Community, Business, and Society With Contemporary Worldwide Trend and Emerging Potentialities in India. In M. Khosrow-Pour, D.B.A. (Ed.), Encyclopedia of Information Science and Technology, Fourth Edition (pp. 4723-4735). Hershey, PA: IGI Global. doi:10.4018/978-1-5225-2255-3.ch410

Pessoa, C. R., & Marques, M. E. (2017). Information Technology and Communication Management in Supply Chain Management. In G. Jamil, A. Soares, & C. Pessoa (Eds.), *Handbook of Research on Information Management for Effective Logistics and Supply Chains* (pp. 23–33). Hershey, PA: IGI Global. doi:10.4018/978-1-5225-0973-8.ch002

Pineda, R. G. (2016). Where the Interaction Is Not: Reflections on the Philosophy of Human-Computer Interaction. *International Journal of Art, Culture and Design Technologies*, 5(1), 1–12. doi:10.4018/IJACDT.2016010101

Pineda, R. G. (2018). Remediating Interaction: Towards a Philosophy of Human-Computer Relationship. In M. Khosrow-Pour (Ed.), *Enhancing Art, Culture, and Design With Technological Integration* (pp. 75–98). Hershey, PA: IGI Global. doi:10.4018/978-1-5225-5023-5.ch004

Poikela, P., & Vuojärvi, H. (2016). Learning ICT-Mediated Communication through Computer-Based Simulations. In M. Cruz-Cunha, I. Miranda, R. Martinho, & R. Rijo (Eds.), *Encyclopedia of E-Health and Telemedicine* (pp. 674–687). Hershey, PA: IGI Global. doi:10.4018/978-1-4666-9978-6.ch052

Qian, Y. (2017). Computer Simulation in Higher Education: Affordances, Opportunities, and Outcomes. In P. Vu, S. Fredrickson, & C. Moore (Eds.), *Handbook of Research on Innovative Pedagogies and Technologies for Online Learning in Higher Education* (pp. 236–262). Hershey, PA: IGI Global. doi:10.4018/978-1-5225-1851-8.ch011

Radant, O., Colomo-Palacios, R., & Stantchev, V. (2016). Factors for the Management of Scarce Human Resources and Highly Skilled Employees in IT-Departments: A Systematic Review. *Journal of Information Technology Research*, 9(1), 65–82. doi:10.4018/JITR.2016010105

Rahman, N. (2016). Toward Achieving Environmental Sustainability in the Computer Industry. *International Journal of Green Computing*, 7(1), 37–54. doi:10.4018/IJGC.2016010103

Rahman, N. (2017). Lessons from a Successful Data Warehousing Project Management. *International Journal of Information Technology Project Management*, 8(4), 30–45. doi:10.4018/IJITPM.2017100103

Rahman, N. (2018). Environmental Sustainability in the Computer Industry for Competitive Advantage. In M. Khosrow-Pour (Ed.), *Green Computing Strategies for Competitive Advantage and Business Sustainability* (pp. 110–130). Hershey, PA: IGI Global. doi:10.4018/978-1-5225-5017-4.ch006

Rajh, A., & Pavetic, T. (2017). Computer Generated Description as the Required Digital Competence in Archival Profession. *International Journal of Digital Literacy and Digital Competence*, 8(1), 36–49. doi:10.4018/IJDLDC.2017010103

Raman, A., & Goyal, D. P. (2017). Extending IMPLEMENT Framework for Enterprise Information Systems Implementation to Information System Innovation. In M. Tavana (Ed.), *Enterprise Information Systems and the Digitalization of Business Functions* (pp. 137–177). Hershey, PA: IGI Global. doi:10.4018/978-1-5225-2382-6.ch007

Rao, Y. S., Rauta, A. K., Saini, H., & Panda, T. C. (2017). Mathematical Model for Cyber Attack in Computer Network. *International Journal of Business Data Communications and Networking, 13*(1), 58–65. doi:10.4018/IJBDCN.2017010105

Rapaport, W. J. (2018). Syntactic Semantics and the Proper Treatment of Computationalism. In M. Danesi (Ed.), *Empirical Research on Semiotics and Visual Rhetoric* (pp. 128–176). Hershey, PA: IGI Global. doi:10.4018/978-1-5225-5622-0. ch007

Raut, R., Priyadarshinee, P., & Jha, M. (2017). Understanding the Mediation Effect of Cloud Computing Adoption in Indian Organization: Integrating TAM-TOE- Risk Model. *International Journal of Service Science, Management, Engineering, and Technology, 8*(3), 40–59. doi:10.4018/IJSSMET.2017070103

Regan, E. A., & Wang, J. (2016). Realizing the Value of EHR Systems Critical Success Factors. *International Journal of Healthcare Information Systems and Informatics, 11*(3), 1–18. doi:10.4018/IJHISI.2016070101

Rezaie, S., Mirabedini, S. J., & Abtahi, A. (2018). Designing a Model for Implementation of Business Intelligence in the Banking Industry. *International Journal of Enterprise Information Systems, 14*(1), 77–103. doi:10.4018/IJEIS.2018010105

Rezende, D. A. (2016). Digital City Projects: Information and Public Services Offered by Chicago (USA) and Curitiba (Brazil). *International Journal of Knowledge Society Research, 7*(3), 16–30. doi:10.4018/IJKSR.2016070102

Rezende, D. A. (2018). Strategic Digital City Projects: Innovative Information and Public Services Offered by Chicago (USA) and Curitiba (Brazil). In M. Lytras, L. Daniela, & A. Visvizi (Eds.), *Enhancing Knowledge Discovery and Innovation in the Digital Era* (pp. 204–223). Hershey, PA: IGI Global. doi:10.4018/978-1-5225-4191-2.ch012

Riabov, V. V. (2016). Teaching Online Computer-Science Courses in LMS and Cloud Environment. *International Journal of Quality Assurance in Engineering and Technology Education, 5*(4), 12–41. doi:10.4018/IJQAETE.2016100102

Ricordel, V., Wang, J., Da Silva, M. P., & Le Callet, P. (2016). 2D and 3D Visual Attention for Computer Vision: Concepts, Measurement, and Modeling. In R. Pal (Ed.), *Innovative Research in Attention Modeling and Computer Vision Applications* (pp. 1–44). Hershey, PA: IGI Global. doi:10.4018/978-1-4666-8723-3.ch001

Rodriguez, A., Rico-Diaz, A. J., Rabuñal, J. R., & Gestal, M. (2017). Fish Tracking with Computer Vision Techniques: An Application to Vertical Slot Fishways. In M. S., & V. V. (Eds.), Multi-Core Computer Vision and Image Processing for Intelligent Applications (pp. 74-104). Hershey, PA: IGI Global. doi:10.4018/978-1-5225-0889-2.ch003

Romero, J. A. (2018). Sustainable Advantages of Business Value of Information Technology. In M. Khosrow-Pour, D.B.A. (Ed.), Encyclopedia of Information Science and Technology, Fourth Edition (pp. 923-929). Hershey, PA: IGI Global. doi:10.4018/978-1-5225-2255-3.ch079

Romero, J. A. (2018). The Always-On Business Model and Competitive Advantage. In N. Bajgoric (Ed.), *Always-On Enterprise Information Systems for Modern Organizations* (pp. 23–40). Hershey, PA: IGI Global. doi:10.4018/978-1-5225-3704-5.ch002

Rosen, Y. (2018). Computer Agent Technologies in Collaborative Learning and Assessment. In M. Khosrow-Pour, D.B.A. (Ed.), Encyclopedia of Information Science and Technology, Fourth Edition (pp. 2402-2410). Hershey, PA: IGI Global. doi:10.4018/978-1-5225-2255-3.ch209

Rosen, Y., & Mosharraf, M. (2016). Computer Agent Technologies in Collaborative Assessments. In Y. Rosen, S. Ferrara, & M. Mosharraf (Eds.), *Handbook of Research on Technology Tools for Real-World Skill Development* (pp. 319–343). Hershey, PA: IGI Global. doi:10.4018/978-1-4666-9441-5.ch012

Roy, D. (2018). Success Factors of Adoption of Mobile Applications in Rural India: Effect of Service Characteristics on Conceptual Model. In M. Khosrow-Pour (Ed.), *Green Computing Strategies for Competitive Advantage and Business Sustainability* (pp. 211–238). Hershey, PA: IGI Global. doi:10.4018/978-1-5225-5017-4.ch010

Ruffin, T. R. (2016). Health Information Technology and Change. In V. Wang (Ed.), *Handbook of Research on Advancing Health Education through Technology* (pp. 259–285). Hershey, PA: IGI Global. doi:10.4018/978-1-4666-9494-1.ch012

Ruffin, T. R. (2016). Health Information Technology and Quality Management. *International Journal of Information Communication Technologies and Human Development*, 8(4), 56–72. doi:10.4018/IJICTHD.2016100105

Ruffin, T. R., & Hawkins, D. P. (2018). Trends in Health Care Information Technology and Informatics. In M. Khosrow-Pour, D.B.A. (Ed.), Encyclopedia of Information Science and Technology, Fourth Edition (pp. 3805-3815). Hershey, PA: IGI Global. doi:10.4018/978-1-5225-2255-3.ch330

Safari, M. R., & Jiang, Q. (2018). The Theory and Practice of IT Governance Maturity and Strategies Alignment: Evidence From Banking Industry. *Journal of Global Information Management, 26*(2), 127–146. doi:10.4018/JGIM.2018040106

Sahin, H. B., & Anagun, S. S. (2018). Educational Computer Games in Math Teaching: A Learning Culture. In E. Toprak & E. Kumtepe (Eds.), *Supporting Multiculturalism in Open and Distance Learning Spaces* (pp. 249–280). Hershey, PA: IGI Global. doi:10.4018/978-1-5225-3076-3.ch013

Sanna, A., & Valpreda, F. (2017). An Assessment of the Impact of a Collaborative Didactic Approach and Students' Background in Teaching Computer Animation. *International Journal of Information and Communication Technology Education, 13*(4), 1–16. doi:10.4018/IJICTE.2017100101

Savita, K., Dominic, P., & Ramayah, T. (2016). The Drivers, Practices and Outcomes of Green Supply Chain Management: Insights from ISO14001 Manufacturing Firms in Malaysia. *International Journal of Information Systems and Supply Chain Management, 9*(2), 35–60. doi:10.4018/IJISSCM.2016040103

Scott, A., Martin, A., & McAlear, F. (2017). Enhancing Participation in Computer Science among Girls of Color: An Examination of a Preparatory AP Computer Science Intervention. In Y. Rankin & J. Thomas (Eds.), *Moving Students of Color from Consumers to Producers of Technology* (pp. 62–84). Hershey, PA: IGI Global. doi:10.4018/978-1-5225-2005-4.ch004

Shahsavandi, E., Mayah, G., & Rahbari, H. (2016). Impact of E-Government on Transparency and Corruption in Iran. In I. Sodhi (Ed.), *Trends, Prospects, and Challenges in Asian E-Governance* (pp. 75–94). Hershey, PA: IGI Global. doi:10.4018/978-1-4666-9536-8.ch004

Siddoo, V., & Wongsai, N. (2017). Factors Influencing the Adoption of ISO/IEC 29110 in Thai Government Projects: A Case Study. *International Journal of Information Technologies and Systems Approach, 10*(1), 22–44. doi:10.4018/IJITSA.2017010102

Sidorkina, I., & Rybakov, A. (2016). Computer-Aided Design as Carrier of Set Development Changes System in E-Course Engineering. In V. Mkrttchian, A. Bershadsky, A. Bozhday, M. Kataev, & S. Kataev (Eds.), *Handbook of Research on Estimation and Control Techniques in E-Learning Systems* (pp. 500–515). Hershey, PA: IGI Global. doi:10.4018/978-1-4666-9489-7.ch035

Sidorkina, I., & Rybakov, A. (2016). Creating Model of E-Course: As an Object of Computer-Aided Design. In V. Mkrttchian, A. Bershadsky, A. Bozhday, M. Kataev, & S. Kataev (Eds.), *Handbook of Research on Estimation and Control Techniques in E-Learning Systems* (pp. 286–297). Hershey, PA: IGI Global. doi:10.4018/978-1-4666-9489-7.ch019

Simões, A. (2017). Using Game Frameworks to Teach Computer Programming. In R. Alexandre Peixoto de Queirós & M. Pinto (Eds.), *Gamification-Based E-Learning Strategies for Computer Programming Education* (pp. 221–236). Hershey, PA: IGI Global. doi:10.4018/978-1-5225-1034-5.ch010

Sllame, A. M. (2017). Integrating LAB Work With Classes in Computer Network Courses. In H. Alphin Jr, R. Chan, & J. Lavine (Eds.), *The Future of Accessibility in International Higher Education* (pp. 253–275). Hershey, PA: IGI Global. doi:10.4018/978-1-5225-2560-8.ch015

Smirnov, A., Ponomarev, A., Shilov, N., Kashevnik, A., & Teslya, N. (2018). Ontology-Based Human-Computer Cloud for Decision Support: Architecture and Applications in Tourism. *International Journal of Embedded and Real-Time Communication Systems*, 9(1), 1–19. doi:10.4018/IJERTCS.2018010101

Smith-Ditizio, A. A., & Smith, A. D. (2018). Computer Fraud Challenges and Its Legal Implications. In M. Khosrow-Pour, D.B.A. (Ed.), Encyclopedia of Information Science and Technology, Fourth Edition (pp. 4837-4848). Hershey, PA: IGI Global. doi:10.4018/978-1-5225-2255-3.ch419

Sohani, S. S. (2016). Job Shadowing in Information Technology Projects: A Source of Competitive Advantage. *International Journal of Information Technology Project Management*, 7(1), 47–57. doi:10.4018/IJITPM.2016010104

Sosnin, P. (2018). Figuratively Semantic Support of Human-Computer Interactions. In *Experience-Based Human-Computer Interactions: Emerging Research and Opportunities* (pp. 244–272). Hershey, PA: IGI Global. doi:10.4018/978-1-5225-2987-3.ch008

Spinelli, R., & Benevolo, C. (2016). From Healthcare Services to E-Health Applications: A Delivery System-Based Taxonomy. In A. Dwivedi (Ed.), *Reshaping Medical Practice and Care with Health Information Systems* (pp. 205–245). Hershey, PA: IGI Global. doi:10.4018/978-1-4666-9870-3.ch007

Srinivasan, S. (2016). Overview of Clinical Trial and Pharmacovigilance Process and Areas of Application of Computer System. In P. Chakraborty & A. Nagal (Eds.), *Software Innovations in Clinical Drug Development and Safety* (pp. 1–13). Hershey, PA: IGI Global. doi:10.4018/978-1-4666-8726-4.ch001

Srisawasdi, N. (2016). Motivating Inquiry-Based Learning Through a Combination of Physical and Virtual Computer-Based Laboratory Experiments in High School Science. In M. Urban & D. Falvo (Eds.), *Improving K-12 STEM Education Outcomes through Technological Integration* (pp. 108–134). Hershey, PA: IGI Global. doi:10.4018/978-1-4666-9616-7.ch006

Stavridi, S. V., & Hamada, D. R. (2016). Children and Youth Librarians: Competencies Required in Technology-Based Environment. In J. Yap, M. Perez, M. Ayson, & G. Entico (Eds.), *Special Library Administration, Standardization and Technological Integration* (pp. 25–50). Hershey, PA: IGI Global. doi:10.4018/978-1-4666-9542-9.ch002

Sung, W., Ahn, J., Kai, S. M., Choi, A., & Black, J. B. (2016). Incorporating Touch-Based Tablets into Classroom Activities: Fostering Children's Computational Thinking through iPad Integrated Instruction. In D. Mentor (Ed.), *Handbook of Research on Mobile Learning in Contemporary Classrooms* (pp. 378–406). Hershey, PA: IGI Global. doi:10.4018/978-1-5225-0251-7.ch019

Syväjärvi, A., Leinonen, J., Kivivirta, V., & Kesti, M. (2017). The Latitude of Information Management in Local Government: Views of Local Government Managers. *International Journal of Electronic Government Research*, *13*(1), 69–85. doi:10.4018/IJEGR.2017010105

Tanque, M., & Foxwell, H. J. (2018). Big Data and Cloud Computing: A Review of Supply Chain Capabilities and Challenges. In A. Prasad (Ed.), *Exploring the Convergence of Big Data and the Internet of Things* (pp. 1–28). Hershey, PA: IGI Global. doi:10.4018/978-1-5225-2947-7.ch001

Teixeira, A., Gomes, A., & Orvalho, J. G. (2017). Auditory Feedback in a Computer Game for Blind People. In T. Issa, P. Kommers, T. Issa, P. Isaías, & T. Issa (Eds.), *Smart Technology Applications in Business Environments* (pp. 134–158). Hershey, PA: IGI Global. doi:10.4018/978-1-5225-2492-2.ch007

Thompson, N., McGill, T., & Murray, D. (2018). Affect-Sensitive Computer Systems. In M. Khosrow-Pour, D.B.A. (Ed.), Encyclopedia of Information Science and Technology, Fourth Edition (pp. 4124-4135). Hershey, PA: IGI Global. doi:10.4018/978-1-5225-2255-3.ch357

Trad, A., & Kalpić, D. (2016). The E-Business Transformation Framework for E-Commerce Control and Monitoring Pattern. In I. Lee (Ed.), *Encyclopedia of E-Commerce Development, Implementation, and Management* (pp. 754–777). Hershey, PA: IGI Global. doi:10.4018/978-1-4666-9787-4.ch053

Triberti, S., Brivio, E., & Galimberti, C. (2018). On Social Presence: Theories, Methodologies, and Guidelines for the Innovative Contexts of Computer-Mediated Learning. In M. Marmon (Ed.), *Enhancing Social Presence in Online Learning Environments* (pp. 20–41). Hershey, PA: IGI Global. doi:10.4018/978-1-5225-3229-3.ch002

Tripathy, B. K. T. R., S., & Mohanty, R. K. (2018). Memetic Algorithms and Their Applications in Computer Science. In S. Dash, B. Tripathy, & A. Rahman (Eds.), Handbook of Research on Modeling, Analysis, and Application of Nature-Inspired Metaheuristic Algorithms (pp. 73-93). Hershey, PA: IGI Global. doi:10.4018/978-1-5225-2857-9.ch004

Turulja, L., & Bajgoric, N. (2017). Human Resource Management IT and Global Economy Perspective: Global Human Resource Information Systems. In M. Khosrow-Pour (Ed.), *Handbook of Research on Technology Adoption, Social Policy, and Global Integration* (pp. 377–394). Hershey, PA: IGI Global. doi:10.4018/978-1-5225-2668-1.ch018

Unwin, D. W., Sanzogni, L., & Sandhu, K. (2017). Developing and Measuring the Business Case for Health Information Technology. In K. Moahi, K. Bwalya, & P. Sebina (Eds.), *Health Information Systems and the Advancement of Medical Practice in Developing Countries* (pp. 262–290). Hershey, PA: IGI Global. doi:10.4018/978-1-5225-2262-1.ch015

Vadhanam, B. R. S., M., Sugumaran, V., V., V., & Ramalingam, V. V. (2017). Computer Vision Based Classification on Commercial Videos. In M. S., & V. V. (Eds.), Multi-Core Computer Vision and Image Processing for Intelligent Applications (pp. 105-135). Hershey, PA: IGI Global. doi:10.4018/978-1-5225-0889-2.ch004

Valverde, R., Torres, B., & Motaghi, H. (2018). A Quantum NeuroIS Data Analytics Architecture for the Usability Evaluation of Learning Management Systems. In S. Bhattacharyya (Ed.), *Quantum-Inspired Intelligent Systems for Multimedia Data Analysis* (pp. 277–299). Hershey, PA: IGI Global. doi:10.4018/978-1-5225-5219-2.ch009

Vassilis, E. (2018). Learning and Teaching Methodology: "1:1 Educational Computing. In K. Koutsopoulos, K. Doukas, & Y. Kotsanis (Eds.), *Handbook of Research on Educational Design and Cloud Computing in Modern Classroom Settings* (pp. 122–155). Hershey, PA: IGI Global. doi:10.4018/978-1-5225-3053-4.ch007

Wadhwani, A. K., Wadhwani, S., & Singh, T. (2016). Computer Aided Diagnosis System for Breast Cancer Detection. In Y. Morsi, A. Shukla, & C. Rathore (Eds.), *Optimizing Assistive Technologies for Aging Populations* (pp. 378–395). Hershey, PA: IGI Global. doi:10.4018/978-1-4666-9530-6.ch015

Wang, L., Wu, Y., & Hu, C. (2016). English Teachers' Practice and Perspectives on Using Educational Computer Games in EIL Context. *International Journal of Technology and Human Interaction*, *12*(3), 33–46. doi:10.4018/IJTHI.2016070103

Watfa, M. K., Majeed, H., & Salahuddin, T. (2016). Computer Based E-Healthcare Clinical Systems: A Comprehensive Survey. *International Journal of Privacy and Health Information Management*, *4*(1), 50–69. doi:10.4018/IJPHIM.2016010104

Weeger, A., & Haase, U. (2016). Taking up Three Challenges to Business-IT Alignment Research by the Use of Activity Theory. *International Journal of IT/ Business Alignment and Governance*, *7*(2), 1-21. doi:10.4018/IJITBAG.2016070101

Wexler, B. E. (2017). Computer-Presented and Physical Brain-Training Exercises for School Children: Improving Executive Functions and Learning. In B. Dubbels (Ed.), *Transforming Gaming and Computer Simulation Technologies across Industries* (pp. 206–224). Hershey, PA: IGI Global. doi:10.4018/978-1-5225-1817-4.ch012

Williams, D. M., Gani, M. O., Addo, I. D., Majumder, A. J., Tamma, C. P., Wang, M., ... Chu, C. (2016). Challenges in Developing Applications for Aging Populations. In Y. Morsi, A. Shukla, & C. Rathore (Eds.), *Optimizing Assistive Technologies for Aging Populations* (pp. 1–21). Hershey, PA: IGI Global. doi:10.4018/978-1-4666-9530-6.ch001

Wimble, M., Singh, H., & Phillips, B. (2018). Understanding Cross-Level Interactions of Firm-Level Information Technology and Industry Environment: A Multilevel Model of Business Value. *Information Resources Management Journal, 31*(1), 1–20. doi:10.4018/IRMJ.2018010101

Wimmer, H., Powell, L., Kilgus, L., & Force, C. (2017). Improving Course Assessment via Web-based Homework. *International Journal of Online Pedagogy and Course Design, 7*(2), 1–19. doi:10.4018/IJOPCD.2017040101

Wong, Y. L., & Siu, K. W. (2018). Assessing Computer-Aided Design Skills. In M. Khosrow-Pour, D.B.A. (Ed.), Encyclopedia of Information Science and Technology, Fourth Edition (pp. 7382-7391). Hershey, PA: IGI Global. doi:10.4018/978-1-5225-2255-3.ch642

Wongsurawat, W., & Shrestha, V. (2018). Information Technology, Globalization, and Local Conditions: Implications for Entrepreneurs in Southeast Asia. In P. Ordóñez de Pablos (Ed.), *Management Strategies and Technology Fluidity in the Asian Business Sector* (pp. 163–176). Hershey, PA: IGI Global. doi:10.4018/978-1-5225-4056-4.ch010

Yang, Y., Zhu, X., Jin, C., & Li, J. J. (2018). Reforming Classroom Education Through a QQ Group: A Pilot Experiment at a Primary School in Shanghai. In H. Spires (Ed.), *Digital Transformation and Innovation in Chinese Education* (pp. 211–231). Hershey, PA: IGI Global. doi:10.4018/978-1-5225-2924-8.ch012

Yilmaz, R., Sezgin, A., Kurnaz, S., & Arslan, Y. Z. (2018). Object-Oriented Programming in Computer Science. In M. Khosrow-Pour, D.B.A. (Ed.), Encyclopedia of Information Science and Technology, Fourth Edition (pp. 7470-7480). Hershey, PA: IGI Global. doi:10.4018/978-1-5225-2255-3.ch650

Yu, L. (2018). From Teaching Software Engineering Locally and Globally to Devising an Internationalized Computer Science Curriculum. In S. Dikli, B. Etheridge, & R. Rawls (Eds.), *Curriculum Internationalization and the Future of Education* (pp. 293–320). Hershey, PA: IGI Global. doi:10.4018/978-1-5225-2791-6.ch016

Yuhua, F. (2018). Computer Information Library Clusters. In M. Khosrow-Pour, D.B.A. (Ed.), Encyclopedia of Information Science and Technology, Fourth Edition (pp. 4399-4403). Hershey, PA: IGI Global. doi:10.4018/978-1-5225-2255-3.ch382

Zare, M. A., Taghavi Fard, M. T., & Hanafizadeh, P. (2016). The Assessment of Outsourcing IT Services using DEA Technique: A Study of Application Outsourcing in Research Centers. *International Journal of Operations Research and Information Systems*, *7*(1), 45–57. doi:10.4018/IJORIS.2016010104

Zhao, J., Wang, Q., Guo, J., Gao, L., & Yang, F. (2016). An Overview on Passive Image Forensics Technology for Automatic Computer Forgery. *International Journal of Digital Crime and Forensics*, *8*(4), 14–25. doi:10.4018/IJDCF.2016100102

Zimeras, S. (2016). Computer Virus Models and Analysis in M-Health IT Systems: Computer Virus Models. In A. Moumtzoglou (Ed.), *M-Health Innovations for Patient-Centered Care* (pp. 284–297). Hershey, PA: IGI Global. doi:10.4018/978-1-4666-9861-1.ch014

Zlatanovska, K. (2016). Hacking and Hacktivism as an Information Communication System Threat. In M. Hadji-Janev & M. Bogdanoski (Eds.), *Handbook of Research on Civil Society and National Security in the Era of Cyber Warfare* (pp. 68–101). Hershey, PA: IGI Global. doi:10.4018/978-1-4666-8793-6.ch004

About the Contributors

Kemal Vatansever was born in Burgaz on August 29, 1979 and grew up into Bursa (Turkey). He studied Business Administration at the university of Osmangazi, Eskişehir (Turkey), from which he graduated in 2002. He received Master (2005) and Ph.D. (2010) degree in Business Administration at Dumlupınar University, Kütahya, Turkey. He worked as an Assistant Professor at the Department of Capital Markets and as a head of department at the same Department, Pamukkale University, Denizli, Turkey. He works as an Assoc. Prof. Dr. at the Alanya Alaaddin Keykubat University in Turkey. His researches focuses on quantitative decision methods, multi criteria decision making, statistics and operational research.

Yakup Akgül was born on March 22, 1977. He studied Department of Information Management at the university of Hacettepe, Ankara (Turkey), from which he graduated in 2001. He received Master (2010) and Ph.D. (2015) in Business Administration at Süleyman Demirel University, Isparta, Turkey. He works as an Ass. Prof. at the Alanya Alaaddin Keykubat University, Alanya/ANTALYA, Turkey.

* * *

Aakash Aakash is a PhD Scholar in the Department of Operational Research, University of Delhi, India since 24 April 2017. He obtained his MPhil degree in Operational Research from the University of Delhi in 2017. He has one year of experience as a Lecturer in Raj Kumar Goel Engineering College, Uttar Pradesh, India. He has written few research papers which have been published in international journals and conference proceedings. His research areas are online marketing and operational research.

Anu G. Aggarwal is working as Professor in the Department of Operational Research, University of Delhi. She obtained her Ph.D., M.Phil and M.Sc. degrees in Operational Research from the University of Delhi in year 2007, 1999 and 1996, respectively. She has published several papers in the area of Marketing Management and Theory of Reliability. Her research interests include modeling and optimization in Consumer Buying Behavior, Innovation-Diffusion modeling and Soft Computing Techniques. She has reviewed many research papers for reputed journals including IEEE Transactions on Engineering Management, International journal of System Science, Int. J. of Production Research, Int. J. of Operational Research etc.

Hasan Dinçer is an Associate Professor of finance at Istanbul Medipol University, Faculty of Economics and Administrative Sciences, Istanbul-Turkey. Dr. Dinçer has BAs in Financial Markets and Investment Management at Marmara University. He received PhD in Finance and Banking with his thesis entitled "The Effect of Changes on the Competitive Strategies of New Service Development in the Banking Sector". He has work experience in finance sector as portfolio specialist and his major academic studies focusing on financial instruments, performance evaluation, and economics. He is the executive editor of the International Journal of Finance and Banking Studies (IJFBS) and the founder member of the Society for the Study of Business and Finance (SSBF).

Burak Efe is a Research Assistant at the Department of Industrial Engineering, Necmettin Erbakan University, Turkey. He received his MS and PhD in Industrial Engineering at Gazi University, Turkey. His current research interests include assembly line balancing, ergonomics, fuzzy logic, multi-criteria decision making, risk assessment.

Cengiz Gazeloğlu completed his undergraduate education in 2010 in the field of statistics at Afyon Kocatepe University. In the same university, he completed his master's degree in applied statistics in 2012. In 2014, he received his PhD degree in applied statistics from Anadolu University. He is currently the head of applied statistics department at Suleyman Demirel University. His areas of expertise include Structural Equation Model, Type II Regression, Data Mining, Fuzzy Logic, Scale Development.

Murat Kemal Keleş gained his B.S. degree from Wood Affairs Industrial Engineering Department at Hacettepe University in 1994 with honorary degree. Until 2002, he worked as a production and planning engineer in the private sector. In 2002, he became a lecturer at Suleyman Demirel University in Isparta. He received his M.S. and Ph.D. degrees from the Department of Business Administration of Süleyman Demirel University in 2007 and 2014, respectively. He is currently working at Keçiborlu Vocational School of Isparta University of Applied Sciences as a Dr. lecturer. His research areas are production management, marketing, planning, entrepreneurship, Technoparks, Technology Transfer Offices, R & D, and Innovation.

Himanshu Sharma is currently pursuing research in Operational Research from University of Delhi. He has obtained his M.Phil and M.Sc. degrees in Operational Research from University of Delhi in the year 2017 and 2015 respectively. His research interest includes marketing models in the area of electronic commerce, mobile commerce, online marketing, multi criteria decision making, path modelling.

Cüneyt Toyganözü is an assistant professor of statistics at the Department of Econometrics, Suleyman Demirel University, Turkey. He studied mathematics for his B.Sc. degree in Turkey after that he had his M.Sc. degree in statistics at Western Michigan University and had M.A. degree in applied statistics at University of Pittsburgh. He granted his Ph.D. in applied mathematics. His research interests are time series analysis, extreme value theory, structural equation modeling and decision theory.

Zeynep Hande Toyganözü has a PhD in Mathematics from Suleyman Demirel University, Turkey and she has been working as a research assistant of functional analysis section at the Department of Mathematics, at the same university. She studies on some convergence types of sequences and sequences of functions. Also, she has some research papers about asymmetric metric spaces which is a subject used in some applied sciences such as information sciences. Recently, she is interested in decision theory and structural equation modeling.

Alptekin Ulutaş is Assistant Professor in International Trade and Logistics Dept. at Cumhuriyet University in Sivas, Turkey. He has taken a PhD degree from University of Wollongong in February 2016. He has been serving as assistant professor at the Faculty of Economics and Administrative Sciences at Cumhuriyet University since June 2017. So far, he has written 7 articles and 11 conference papers in total. His research area is optimization and multi-criteria decision making, fuzzy and stochastic programming.

Serhat Yüksel is associate professor of finance in İstanbul Medipol University. Before this position, he worked as a senior internal auditor for seven years in Finansbank, Istanbul-Turkey and 1 year in Konya Food and Agriculture University as an assistant professor. Dr. Yüksel has a BS in Business Administration (in English) from Yeditepe University (2006) with full scholarship. He got his master degree from the economics in Boğaziçi University (2008). He also has a PhD in Banking from Marmara University (2015). His research interests lie in banking, finance and financial crisis. He has more than 70 publications (books, book chapters, scientific articles, etc.).

Index

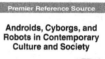

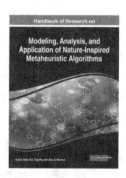

Ensure Quality Research is Introduced to the Academic Community

Become an IGI Global Reviewer for Authored Book Projects

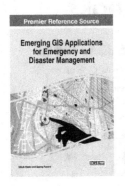

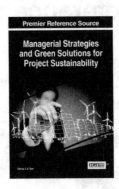

The overall success of an authored book project is dependent on quality and timely reviews.

In this competitive age of scholarly publishing, constructive and timely feedback significantly expedites the turnaround time of manuscripts from submission to acceptance, allowing the publication and discovery of forward-thinking research at a much more expeditious rate. Several IGI Global authored book projects are currently seeking highly qualified experts in the field to fill vacancies on their respective editorial review boards:

Applications may be sent to:
development@igi-global.com

Applicants must have a doctorate (or an equivalent degree) as well as publishing and reviewing experience. Reviewers are asked to write reviews in a timely, collegial, and constructive manner. All reviewers will begin their role on an ad-hoc basis for a period of one year, and upon successful completion of this term can be considered for full editorial review board status, with the potential for a subsequent promotion to Associate Editor.

If you have a colleague that may be interested in this opportunity,
we encourage you to share this information with them.